Adventures of a Louisiana Birder

ADVENTURES

~~~~ OF ~~~~

A LOUISIANA

BIRDER

1 YEAR ∗ 2 WINGS ∗ 300 SPECIES

MARYBETH LIMA

WITH A NEW AFTERWORD
BY THE AUTHOR

Louisiana State University Press
Baton Rouge

Published by Louisiana State University Press
lsupress.org

Louisiana Paperback Edition, 2023

Designer: Michelle A. Neustrom
Typeface: Sentinel

Map by Lynn Hathaway
Illustrations by Aaron Hargrove
Cover photo by J. V. Remsen

Library of Congress Cataloging-in-Publication Data
Names: Lima, Marybeth, 1965– author.
Title: Adventures of a Louisiana birder : one year, two wings, three
    hundred species / Marybeth Lima.
Description: Baton Rouge : Louisiana State University Press, [2019] |
    Includes bibliographical references and index.
Identifiers: LCCN 2018046200 | ISBN 978-0-8071-7137-0 (cloth : alk.
    paper) ISBN 978-0-8071-7955-0 (paperback) | ISBN 978-0-8071-7158-5
    (pdf) | ISBN 978-0-8071-7159-2 (epub)
Subjects: LCSH: Lima, Marybeth, 1965– | Bird watchers—Louisiana—
    Biography. | Bird watching—Louisiana. | Birds—Louisiana.
Classification: LCC QL684.L8 L56 2019 | DDC 598.072/3409763—dc23
LC record available at https://lccn.loc.gov/2018046200

This one is for all you mommas out there, two in particular:
Kathleen (Kay) Florence Rogers and Mary Eleanor Hathaway

CONTENTS

PREFACE

When I began writing this book, my main purpose was to share stories about birds, birders, and Louisiana, to shine a light on these communities and places. My hope was that some random birders living outside the state might read the book and think to themselves, "Wow, I really want to visit Louisiana to bird. I think I would have a wonderful time." Louisiana is, I humbly submit, one of the best states for birding in the country, and among the most underappreciated. Our official state checklist, which includes all bird species seen within our borders, numbers 482 and counting.[1] Louisiana's species diversity is high in part because we have portions of two of the nation's four major migratory flyways (Mississippi and Central) located within the state. We also sport 397 miles of coastline, and although our pelagic (ocean) bird species diversity is nothing like what you'd encounter in California or New England, it is still respectable enough to contribute substantially to our state list.

Louisiana offers great birding year-round. One can see almost every North American species of duck and sparrow in the winter. Spring migration colors start flying through in late March and keep birders of all stripes spellbound until mid- to late-May. The sweltering summer is our slow season, although the coastline is a wonderful reprieve from the heat and yields a number of shorebird and tern species. Also, a post-breeding population of Wood Storks, mostly from Mexico, heads over to hang out in south Louisiana during the summer, and some of our intrepid birding souls manage to find summer rarities like the Ruff or Gray Kingbird. Fall migration is the season of understated color and greater challenges, as the birds would rather blend in than stand out. And then, back toward winter, American White Pelicans show up in droves at the LSU lakes and bring out half the citizens of Baton Rouge to see them.

During the almost five years in which I wrote this book, the contours of near death and death intertwined with my birding. As a result, I added two additional goals: to illustrate the ways in which birds and birding (and by extension, any beloved pursuit) can help one get through tough times, and to share the story of the end of a person's life in the hopes that the experiences that come with it might be helpful to others.

I am not a professional birder, far from it. I am more an active amateur—which isn't to say I'm not entirely consumed. It's just that my talent for birding doesn't match my passion (although my mom thinks it does—more on that later). Birds and the people who are passionate about them are intensely interesting to me—interesting and fun and magical and crazy and idiosyncratic all at the same time. Birding offers a perspective on the human condition, at the intersection of people and birds. Birding is also about communities, both human and avian, contained in the larger ecosystem in which we all reside.

The stories, rituals, and customs at disparate intersections have been the focus of my professional life (intersections of biology and engineering, of university and community). Birds help me understand the world and make me a better person, a person passionately interested in the world being a fair, just place for all its inhabitants, particularly ones with wings and beaks. Hopefully I am not plagiarizing myself by ending this preface with exactly the same sentence I used in my book *Building Playgrounds, Engaging Communities*: I hope that you enjoy reading this book as much as I enjoyed writing it.

Adventures of a Louisiana Birder

Plain Dealing

Shreveport

Cross Lake

Monroe

A birder's view
of Louisiana

N

W ← → E

S

Roadrunner
Loop

Turf Grass
Road

Johnson's
Bayou

Home-base
♥ aka
Baton Rouge

Folsom

Lake
Pontchartrain

New
Orleans

Cameron

Cutoff

Venice

Lighthouse
Road

Peveto
Woods

Four
Magic
Miles

Golden
Meadow

Grand
Isle

LISTING TOWARD LISTING

The truck peeled backward down the dirt road and angled in uncomfortably close to my rear bumper. The man who jauntily exited and headed for my passenger window looked a little like a Bantam Rooster.

"Watch y'all doin'?" he demanded.

"A Christmas Bird Count, sir," I answered. "We count the birds out here in rice country on this day each year."

"Ah," he said, visibly relaxing and blooming a smile. "So, what have you seen so far?"

"Lots of geese, but duck numbers this year are pretty low."

"You right about that," he responded. "It's on account of Wildlife and Fisheries —they been feeding the ducks out at Lacassine National Wildlife Refuge. It kind of isn't fair. Wildlife and Fisheries encourages us to hunt and we all go out and buy our duck stamps, but in the middle of duck season they ring the dinner bell for the ducks in a place we're not allowed to hunt."

"Ah," I said.

"Not only that, but that blasted crop duster went through here this morning."

"Yes, it flew right over our heads a few times." We'd been watching two Vermilion Flycatchers when the biplane first motored overhead. Although the brilliant red, adult male flycatchers stood their ground during the plane's closest passes, many other birds had flushed and our team had tried to count them as they scattered.

"That thing scared off whatever few ducks were left. Anyway, I watch stuff around here. What do y'all want to see?"

"Everything."

"Y'all seen the eagles yet?"

"Yes, in the fields off Highway 335."

Nodding, he said, "How 'bout the cranes?"

"Which ones?" In rural Louisiana, crane is something of a generic term, the same way that coke is generic for a soft drink of any flavor. A crane might be a Sandhill Crane, but it could also mean an egret or heron species.

"Whoopers," he said, "the big ones. I haven't seen them in awhile, but they used to hang out together, three of 'em, on this very road you're on now—go down farther, past those trees up there, and search the fields. I sure hope they're okay. I try to watch out for them and make sure that no one shoots them."

Another truck was attempting to traverse the road and the man's truck was blocking it, so he said his goodbyes.

Some twenty minutes later and about three-quarters of a mile down the road, my entire Christmas Bird Count (CBC) team drew in an excited, collective breath when we viewed three Whooping Cranes foraging in a rice field about a quarter mile north of the road. Two were bent over, slowly probing the ground, while the third stood erect; I viewed it eye-to-eye, because this beautiful all-white bird with red crown accents stood as tall as I did. The product of a six-year, concerted reintroduction effort,[1] these individuals were among the seventy-two total whoopers in the state. We reported the presence of the cranes, but not their location, to ensure that the cranes were not further disturbed by humans.

Place can teach you things. One of the things Louisiana has taught me about is birds. Sometimes you can clearly trace the path of a hobby from childhood to adulthood, a hobby that "maps," if you will. For example, my wife, Lynn Hathaway, spent a large part of her childhood at her daddy's knee, and he was a fix-it guy. He taught her everything, and as a result Lynn likes to tinker now and can fix just about anything, which is an amazing perk for me. I may be an engineer, but I am definitely not what one would call mechanically inclined. Anyway, my birding hobby, or to quote the infamous words of author Mark Obmascik, my "fowl obsession," doesn't map directly from childhood to adulthood.

If I think about it, signposts along the way hinted that birds would find a place in my heart, because I have many childhood memories about nature and specific memories that involve birds. My parents taught my brother and me about the natural world while we were growing up—whether it was bacteria in pond water that my dad took us to collect and observe under my microscope, or the names of various rocks, plants, trees, shells, and yes, some birds that my mom taught us. One of my earliest memories is of me and my parents watching spellbound as a praying mantis ate a grasshopper.

When we lived in Nashua, New Hampshire, in the late 1960s and early 1970s, my mom sprinkled birdseed on the picnic table in our backyard and pointed out the Blue Jays, Northern Cardinals, and Black-capped Chickadees that came to feed. I remember standing outside without moving for forty-five minutes in frigid temperatures with my mom while we watched a Great Blue Heron fishing in a brook in Oswego, New York; we had gotten sidetracked from an after-Thanksgiving dinner walk with family. The silhouette of that bird patiently fishing against a sky that morphed from pink to purple to midnight blue is one I will never forget.

We vacationed in Massachusetts every summer while I grew up. During family walks along the beach, we'd always point out "the big sandpipers" and "the little sandpipers." And yes, we thought that there were only two kinds, Willets and Sanderlings, respectively. Although I didn't know the name of the bird that made the call until years later, the sound of the Common Tern was part of my quintessential summer vacation memories, the same way that the call of the Fish Crow was a reminder of the spring breaks I spent in Florida during college. So, there were signposts (if not clear epiphanies) of my future birding adventures.

I am lucky enough to have run with a group of ladies a generation older than me from the time I moved to Baton Rouge in 1996. Several years after I started running with them, the ladies got into bird-watching. Their conversations about the birds we encountered while running fired my interest. There were the birds we'd see pretty much every week, like the Carolina Wren, Northern Mockingbird, and Northern Cardinal, but then there were others we saw or heard only occasionally, like the Eastern Kingbird or Eastern Towhee. The birding leader of the ladies is Joan Nicolosi; she and her husband, Joe, own a camp on Grand Isle, a barrier island off the coast of Louisiana and one of the best places in the state to bird. Joan and Joe were generous enough to share the camp with all of us for birding purposes.

In 2000, a pair of binoculars for Christmas sent me off to the races. Early in my birding days, I attended monthly birding walks at Bluebonnet Swamp Nature Center in Baton Rouge; the walks through the 105-acre swamp and bottomland hardwood forest area were led by Harriett Pooler, a strong birder by sight, and Beverly Landaiche, a volunteer at the center, who birded primarily by ear. I loved it when the two of them guided together because I could learn the basics of birding through two senses at once. Although I love seeing birds and can attest to the frustration of hearing a bird you've never seen, I am especially drawn to bird song.

I bird-watched for five years without writing anything down, and for another five with occasional lists for when I did something "serious." Joan and I went to a Louisiana Ornithological Society (LOS) meeting in New Orleans in 2007, and several months later the two of us dragged along the ladies and their husbands on a spring migration trip to High Island, a small coastal community near Galveston with an appropriately Texas-sized reputation for birds. Until 2010, I was happy to call a sparrow a little brown job and never bother to go further with identification. But something changed over time; I got increasingly interested in birds, even sparrows—especially sparrows, actually, because I knew so little about them. In so doing, I shifted from bird-watching to the more serious pursuit of birding.

In 2010, I hired my first-ever birding guide when Lynn and I took a trip to New Mexico with our friend Linda Lee. We spent a day with Bill West, who took us to Santa Fe National Forest and showed us birds I'd never even heard of, like the American Dipper and the Williamson's Sapsucker. The latter was particularly memorable because Bill showed us a nesting pair of these woodpeckers, and the females and males look completely different from each other, a phenomenon known as sexual dimorphism. In addition, the babies looked distinctly different than their parents. It was a jaw-dropping experience to watch the pair feed their babies in a nest hole about twenty feet from where we stood. Bill's knowledge of birding amazed me, and I resolved to see if I could become as good of a birder as Bill.

In 2011, I finally decided to take the advice of Joan and the ladies and go to the Rio Grande Valley Birding Festival (RGVBF) in Texas. They had gone in 2007, but because of my teaching schedule I hadn't been able to go with them. The ladies had raved about that festival for years. By 2011 my schedule had changed substantially enough and I had gotten serious enough about birding to book a trip. I took my momma with me; she had continued to appreciate birds throughout her working life.

My mom worked at the public library in Grand Island, New York, for fifteen years; every spring she put chairs over nests that Killdeer had constructed on the library grounds and made sure that the public stayed away from them. She loved watching Red-tailed Hawks on her drive to work; once, she shared her amazement at seeing a Snowy Owl on this same drive. When she retired and

moved south to coastal Mississippi, my mom decided to take up birding more seriously. She joined the Bushwhackers, an informal birding club started by the late legendary Mississippi birder Judy Toups. Instead of watching only the birds that came across her path, my momma started taking trips to see them.

Our first trip during the RGVBF was the big day van tour. On this outing, teams of six birders, two birding guides, and two local guides who know how to get to all the birding spots ride in each of six or so vans, and the vans are in friendly competition. The van that tallies the highest number of species seen between 6:00 A.M. and 4:30 P.M. wins the competition and bragging rights. (Big days usually last for twenty-four hours, but this festival sported a shorter competition period.)

This day was one of the most amazing I have had as a birder. We put 250 miles on the van as we picked off spectacular birding area after spectacular birding area—Estero Llano Grande State Park, Laguna Madre, Bentsen-Rio Grande State Park, and so on. I wound up seeing more than forty birds I'd never seen before, and my jaw dropped several times at some of the most wondrous birding sights I'd ever witnessed: An adult White-tailed Hawk atop a telephone pole at close range; seventy-five Buff-bellied Hummingbirds feeding in a small field of Turk's Cap; and an Aplomado Falcon perched at eye-level on the post of a barbed wire fence, with a Cassin's Sparrow balancing on the barbed wire right below it. I have yet to see a picture or drawing of an Aplomado Falcon that comes close to how majestic this bird is in real life. The mix of colors (yellow, orange, black, gray, and white), along with bold lines and nuanced streaking, make the bird seem like a moving impressionist painting. We finished the day with 150 bird species and came in second place to the winning van, which had 153. After that big day with guides Andy Bankert and Michael Hilchey, I was totally hooked. I began my ascent (or descent, depending on whom you ask) into bird nerddom.

After the RGVBF, I got inspired: I compiled my years of "important" lists—including several trips to Grand Isle courtesy of Joan and Joe, the LOS and High Island trips, the day in New Mexico with Bill West, occasional day trips to bird, lists of birds that had crossed my path during trips I had taken to places like Hawaii, California, and Grand Cayman, as well as things I could remember from childhood—into my birding life list. It had about 350 birds on it. In creating this list, I joined the legion of birders who keep a life list, which consists of all the species of wild birds encountered in their lives.

The other thing I took with me from that trip at the RGVBF was a driving desire to see the movie *The Big Year,* which had just been released. The author of the book upon which the movie was based, Mark Obmascik, was a keynote speaker at the festival. Greg Miller, one of the birders featured in the book and movie, was also on hand at the festival.[2] My mom and I had read the book, which is about three birders trying to see a record number of bird species in North America in a single year; hearing Greg and Mark talk about the movie got us excited to see it. I was even more thrilled because during that very first morning in Harlingen, Texas, at the Best Western that netted birders like us by providing a predawn breakfast, Greg Miller sat down at the table next to us at about 5:15 A.M. I read his festival name tag and said, "You're Greg Miller? *The* Greg Miller?"

He said yes in his unassuming way—I was an instant groupie. Having Greg Miller sit next to you for breakfast is like having Steven Tyler sit next to you in a diner if you're a diehard rock fan, or seeing Denzel Washington if you're big into movies. Greg had been hired as a consultant for the making of the movie, in which his character was played by Jack Black. Jack wasn't a birder, so Greg took him out birding so that he'd be able to "look the part." Greg showed Jack a Red-winged Blackbird, and Jack was watching it through his binoculars and said, "I see it, but I don't understand why it's called a Red-winged Blackbird." Just then, the male opened his wings wide and took flight—Jack continued to watch the bird and said, "Ohhhh . . . like, I totally get it, man."

Unfortunately, the movie didn't do well at the box office. It migrated through Baton Rouge like a Cape May Warbler comes through Louisiana in the spring—here and gone in several weeks, and not available in every location. When I checked movie listings upon returning from the RGVBF, *The Big Year* was no longer showing in Baton Rouge. It was still playing in Slidell, a ninety-minute drive east of Baton Rouge and close to one of the outdoor places that Lynn and I like to explore.

The kayak launch at Irish Bayou Lagoon, which leads into Bayou Sauvage

National Wildlife Refuge, is a great place for Lynn and me to practice our respective passions at the same time. Lynn loves to fish from a kayak, and this area provides excellent habitat for the saltwater inshore species she endeavors to catch, including Redfish, Speckled Trout, and Flounder. I enjoy the same habitats for the birds that they hold, and birding in a kayak is really fun because it's a great way to get eye-to-eye with birds that skulk in marsh grass. Approximately two miles from the kayak launching area, South Point is a favored stop for both of us. The railroad bridge that crosses the water there offers structure attractive to fish, and the fact that it is a land mass that juts out into a five-mile stretch of open water makes it a funnel for birds during migration and in inclement weather. Lynn and I made a deal—we spent the day kayaking and then drove twenty minutes to a theater in Slidell to see the movie. It was a nice day on the water for both of us; Lynn caught several bass, and I saw a raft of hundreds of Bufflehead.

The movie was okay, but it wasn't as good as the book, nothing new there. *But* the movie had a very important, positive impact on my life, because as we walked out of the theater Lynn said, "You never told me that birding could be a sport and that it could be fast paced. I'd actually bird more often with you if you didn't feel the need to hang out for twenty minutes with a sparrow. How about we do a big year in Louisiana in 2012?"

She didn't have to ask me twice! I readily agreed. This year-long adventure effectively grew my hobby to obsessive proportions. If I'd been listing toward listing up to this point, our Louisiana big year catapulted me straight into utter bird nerddom.

We sat down and hashed out the rules of our big year before starting. We both needed to see the same bird in order for it to count. If one of us was sure about the identification of a bird and the other was not, the bird didn't go on the list. And while we made notations about the birds we heard and identified by sound only, unless we actually saw them, they didn't go on the list.

The plan was for us to start on January 1, like normal birders do, but Lynn surprised me by announcing on the evening of Thursday, December 8, 2011, that we would start our big year on my birthday, which was the next day. Lynn got one personal day off per year in her job in the Ascension Parish School System, and she took it to drive us to Lacassine National Wildlife Refuge (NWR), about 120 miles southwest of Baton Rouge. We'd never been there, but our initial research suggested it was great for birding. We packed up the truck early on the morning of the 9th and got our first two birds of the year at our feeder, the Mourning Dove and the House Sparrow. We traveled to Lacassine via rice country. The rice had been harvested, so the fields were bare, but the rice kernels left behind are a great boon to some bird species.

Huge flocks of geese filled the rice fields—I'd never seen anything like it. We stopped at several points to observe massive flocks of Snow Geese, with a few smaller Ross's Geese mixed in, and Greater White-fronted Geese. At one point, a flock of hundreds of geese took flight together. The whoosh they made when they lifted off was so loud that it sounded like someone had lit a match and thrown it into an impossibly wide river of gasoline—the sound was so beautiful, I actually cried. Lacassine was everything I'd hoped for and more; the wildlife refuge was massive and included a large freshwater wetland as well as access to several ridges with mature tree lines. We birded the west and east sides of Lacassine, and by the end of the day we had notched fifty-six birds on our list, including the Glossy Ibis, which I'd never seen before.

We decided to stay closer to home the next day by starting at Capitol Lakes, in the middle of downtown Baton Rouge, to look for ducks. Upon arriving, we ran into a man whose name I no longer remember—he had a Cooper's Hawk queued up in his scope that he shared with us (bird number 59). I talked about trying to see lots of different species of birds (I wasn't ready to admit big year ambitions yet), and he said we had to connect with Steve Cardiff and Donna Dittmann because they had different species of wintering hummingbirds in their yard. When he mentioned that they worked at LSU, I figured that this was an "in," because I work at LSU too. As it turned out, we didn't need any kind of "in," because all Steve and Donna need to know is that you're interested in birds. I emailed them later on Saturday, after we returned from birding South Farm, a wetland and bottomland hardwood forest area managed by the Army Corps of Engineers about thirty miles west of Baton Rouge. We were in their yard in St. Gabriel the very next morning, where we picked up Black-chinned, Buff-bellied, and Rufous Hummingbirds in quick succession, along with a bonus Hairy Woodpecker. We ended our first weekend with eighty-seven birds, 31 percent of the total we would get for the entire year.

We began our big year somewhat in the dark about how it really works. Seeing the movie *The Big Year* is one thing; actually attempting one is quite another, even as a much scaled-down venture. During that first weekend I heard twice about the listserv LA-BIRD, once from the Cooper's Hawk scope guy and then from Donna and Steve. It took one more nudge from Jane Patterson before I finally signed up in early February. Joining LA-BIRD was the smartest thing I did from a strategic standpoint. Research through bird books and guides can only get you so far; there's nothing like a close to real-time recital of which species are where. LA-BIRD provides this information. It is a listserv on which birders post information regarding their bird sightings in Louisiana and is especially useful for unusual or rare bird reports. Although I hadn't met many of the birders who routinely posted their lists on LA-BIRD, I almost felt like I knew them, and I am indebted to many. Because of them and LA-BIRD, we got so much further in our big year than I thought we would. We had set a modest goal of two hundred species, and if it hadn't been for LA-BIRD, that's probably about where we would have finished.

In late January we attended the winter LOS meeting in Lake Charles. Other than Sabine NWR, I was unfamiliar with southwest Louisiana hot spots. The day-long field trip we took during the LOS meeting with guides Gene Barnett and Bill Gover added nine birds to our list, and the knowledge base they provided in terms of places to bird was immensely useful. Our first stop of the day was at Turf Grass Road, a spot about fifteen miles east of Lake Charles, in Jefferson Davis Parish.[3] Two days previously, Gene had seen an American Pipit and a Horned Lark there. Although we saw neither species on that crisp morning, I immediately fell in love with the location. The turfgrass farm was as wide as my line of sight in easterly and westerly directions, and the relatively low grass line made it easy to see birds standing in the fields. The roads surrounding the sod farm were intermittently tree-lined and fully "power-lined," giving passerines plenty of places to perch. A landfill that the birders called "Mount Trashmore" rose up from the flat landscape several miles to the east; although we didn't stop there, the group told us that the landfill attracted gulls and raptors and was worth birding when there was time. Lynn and I returned to Turf Grass Road six times throughout the year, obtaining numerous birds for our list, including Upland Sandpiper and Sprague's Pipit.

We birded frequently throughout the spring and picked up a number of species at places like the Atchafalaya basin, the largest wetland and swamp area in the United States (located only thirty miles from our house); Braithwaite, a small community southeast of New Orleans; and Big Branch Marsh NWR, which hugs the north shore of Lake Pontchartrain some forty-five miles northeast of New Orleans.

Joan invited us to Grand Isle in mid-April. Although it was a slow weekend for spring migrants, we managed to pick up twenty-two birds for our list, including a Virginia Rail at the Exxon fields that Lynn "whispered" out of the marsh grass lining the ditch. She just "had a feeling" about that corner, so we sat in the truck and waited; within five minutes a rail came out and crept across the gravel road into one of the ditches that lined the grassy fields and marsh area named for the company that used to own them. We left Grand Isle on April 16 with 193 birds on the list. We decided to change our big year goal to 220 birds.

Then came Ed. I had never met Ed Wallace before the spring LOS meeting, when he led a day-long field trip to Cameron Parish hot spots on April 28. When it comes to birds, all I can say is that Ed kicks ass—there's just no other way to put it. Lynn and I stuck close to Ed throughout the day because it was a large group, and you figure out quickly that in a large group, if you can stay close to the guide, you'll see the most birds. Cameron Parish is the most southwestern parish in Louisiana and boasts the highest bird diversity in the state; 404 bird species have been logged in this parish alone.[4]

At midafternoon we drove to Lighthouse Road, two miles from the Texas state line and privately owned by Cheniere Energy. Luckily, the company allows birders onto the property, at least those who have the combination to the access gate. I'd never been on Lighthouse Road before and was amazed at the site after we unlocked the rusty cattle gate and relocked it behind us. The dirt road is so narrow that it's functionally a one-way street, and initially we traveled due east with a tree ridge on the south side of the road and a hill with high grass and thicket to the north. Birds kept flying right in front of us, including Yellow-billed Cuckoos and Scissor-tailed Flycatchers, along with bunches of Indigo Buntings and Common Yellowthroats.

After about a half mile the habitat on both sides of the road opened out into coastal marsh with lots of healthy marsh grass, and to the south bayous and beach flats leading into the Gulf were visible. Lynn immediately began salivating over the bayous, which appeared to be filled with fish (and of course, fishing was strictly off limits). We eventually wound through the coastal marsh, past some mud flats on the right and a levee on the left, and then parked at the end of the road in a makeshift grassy parking lot.

After exiting our vehicles, many participants were interested in the Sabine Pass Lighthouse, abandoned but still standing guard a few hundred yards away. These birders went along with co-leader Linda Stewart Knight to investigate the structure more fully. Ed said, almost to himself, "Well, I'm going to keep birding."

He headed for the high grass and low tree line immediately in front of the parking area, and in the opposite direction of the lighthouse. Lynn and I went with him. While the three of us picked a mini-trail through waist-high grass, we told Ed that we were doing a big year—it was the first time we had said it out loud to anyone other than our nonbirding friends. Ed immediately got excited— "I am keeping a year list too," he told us. "Let's see if we can add anything to y'all's list or mine." We saw a Painted Bunting (old news) and then Ed said, "Do y'all want to see a Western Kingbird?"

"*Yes!*" That was a new bird for our list, and in quick succession we found three. The rest of the birding crew joined us, and we reveled in the kingbirds. At the end of the day with Ed, our list stood at 219 birds. We decided to re-up our big year goal to 240. Best of all, we had Ed on speed dial. He told us that if we needed any advice on finding particular birds, he would be happy to provide it. We took him up on that offer many, many times in the ensuing eight months.

The big year was a joyful undertaking in a global sense, but there were definite high points along the way. My friend Roxanne Dill said, "You were so lucky!" when I relayed the story of how we landed the Glaucous Gull on December 6, at the close of our big year journey. We were in New Orleans chasing the Monk Parakeet, and our quest was going more slowly than anticipated because we thoroughly checked the two places in which we'd seen them in years past and none were there. A quick text to Ed netted us three additional locations in which to search for the bird, and we were closest to City Park, so we headed for Tad Gormley Stadium, where we saw several pairs of Monk Parakeets, one pair per stadium light fixture, each with a nest in the bottom of the fixture structures. While searching, I kept checking my cell phone for LA-BIRD posts, and David Muth posted that he'd just seen a Glaucous Gull at Seabrook, a harbor on the south edge of Lake Pontchartrain, within the city limits of New Orleans. A follow-up email to David clued us in on where to look once we got to Seabrook, and another text to Ed gave us specific directions on how to get there. Between the two of them, we had the Glaucous, a bird I never expected to get, up close and personal less than an hour after David had posted. Also incredibly lucky was the Say's Phoebe we picked up at the very beginning of our big year on December 10 at South Farm. The bird sat in a leafless tree without moving so that we could get the ten-minute-long look necessary to confirm that this was indeed a bird species that we'd only seen in New Mexico before then.

Highway 82 is a picturesque 143-mile two-lane that runs from the Louisiana–Texas state line to Youngsville, just south of Lafayette. Most of the route runs parallel to the Gulf of Mexico and provides access to tiny towns that are largely unknown but legendary for Louisiana birders, including Johnson's Bayou, Cameron, and Holly Beach. The road is fantastic for birding, though not exactly conducive to it; you have to pull off the side of the highway with caution because its shoulders are thin or nonexistent. There is something extra special about the birding immediately to the west of Holly Beach, with beach to the south of the highway and meadow and power line to the north. The area between mile markers 21 and 25 seems to hold an outsized number of birds and rarities, so I nicknamed this stretch of the highway "Four Magic Miles." A lucky for us White-winged Scoter was mixed in with a raft of Lesser Scaup at Four Magic Miles in January.

In addition to the lucky bird sightings were images seared in my memory that I don't think I'll ever forget. Six Swallow-tailed Kites soaring together just as we came off I-510 while headed for Braithwaite in March. Because of their position relative to the raised road, it almost seemed as if our truck was gliding with them, and then, as we descended off the interstate, it was as if all six lifted high on the thermals upon which they were coasting. Donna and Steve tried to get us the Eastern Whip-poor-will twice in their backyard; although we only heard the bird the first time we tried in the spring, we returned at the tail end of our year and they hiked us out to the appointed place where they regularly observed whips. After about twenty minutes of concerted searching, a Whip-poor-will flew clearly into view, landed on a nearby tree branch, and looked down at us. Steve put a spotlight on the bird and it was just gorgeous, an extra special treat for me because I'd heard them my entire life and had never seen one. We had already seen Crested Caracaras twice during our year, but the third one we viewed on the last day of our big year was absolutely majestic. We drove by it perched on a roadside fence post on Fruge Road in southwest Louisiana; as we slowed to watch it, the bird flew low over a field and then perched on a fence post at the back of the field, still very close but with its back to us and looking right at us over its shoulder—the perfect portrait of a perfect species. It was the only time all year I wished I had a camera, to capture its blue-gray beak, red face, and black body.

Our best bird of the year was the Burrowing Owl. Jane Patterson gave us exact—and I mean exact—directions to the Secret Place. We went there on a 3.5-hour-each-way day trip, with seeing the owl as our singular goal. Even with Jane's exact directions, we still had to turn around on Highway 82 a couple of times before we were sure that we had the correct dirt road and cattle gate, approximately nine miles east of the Texas state line. When we pulled up to the trailer check-in point, the woman inside stuck her head out, took one look at us, and said, "Y'all birders" (not a question). When we replied in the affirmative, she waved us through with that look you get sometimes when birding, that "Oh man, are they weird" vibe.

While Jane's directions seemed somewhat unclear in Baton Rouge (follow the oil pipe?), they were perfectly clear and easy to follow once we were at the appointed location. The owl was supposed to be by the first drainpipe under the road just after the oil pipe veered right. We stopped, approached slowly, and looked, but nothing. We then proceeded to the second drainpipe and repeated our careful scan—still nothing. As we scanned the last drainpipe with our binoculars from a distance, I thought I saw the opening of one end of the pipe move. The colors created a brown and green camouflage pattern, but the pattern seemed to move. I kept looking, and all of a sudden what I was seeing became clear. Some grass, some brown-gray feather down—and a big yellow eye!

To get a better angle on the pipe opening, we drove closer, parked, got out our gear, and slowly picked our way across a muddy field filled with suitcase-size cowpatties. Sure enough, when we looked through our binoculars the Burrowing Owl was standing in front of the pipe, a small football with luminous eyes and thick yellow legs. It was absolutely beautiful—neither of us had ever seen a Burrowing Owl before. Lynn queued up the bird in the scope and we observed it up close. The owl seemed to be enjoying the sunny, windy day, its face the picture of contentment while the wind ruffled its feathers. He seemed like a sentry, but a friendly one, as he surveyed his surroundings occasionally by moving only his neck. That owl was breathtaking, as was the entire scene. To the south, we could see the Gulf in the distance, and the windblown landscape made the air seem to shimmer, smelling sweet and clean, surprisingly not like cowpatties. The cows were nearby, feeding contentedly and quietly ignoring us. It felt as if we had dropped into a parallel universe. Perhaps the best thing about birding is being transported absolutely into the moment, in touch with all your senses, out in nature, and in perfect harmony with the earth, the ecosystem, and all its inhabitants. We eventually packed up and left, watching for the Harris's Sparrows that Jane had told us about, although they were not at the appointed location.

We did pick up the Brewer's Blackbird, the only time we would see these all year. We never did get a Harris's Sparrow.

Our most magical birding day of the year was April 29, the day after the LOS spring meeting, when Ed led us and we added seventeen new birds to our list. We spent the night before in the Cameron Motel, and in the morning we decided to see if we could pick up a couple of birds based on tidbits we'd gotten the previous day. During the LOS field trip, Ed had taken the group to the Cameron jetty to look for the Long-tailed Duck that had been seen there, and though we added Whimbrel and Clapper Rail to our list, the duck was nowhere to be found. This next day, we drove the five minutes from the hotel to the jetty and headed for the observation area with our scope. Luckily for us, there were about ten birders already at the jetty and almost as many scopes available. Someone sighted the duck not even five minutes after we arrived. What had been an unsuccessful quest for a target species the day before turned into an easy "get" the very next morning.

During the LOS field trip, Lynn overheard two birders talking about how someone had seen a Purple Gallinule at Lacassine NWR, so we decided that we'd try for that bird while making a few strategic stops on the way. We went to Peveto Woods Sanctuary first, just on the chance it had new goodies for us, and as luck would have it, we both got a fantastic look at a Lesser Nighthawk. The day before, both Lesser and Common Nighthawks had been spotted in the forty-acre oak chenier.[5] We had turned a trail corner and Lynn had gotten a great look at what she was sure was a Lesser Nighthawk; Ed had gotten a quick look, but not good enough to tell which species. Another birder with a strong vantage point like Lynn said that it was indeed a Lesser Nighthawk. I was behind Lynn and Ed, and all I saw was a brown streak. I couldn't even tell it was a nighthawk, so it didn't count for our list. On our April 29 trip, we were in the same vicinity as the day before when a nighthawk darted out of the low branch of a tree and flew absolutely clearly in a large, sweeping S-pattern before hiding in another tree. This time, we both got great looks at it, and its color and the placement of the cream-colored bar adjacent to the bird's wingtips made both of us confident in the identification of this bird as a Lesser Nighthawk. It wasn't even 10:00 A.M. and we already had two new list birds, and lifers (birds we observed for the first time ever), for the day.

We then headed for Lacassine NWR via Turf Grass Road. We'd stopped at Turf Grass on Friday on our way down to Cameron and had seen an Upland Sandpiper. I thought I had also seen a Buff-breasted Sandpiper; I watched through the scope as one hopped away from me and then down into a rut in one of the turfgrass fields, but it never came back out. Lynn hadn't seen the bird, and I didn't claim a positive ID since I only saw the back and wanted a better look at it from other angles. I called out our intention to see the Buff-breasted Sandpiper as we drove down Turf Grass Road toward the grass fields. It took a little searching, but after seeing several more Upland Sandpipers and a passel of Black-bellied Plovers, we scoped a Buff-breasted Sandpiper, and it gave us plenty of angles from which to view it. We did the "new lifer bird dance," packed it in, and headed for a specific part of Lacassine NWR called Pool Unit D. This portion of the NWR is a famous bird magnet, sporting wetlands, coastal marshes, large expanses of shallow water, an observation tower, and several hundred yards of tree line in various places around the unit. A drive through this three-mile area netted us six Purple Gallinules.

We had enough time to hike the wooded trail on the east side of the refuge, which was, unlike the rest of the day, pretty dull in terms of birds. We observed the usual suspects—cardinals, Carolina Wrens, and one incessantly calling male Painted Bunting—but we hiked almost the entire trail with few birds. We were one hundred yards from the end of the trail when I heard a bird moving in the underbrush; we stopped and crept forward stealthily to see if we could locate it. The bird popped up from the ground, landed on a low branch, and sat in the open without moving. It was an Ovenbird, a species that I had searched for in vain for years and had never seen. My searches for the Ovenbird always seemed to yield Hooded Warblers and Louisiana and Northern Waterthrushes, but never the Ovenbird. And here it perched, showing off.

We headed home and then took the Whiskey Bay exit, in the heart of the Atchafalaya basin, with enough daylight left to ride up Highway 975 and get out and walk at several strategic locations along the tree-lined gravel road; in an hour we had added the Yellow-breasted Chat and Tennessee and Kentucky Warblers to our list. On April 29, it seemed as if every bird we sought we found, and we didn't have to work hard at all—they seemed to come to us instead of the other way around. Even the relatively quiet woods in Lacassine yielded a long sought-after bird. It was a most awesome day in every sense of the word.

A couple weeks later we were also lucky enough to hit a "fallout," a phenomenon in which bad weather will stop the flights of migrating birds, which will land until weather improves. If they experience such weather while migrating over water, birds will stop at the first land they encounter. Because many birds migrate simultaneously, fallouts represent a great opportunity to see lots of birds in a concentrated area. Strong storms in southwest Louisiana on May 12 and into the morning of May 13 created conditions that we thought would be excellent for birding, so we headed for Peveto on the morning of the 13th. As soon as we entered the woods we got a Blue-headed Vireo, a bird we had missed to that point. It was a good omen. Droves of Swainson's Thrushes bunched low around the trees, and we added that bird to our list as well. As we moved farther into the woods, we ran into two young men who were stoked because they'd seen a Yellow-green Vireo—they'd also seen Bay-breasted and Blackburnian Warblers in specific trees that they pointed out to us. We tackled the trees and finally got an American Redstart (I'd seen one during the spring LOS trip but Lynn had not) and a Chestnut-sided Warbler. Although we missed the Yellow-green Vireo and both warbler species mentioned by the birders, Peveto was vireo heaven for us because we finally "cleaned up" on them by getting Philadelphia, Warbling, Yellow-throated, and Red-eyed in quick succession (I'd seen the latter the month before in the Atchafalaya, but Lynn hadn't). Yellow-billed Cuckoos were *everywhere*. It seemed like someone had opened a faucet of them in the woods.

We left after a couple of hours to try some beach locations for species like Black Tern, American Oystercatcher, and Snowy Plover. Although we didn't get any of these, Lynn had a chance to fish on Holly Beach, where we picked up Common Nighthawk as two were chasing each other up and down the beach, calling the entire time. The fishing wasn't great, and after another couple of hours we decided to hit Peveto one more time to see if we could pick up anything else before heading for the long ride home.

The faucet was still spewing Yellow-billed Cuckoos and now Black-and-white Warblers as well. We went back to the appointed warbler trees and after some searching located a Bay-breasted Warbler. The male was so colorful that I got goose bumps while watching him. We kept on searching for the Blackburnian, challenged by twilight, when we finally, finally saw one. I had never seen a Blackburnian Warbler before; they look like tiny fireballs or mini-tigers with wings. We decided to call it quits after that, almost tripping over more Swainson's Thrushes as we left. This was our best day at Peveto. We added fifteen new birds to our list and were at 244, once again eclipsing our new goal. Lynn and I decided to up the ante to our final target of 275 birds.

The best birding trip of our year was to Grand Isle on July 1. This was not the best trip because of the birds or the weather, which was hot, hot, hot. Ed had come down with his son, Sean, to meet us. He was looking for a Grand Isle rarity like a Shiny Cowbird or a Gray Kingbird. We birded throughout the morning with Joan, finding nothing we didn't already have. Joe and Joan had generously offered to take all of us out on their boat, so at mid-morning we quit land birding and took to the water. Joe had recently seen American Oystercatchers on islands out in the Gulf while fishing, so he took us out to see the bird, which we needed. The boat provided a welcome respite from the oppressive heat, and although we saw lots of gulls and terns, the tide was high and the oystercatchers were nowhere to be found because their sand and oyster bars were covered with water. I was disappointed, because I never tired of seeing these crow-sized, boldly patterned, high contrast black-and-white shorebirds with bright orange bills. Nationally renowned shorebird expert Kevin Karlson once described the American Oystercatcher as "The bird wearing a tuxedo and smoking a carrot."[6] These birds were not hard to miss if present, but their presence proved fleeting.

After the boat ride, the group (sans Joe) headed back to the woods to bird, and at about 2:00 in the afternoon we overheated to the point that we were finished. As we were leaving the woods, Lynn and I flushed out a bird that Ed saw behind us. He located the bird, and although it was a quick look, we all saw the Yellow-throated Warbler, which we didn't have to that point; it was our first new bird of the day. Ed didn't get a bird that day. We said our goodbyes, and Lynn and I headed back to Joan and Joe's and the air-conditioning. We packed up to head home and decided to hit Elmer's Island Wildlife Refuge, a stretch of beach across Caminada Pass just southwest of Grand Isle, before leaving—maybe we could get the Snowy Plover that had eluded us to this point. Although I didn't know it, July 1 would be the last time we were on Elmer's Island in 2012 because recurring oil slicks from the BP oil spill on April 20, 2011, shut the beach intermittently for the rest of the year, and it was closed each time we returned.

We birded the marshes and mudflats up the gravel road toward the beach from our truck, and then the beach itself; along the way we saw plenty of Black-bellied Plovers and Laughing Gulls, but no Snowy Plovers. We made it out to the end of the beach, and Lynn turned the truck around toward home. There were six or seven people hanging out on a spit of beach at the end of the line. Lynn stopped the truck and said, "That woman looks a little upset."

The woman looked okay to me. I was ready to get on the road and go home with our one new bird for the day (which was starting to feel like a major accomplishment), but Lynn stopped the truck, rolled down the window, and listened. The woman who seemed upset to Lynn and not to me was talking to a guy with a kayak, and then she saw us stopped and walked over. Lynn was right, the woman was crying when she reached our truck.

"My boyfriend," she said, "we were standing in the water together, and it wasn't even that deep, I mean, I was only up to my knees, but the water was pulling so hard. I looked over to tell him that I wasn't comfortable and wanted to go back to shore, but he was gone, just gone, and now we can't find him."

"How long has he been gone?" Lynn asked.

"About 20 minutes."

Lynn and I immediately got out of the truck and joined the other folks who were looking out over the water, including the kayaker, who was ready to launch, but who didn't have a direction in which to paddle for a rescue. It was easy to see the rip currents, because at this spit of beach two different water streams were coming together—the fast current flowing outward was evident, and I followed its direction from the brown, shallow water out to deep blue. Lynn and I were armed with one thing that the other searchers were not: binoculars. We scoured the water for a couple of minutes. I was starting to lose hope when I saw the man come up out of the water—he seemed to be calling and one arm was raised up high for us to see. He was bobbing in the water, just beyond the rip current, and he was way out, so far out that he couldn't be seen with the naked eye.

I screamed—I screamed like I haven't since I was a kid—I think I screamed louder than I ever have in my life. "*I GOT HIM!*"

I kept one hand steady on my binoculars so that I wouldn't lose him in my field of vision, and I lined up my other arm in a direct path so that the kayaker could see where I was pointing. He launched immediately and started paddling out to save the guy. But the guy was clearly not in control out there—he slipped back under the water and I couldn't find him. Lynn was standing next to me, and

I told her that I'd lost him. We both kept looking, and a minute later it was Lynn screaming, as loudly as I just had, *"THERE HE IS!"* Her arm was pointing two degrees south of mine, and when I followed her arm and refocused my gaze, he was back on the surface of the water, obviously tired and fighting to stay afloat.

The kayaker kept looking at Lynn's arm and mine and after a few minutes was more than halfway out to the guy when three jet skiers entered the picture. They were barreling toward where the guy flailed in the water but clearly were not aware of his presence there, and no wonder. Why would any swimmer be four hundred yards offshore in an area where only boats and jet skis would venture? Everyone on the beach screamed at the jet skiers, but they were so far away and their motors so loud that they couldn't hear us, despite the fact that we made quite a sound, the six or seven of us keening into the wind, trying in vain for our collective voices to carry across the water.

The kayaker saved the day, and probably the guy, at this point. He paddled furiously until the jet skiers got critically close to the guy, and then he held his paddle in the air and pumped it, trying to get the attention of the jet skiers. Lynn and I watched breathlessly through our binoculars as the jet skiers got close to the guy, but not close enough that they saw him (or ran over him). After about thirty seconds, one of the jet skiers saw the kayaker. He signaled to the other two skiers and all three rode slowly toward the kayaker, who by this point was pointing at the flailing guy. One jet skier finally saw the guy and carefully drove over to him. The kayaker kept coming and eventually reached the wayward swimmer, who was so tired that it took a good five minutes for the jet skier and the kayaker to help the guy out of the water and onto the jet ski. The guy's girlfriend was right next to me and kept asking, "What's happening?" I gave her the blow-by-blow, that they had him and that he was okay, but I didn't want to give her my binoculars until the guy was actually safely on the jet ski; he was so tired that he fell off twice.

When he finally got situated on the jet ski, I handed the woman my binoculars so that she could watch him being driven in. Her breath had quit hitching by the time the craft and its two passengers reached the shore. She handed back my binoculars and went to meet him in the water. He walked out and hugged her, clearly exhausted, but also clearly okay. The kayaker made it back to shore and we got into the truck to leave. As we did so, one of the girl's friends came over to our truck. "Thanks," she said. And that was that. We left the beach, no Snowy Plovers on the way in and none on the way out.

I think a lot about communities and the way that each of us is a member of many different communities. On the beach that day, we were members of an impromptu community, one in which the chips were down and a life was on the line. We didn't know each other, but that didn't matter, because relationships weren't the point. We had among us the equipment and tools necessary to save the guy—the girlfriend, who was thoughtful enough to recruit other people on the beach to assist, the kayaker, and us, who just happened to be there in hopes of a Snowy Plover.

Lynn was astute enough to recognize that the woman was upset. If it had been me driving the truck, I would have kept going. I like to think that on July 1 this couple of bird nerds and our binoculars helped to save a guy's life, and that in essence it was a bird, the elusive Snowy Plover, that helped to save the guy too. That was our best birding trip. We didn't successfully sight the plover, but we sighted the victim of a riptide, and because of the collective action of an impromptu community on the beach, he was ultimately the survivor of a riptide.

* * * * *

There were many joyful parts of our big year, but also some notably not so joyful parts. For example, deerflies. I recognize the importance of biodiversity and the fact that all native species in an ecosystem have an important niche, but I find it really, really hard to appreciate deerflies. They are formidable creatures that pack a punch of misery completely out of proportion to their small stature. Bug spray simply does not work on them—doesn't slow them one iota. Additionally, they are adept at finding the only uncovered skin you have and biting you silly, and trying to cover yourself entirely in the summer months when they are at their zenith is uncomfortable to start with. Deerflies cut short two of our Peveto trips and made several others distinctly uncomfortable.

We had nemesis birds, those we searched for high and low but never found. One notable nemesis was the Wood Thrush. It seemed that getting this bird should have been easy. We got the more difficult to find Gray-cheeked Thrush, but not the Wood Thrush. Wood Thrushes were sighted in Peveto the same day we were in the woods in both spring and fall, and we didn't see them either time. We took a trip to the Atchafalaya basin in early June just to get this bird. Maybe we were too late in the morning (8:00 A.M.), but we hiked into the woods in at least four different places, played the Wood Thrush call, got immediate, multiple callbacks from Wood Thrushes at all locations, but no bird came close enough to observe.

Our other nemesis bird was the Snowy Plover. The bird that helped to save the guy caught in the riptide was nowhere to be found. What made this failure extra hard to accept was the fact that I saw it every time I went to Dauphin Island, Alabama. We own a small condo on Dauphin Island that is about a five-minute walk from the beach, and every time I birded the beach I saw at least one, and frequently several. The Snowy Plover almost felt like a yard bird in Alabama, they were so common. That's a great thing to be able to say about a near-threatened species, but it made for a frustrating bird in Louisiana.

Then there was the bird that made me feel like a loser: the House Wren. In the wintertime in Louisiana, and somewhat into the spring, almost every trip checklist includes at least one House Wren—and why not? Although they frequently take cover in thickets, House Wrens are so loud that they're easy to find, and they're not overly shy. They will leave cover to investigate pishing, which is a noise that you make with your mouth to entice birds to show themselves. It sounds like the word "pish" and says to birds, "Hey, come check me out!" Occasionally, House Wrens sit out to sing and chatter. Once you get into October, the bird once again starts showing up on almost every list. We missed this bird in our frequent travels, we missed it all winter and all spring, although we got it on Dauphin Island in April and in mid-October. I finally, finally saw one on Recovery Road, a remote, bird-filled strip of asphalt off Highway 90 and across the street from the Ridge Trail of Bayou Sauvage NWR, but Lynn missed it (it was a very quick flit in between branches within a thicket). I heaved a huge sigh of relief when, on October 21, we got one after someone posted that they saw a House Wren on the walking path near the Pennington Biomedical Research Center on Perkins Road in Baton Rouge. We drove all over the state of Louisiana without seeing the House Wren, and finally got the bird forty-eight days before the end of our big year about two miles from where we live. Interestingly, we saw House Wrens several times after that, but it sure took a long time to sight that initial individual.

Of course, there had to be birds Lynn saw that I didn't, and birds I saw that Lynn didn't. One time we pulled in to Peveto, and nature called, so Lynn stopped for me at the Porta Potty and birded for not even two minutes without me. When I exited the Porta Potty, she told me to double-time over to the scrubby area where she was standing. As soon as I did, the bird dipped and I had missed a Canada Warbler. She also had a quick look at a Blue-winged Warbler at Peveto that I missed. What can I say? She has better eyes and a bigger bladder than me. Early one morning when she was near her school in rural Darrow, Louisiana, she saw an Eastern Screech-Owl.

I had two birds that Lynn didn't. I had a conference in Houston in late February, and I stopped at the Turf Grass Road area on the drive over to see if I could locate the two rare birds that everyone on LA-BIRD was talking about on Miller Oilfield Road: the Lark Bunting and the Green-tailed Towhee. Even though they wouldn't count for our year list, I had never seen either species in the state and was thus interested in locating them. I was the only vehicle around for miles and was birding my way over to the third telephone pole from the intersection of Oilfield Road and Miller Oilfield Road when a vehicle came up behind me. The driver was Christine Kooi, whom I knew from birding and from LSU. We headed for the appointed telephone pole together, and after just a few minutes of watching a bunch of Savannah Sparrows, out popped the Green-tailed Towhee. We stayed a little longer for the bunting, but Christine had to head back to Baton Rouge and I decided to try to find huge, mixed flocks of blackbirds in hopes of locating a Yellow-headed Blackbird. I drove around for forty-five minutes and was successful in locating two large blackbird flocks, but no Yellow-headed Blackbird. I headed back to the telephone pole once more before getting back on the road for Houston. This time the Green-tailed Towhee was gone, but the Lark Bunting came out of the bushes after just a couple of minutes.

During our big year, we also had some not so good luck. When a Ruff was reported on Illinois Plant Road, just North of Lacassine NWR, on July 28, we went searching for it the very next day. All we found was Ed, Sean, and two other birders who had been looking for the bird unsuccessfully for three hours. We all continued to search in vain for the Ruff, which was spotted by another birder on Illinois Plant Road the next day, and then no one saw it again the rest of the year.

We had a weekend trip planned to Cameron in late August and got all the way to Peveto woods in driving rain before making the decision to reverse direction and go straight to Dauphin Island, because Hurricane Isaac was coming and we needed to prepare. We didn't even exit the truck to bird. For half of our big year, remnants of the BP oil spill shut Elmer's Island, which is excellent habitat for seeing the Snowy Plover. On our last day of searching, we were barred from Lighthouse Road by a security guard, limiting our opportunities for spotting this bird.

During the fall LOS meeting, Ed was leading a group of us in Peveto when Jane Patterson called, "Marybeth, BT Green!" from a few hundred feet away. Lynn and I peeled away from the group and for a few minutes joined Jane, Christine, and Melanie Driscoll as we watched a particularly cooperative Black-throated Green Warbler work the trees in front of us. I was very excited to get this bird, which had managed to elude us until this point. When we re-joined Ed, he told us that the entire group had seen an Ash-throated Flycatcher, another bird that we were missing. Ed kindly spent an extra thirty minutes in Peveto trying to re-locate it for us, but it never appeared again. We took another couple of cracks at finding the Ash-throated Flycatcher on Recovery Road late in the year but were thwarted by duck hunting season. Trigger-happy hunters, including an approximately eleven-year-old boy toting a fully automatic rifle, walked right by us on the road and proceeded to fire more than fifty rounds so close to us that there was nary a bird to be found. We left the woods quickly that day and never did find an Ash-throated Flycatcher.

The most embarrassing moment of the big year occurred in September in

Cameron. We had stopped at the Shell station to gas up the truck, and I got the pump started and then went upstairs to get drinks. I was so enthralled with my Gatorade that I forgot to remove the nozzle from the gas tank. We were reminded quickly when we pulled away from the gas station and heard a loud crash. We both jumped out of the vehicle immediately; Lynn grabbed the gas hose and folded it hard to stanch the flow of gasoline while I made a mad dash upstairs to get the attendant. The dispenser had actually detached from the hose and I was envisioning an expensive repair, but the attendant screwed the nozzle back onto the hose while Lynn had her finger on a temporary shut off valve and I held the hose. We stunk like the Indy 500 but only had to pay for the extra gas that had flowed out of the hose. Oops!

* * * * *

We started our big year on December 9, 2011, and finished on December 8, 2012. During this 365-day span, we took sixty-one trips in the state and put 11,626 miles on our truck. We spent $2,616 on gas, including the extra $25 that came from the broken nozzle. The most birds we added to our list on a single day was fifty-six, on the first day of our big year. The fewest we added during a trip was zero, and that happened on eleven trips, including our longest dry streak of five consecutive trips with no birds: between the King Rail we saw in our kayaks on the south shore of Lake Pontchartrain on September 9 and the Wilson's Warbler spotted on Recovery Road on October 5.

The big year taught me a lot about a lot of things. First and foremost, it taught me a ton about birds. I joked with Lynn at the start our big year that she'd know everything I knew within six months. I suspect that this actually happened; however, I doubled my own knowledge between day one and day 365. Getting out there often is everything. While it's great to do research and play probability as much as possible, if you get out a lot, eventually you can luck into something occasional or even rare. If you think you don't know enough about birds to try a big year, I highly recommend doing one anyway. In the end, it really doesn't matter how far you get. The best thing about the big year as I look back on it now is not the number of species we saw. It's all the awesome memories I compiled and things I learned along the way.

We didn't learn that three hundred birds was the minimum target number of a big year in Louisiana until we were partway through. I thought that if we ever did one again, and I suspected that we would, we would start with the goal of three hundred. I asked Lynn what she would have done differently, and she answered, "We shouldn't have said, 'Well, we'll get the bird later.' Stay and get it *now*." It was easy to do that in April and June when we were searching for birds like the Wood Thrush—we'll get it later, we said. In that case and a couple of notable others, we never did.

Next time, we'd go to north Louisiana for some birds that seem relatively straightforward, such as the White-breasted Nuthatch and Lapland Longspur. We didn't bird north of Krotz Springs all year long and in effect did a big year in the southern half of the state. Because we weren't on LA-BIRD from day one, we missed out on chasing any "presents" courtesy of the Christmas Bird Count. And although I intended to book a charter boat to get some pelagic species off the coast of Louisiana, I was busy enough with work during the late summer and fall that I let that opportunity pass us by. I'm thinking that such a trip would have netted us at least three extra species.

I learned to never give up on a bird. Joan and Joe took us out for the American Oystercatcher on their boat a second time in November, and we still didn't find one. On our last weekend, we headed for Cameron with visions of Snowy Plovers, oystercatchers, and gannets dancing in our heads. Hours before we left, Joe and Joan texted us to tell us that they had just seen a pair of oystercatchers at their boat slip and invited us to come chase them for this last weekend in our year. They also offered up the boat too, in case the birds had moved on from the boat slip. We stuck with our original plan of Cameron, thinking that some of the other species we were still chasing would be more probable there, such as the Ash-throated Flycatcher, Black Scoter, Common Goldeneye, and Long-billed Curlew.

We searched high and low all day for something new, anything new, and found nothing. We birded Four Magic Miles and then headed farther down Highway 82 toward the Texas state line. After being thwarted by the security guard at

Lighthouse Road, Lynn remembered Ed saying that the only place he'd ever seen oystercatchers in Louisiana was the marshy area and shell bars along the road just inside the Louisiana state line. We continued west, and with the bridge to Texas upon us and about an hour of daylight left, Lynn looked to the south and said, "Hmm, I think I see a black and white bird the right size in the distance."

She pulled over to the side of the road, queued up the scope, looked into it, and started dancing. I looked and sure enough, a pair sat on a shell bar, right near an avocet. We had chased the American Oystercatcher all year long—we saw it a dozen times on Dauphin Island, but not in all the time we looked in southwest Louisiana or on Grand Isle. The oystercatcher was the only new bird we added on the last day of our big year, but a very apropos, almost nemesis bird, and our 280th species.

I learned that there are wild places in Louisiana, places with no restaurants within a twenty-five-mile radius, a fact I found quite comforting. I also learned that while birding, one can build up an appetite, an appetite that peanut butter sandwiches, fruit, and snacks cannot satisfy. When this happens, a Hunt Brothers pizza, baked while you wait at most rural gas stations in Louisiana, tastes better than any gourmet meal.

I've learned that in some cases perspective is everything. For example, in September my cousin's son took me birding for the afternoon in Massachusetts at Horseneck Beach, where he'd been a lifeguard that summer. On the ride to the beach we passed twelve Wild Turkeys feeding together in the grass immediately adjacent to the road.

"Oh, it's turkeys," Roger uttered with disdain.

I was thrilled. South Louisiana doesn't have many turkeys, with the exception of those in the Atchafalaya basin. Even there, turkeys are not easy to find because they can spread out across the basin's 931 square miles with almost no road access. The Atchafalaya is so wild that the original 1917 movie *Tarzan of the Apes* was filmed there, and an urban legend persists that some of the monkeys and apes used during this film escaped and that it is possible to run into their descendants in the Atchafalaya today.[7] I suspect another reason that we don't see turkeys often is that turkey hunting is one of the reasons that Louisiana is considered a Sportsman's Paradise. I have seen a turkey exactly once in Louisiana in all my years of birding. When Lynn was fishing on a bridge in the Atchafalaya NWR, one flew low over the Little Alabama River and landed about fifty feet from us. We enjoyed watching him walk around among the trees, close to the river bank, as the sun went down and dusk approached. After ten or fifteen minutes, it flew on. Other than that brief summer encounter, that was it. So for me, one turkey was a treat, and twelve was a major gift.

"So, you see turkeys often?" I asked Roger.

"All the time," was his grim reply.

We reached the beach shortly after encountering the turkeys. While walking across the sand, Roger pointed and asked, "What kind of bird is that?"

When I told him it was a Great Black-backed Gull, he said, "My friends and I call that bird the kingpin."

"Why?"

"Because we think it's the best looking bird on the beach."

A couple of months later, my friend Roxanne talked about the gull that scared the living daylights out of her and her daughter and son-in-law while they were visiting Ireland.

"It's this huge, mean-looking gull that seems like it could tear you to pieces," is how she described it. "It tried to break into our place." When I showed her a picture of the Great Black-backed Gull, she screamed, "Oh, that's it, that's the scary bird!"

In these cases, whether the turkey is a gift or a trash bird, or whether the Great Black-backed Gull is a predator or the best looking bird on the beach, is just a matter of perspective.

Finally, I learned more about the wonderful community of birders in the state of Louisiana. Phil Stouffer, a man I knew previously only in a work context at LSU, is also a sparrow expert. He gave us several surefire locations for birds like Henslow's and LeConte's Sparrows, places where they were the only sparrows present, which made identification more straightforward. He also did his best to send us to locations likely for birds we didn't have on our list. Without ever meeting me, Dennis Demcheck gave me directions to his house, his cell phone number, his home phone number, and access to his backyard to see the Broad-tailed Hummingbird spending the winter there, just because I asked. Steve and Donna let us crash their yard three times and provided guided tours through it, which resulted in six of their yard birds on our year list; they also organized the Yellow Rails and Rice Festival, which allowed us to add Sprague's Pipit, Yellow Rail, and Swainson's Hawk. Jane Patterson got us the Calliope Hummingbird, the Burrowing Owl, and the Black-throated Green Warbler. And of course, Ed Wallace helped us put about twenty-five birds on our list.

I experienced birding in a lot of contexts in 2012. Mostly it was for the sheer fun of it; Lynn and I had a lot of laughs and were in awe of nature many times. Other times it was serious, like during the riptide. In every context, birding provided that "in the moment" connection to nature that is ultimately life-affirming, a natural resonance that rings true through heart and soul.

* * * * *

Lynn kept telling me throughout 2012 that once our big year was finished I would continue the pace at which we'd been birding. I told her that I wouldn't because it was too consuming. It turns out that we were both right. Although I haven't birded at the same frequency since the big year, I bird a lot more than I did before the undertaking and with more passion than ever. So, here I perch today; I experienced the process of listing toward listing, and I now embrace my fully developed lister, bird nerd self. You might wonder what a lister is. The concept is explained well by my LSU colleague Carol O'Neil, who served as a graduate teaching assistant in ornithology at the University of Arizona in Tucson, a birding mecca if there ever was one.

"Oh, so you're a lister?" she said when I talked about a big day trip. She asked this question in the same tone as when she said in a previous conversation, "So you're a taster?" The answer is yes, I'm a taster. I don't like bitter foods. I hate collard greens and mustard greens, and I put Splenda on my corn bread—to which any self-respecting southerner would say, "Oh, bless her heart," in the tone reserved for those beyond help. I get that tone a lot when I talk about birds now. And yes, I'm a lister, a birder who keeps lists of birds. I have my life list, two state lists (Louisiana and Alabama), individual parish lists, and specific location lists. I have a list of all the birds I've seen in my yard, and I keep a list of North American birds that is important to me because my goal is to see seven hundred.

I will drop everything whenever possible to chase a relative rarity or a bird I haven't seen. For this behavior, I endure good-natured teasing from my friend Carol Lee Moore, who always says, "I don't understand what the sport is when someone else reports a bird somewhere in the state and you jump in the truck and go to see it. Why do you get so excited about that? You didn't discover it, you're coming behind everyone. And you need exact directions to get there—I mean really, where's the sport in *that*? I can kind of understand if you find the rare bird and report it to everyone else, but this chasing stuff that people have already seen—it's easier than an Easter egg hunt."

On the other end of the spectrum, I endure genuine but somewhat misplaced matriarchal adoration regarding my birding ability. I have a realistic sense of my birding skill; I'm decent but not even close to great. I want to be scary good, but sometimes I'm just scary. I once thought that a juvenile robin was a rare bird I had never seen before, even as Lynn rolled her eyes and kept telling me, "Baby robin!" In early morning light I once identified a flyover House Sparrow as a Vermilion Flycatcher. I miscalled a long-tailed Northern Mockingbird as a Scissor-tailed Flycatcher, and three hours later I called a short-tailed scissor-tail a mockingbird. These are just a few in a miles-long list of mistaken calls on my part. Misidentifications are great because I make every attempt to learn from them, but I still have holes in my knowledge. Not according to my momma, though. If I call Cooper's Hawk, she waxes poetic about my ability to tell one apart from a Sharp-shinned Hawk, every time. If we are in the woods together and I identify a Great Crested Flycatcher from its "wheep" call, she vociferously compliments "my amazing ear." The call of the Great Crested Flycatcher is distinctive and easy to learn even if you are not a birder. No matter. When my mom believes something, she believes it with every fiber of her being. Momma thinks I'm great birder. And that is that.

I try really hard not to think about the birds I missed identifying as a kid in Nashua, New Hampshire, because I am confident that Common Redpolls, Hoary Redpolls, and Pine Grosbeaks were among the birds that came to the picnic table to feed in our backyard. At this moment, those species are not on my life list. I try not to think about all the birds I missed in Massachusetts, and all the times I've been whale watching and noticed seabirds with funny-looking hooked beaks hanging around our boat. Or the two trips I took to the Tucson area before I became a birder, not to mention trips to Seattle, west Texas, Oregon, and Minnesota.

I used to run marathons and was struck by a comment that someone once made about running them—that it's one of the only sporting events in which Olympic athletes run the same race with everyday folks who are just trying to finish, and how it's a wonderful thing that so many people with the same interest can participate together in the same event, even if their talent level is vastly different. Birding is like that too. Whether you are a backyard birder, a beginner, a casual birder, or an ornithologist—even if you're not a birder at all, but interested in the topic—no matter what level, it's your love of the activity that binds you together. The birders in this state, from bare-bones beginners to among the best ornithologists in the world, comprise an absolutely amazing community.

There is cooperation and competition, lifer dances, the elation of finding rare birds, and the crush when you miss them. There are nemesis birds, embarrassing misidentifications, and the need for photographic proof. Somewhere in this roiling confluence of birders, place, and birds, the center of my heart sings with utter abandon.

FOR THE LOVE OF IT

"When you go out and look at birds, what are you looking at? Why do you like it? Is it the colors of the birds?" My friend Tee Knight asked the questions that nonbirders ask me most.

"Well, you certainly see the colors of the birds, but I like to hear their calls and watch what they do. Take Brown Pelicans—yes, I see them frequently, but they do so many things. They glide up in the air a few at a time in long lines or in V-formation, or they dive bomb into the water and then sit on the water's surface and eat the fish they bombed for; other times, they fly in low straight lines, barely over the waves. They're really fun to watch. Sometimes I'll be watching and something completely unexpected will happen. Once I was watching a Brown Pelican sitting on the water and a gull came down and landed on its head! And the pelican didn't mind, it just sat there on the water's surface, completely happy to swim around with another bird perched on its head. I am not sure if I can completely explain it; birding just makes me really happy."

Tee was nodding, "Okay, I think I got you. I do the same thing myself. I man watch! And it's not a lustful thing, it's just me sitting around and watching the men go by. And I might think to myself, oh, that's a beautiful shirt he's wearing, or look at the way his chest shows through that T-shirt, or wow, he's got such a pretty nose—the way you might say a bird has a pretty beak."

Parallels between birding and man-watching notwithstanding, the confluence of adventure, exploration, challenge, people, nature, song, and place make birding alluring to me. And I am not alone. In Louisiana, the reasons that people bird are many, and the ways in which they bird are memorable. The state vernacular includes the word lagniappe, which means a little extra for free. Louisiana birding lagniappe takes many forms.

For example, I've never had a cup of coffee with Steve and Donna, but I know that they drink creamer in their coffee—lots of it—and that they've been drinking coffee for a long time. I know that because red caps from Nestle's coffee creamer bottles are everywhere in their yard. It's hard to believe that hundreds of red coffee tops could look like art, but in Donna and Steve's yard the caps are arranged so that they blend in with the diverse plant life at the same time they scream out to hummingbirds, "food *here*." Steve and Donna surround with creamer caps every one of the dozen-plus hummingbird feeders in the yard, as well as every hummingbird friendly plant. The patterns are swirly and lead to the center of a circle where the feeder is, almost like a logarithmic spiral. Fly down the wormhole and you will reach Steve and Donna's version of Hummer in Wonderland. This lagniappe effort on their part brings the hummingbirds.

A visit to their yard in the wintertime, like the one Lynn and I took during our Louisiana big year, will typically yield four species of hummingbirds: hearty overwintering Ruby-throated, Buff-bellied, Rufous, and Black-chinned Hummingbirds. Occasionally they get a Broad-tailed or Calliope. Most hummers that show up in the yard are banded[1] and given a name. Each year, Steve and Donna choose a theme, and then choose names that pertain to that theme, starting with *A* and proceeding down the alphabet as the birds present themselves.

Some birders are driven by a love of sound. Terry Davis is one such birder. He has discovered a number of new bird species in the Shreveport area in the northwest corner of Louisiana. As a birder with a highly talented ear, Terry spent many an hour listening to recordings of birds, learning not just the eastern species that tend to dominate our state, but some of the western species as well. He then carefully and regularly drove every roadway in the area with his windows down, listening to whatever was there. In the process, Terry found that though a rare occurrence, western species of birds, like Cassin's Sparrow, Gray Flycatcher, and Dusky-capped Flycatcher, sneak into the Ark-La-Tex region, including the northwestern corner of Louisiana.

Terry's love of sound is not confined to just listening to birds. He likes to record bird songs for inclusion on xeno-canto, a website where birders can share their recordings. Terry's passion for collecting sound was evident during a winter LOS meeting in Shreveport, in which he was the leader for a field trip at the Shreveport airport. His travels in locating various birds had led him to the airport. (He had a friend who worked there and who negotiated with officials to allow Terry access to the airport fields, far enough away from the runways to be safe for him and the passengers, but within the bounds of the airport itself.) Terry had discovered winter flocks of Smith's Longspurs in those fields and was leading an LOS field trip to see them in the only location in the state known to contain Smith's on a regular basis.

The twenty or so of us, including me, Lynn, and my mom, caravanned to a staff entrance to the airport, where we each showed identification to enter and were given an appointed location in which to park. Terry's airport employee friend was sick, so another airport employee named Daniel accompanied us to make sure that we didn't wander into restricted territory. Daniel was not a birder. He was friendly, but it was clear that he thought we were all weird, a feeling that seemed to increase as the afternoon went on.

Terry was excited and immediately set out toward the last place he had seen the Smith's Longspurs; we walked about a third of a mile to get to the appointed field, stopping along the way to observe Savannah and LeConte's Sparrows. The grass fields were not overgrown, but it was tough walking because the ground was pockmarked and uneven. Once we reached the right field, Terry organized us into a single line with about twenty feet between each of us. Our job was to step slowly and deliberately across the field, at the same speed, in a single line. The configuration reminded me of something I'd see on TV in which volunteers search a natural area for a body. Lucky for us, we were after live birds and not dead humans.

Before we set off on our journey across the field together, Terry explained that Smith's Longspurs typically spend time in flocks and that when disturbed they call while rising up out of the grass, fly in large circles overhead, often still calling, and then drop precipitously back into the grass as a group, usually near the spot from which they took flight. If we were able to locate a flock of the long-spurs, he said, we should be able to engage them a number of times so that every-one could get a look at them, which was not easy because of their tendency to hunker down in the grass when grounded and their constant movement when in flight. With these instructions and explanations, we were off. I had Lynn to my right and Ed Wallace to my left. Collectively, we were an impressive sight, with the group of us able to traverse an approximately four hundred-foot-wide span.

We walked for about ten minutes before a flock of a dozen or so Smith's Longspurs let loose on their rattle calls and rose up out of the field, organizing into formation before taking off on their circular flight pattern about twenty-five feet above the ground. The flock took flight approximately one hundred feet to the right of where I stood. "There they are!" Terry said excitedly while we all tried to get our binoculars on them. The Smith's were airborne for about two minutes, during which time I was able to get a couple of quick views of the mot-tled brown birds with partly white faces. When they landed, Terry reformed and redirected the trajectory of our line so that we could find them again.

The second time they launched, I was lucky for two reasons: first, because they rose right in front of me, and second, because Ed was nearby. As the birds propelled vertically past our line of sight, Ed called out, "I think I've got Chestnut-collared!"

Because I was essentially at Ed's vantage point, I looked quickly to see that, indeed, a similarly shaped but darker bird was with the Smith's. Terry took a few seconds to look himself before whooping and announcing the presence of a Chestnut-collared Longspur mixed in with the flock. We proceeded to re-find and re-launch that flock another couple of times before concluding that the "gang of fourteen" consisted of twelve Smith's Longspurs and two Chestnut-collared Longspurs. Both were lifers for me, and the Chestnut-collared was a rarity, only the ninth state record of the bird. During these successive en-gagements, all birders in the group were able to get views of each species of longspur. My mom was excited when she got a brief but decent look at the Chestnut-collared.

"Okay," Terry said, "now I'm going to tape these birds! I was excited to get additional recordings of the Smith's, but I gotta have recordings of the Chestnut-collared! Y'all need to be quiet, okay?"

We re-formed the line again with Terry's recorder going. After a couple of minutes of walking, two birders exchanged brief, friendly words, and Terry promptly told them to can it. We kept walking deliberately, the only sounds being our feet hitting the uneven grass surface and an occasional grunt from Daniel, who seemed unaccustomed to exercise and was struggling to keep up with us. After a couple of minutes the flock rose again, calling. Terry stood at the end of our line, near the birds, holding his microphone high into the sky to capture the sounds. He shut off the recording and, without checking it, told us to get back in line and find them again. We obeyed and proceeded in the direction in which the birds had landed. This time, finding them took a little longer and several birders once again began a conversation. (I could understand that. Once you've seen the target bird you're after a few times, and a lagniappe state rarity on top of it, it's normal to want to talk.)

"Will y'all please shut up? I'm taping!" Terry rebuked.

The birders grumbled but complied, and after another couple of minutes the flock lifted up on their final human-inspired journey of the day. Terry again held the recorder high—the simultaneous anticipation and concern on his face looked an awful lot like praying—praying that he could capture those calls. After they landed, he shut off the recorder, held the box to his ear, and listened. Other birders took this opportunity to commence long overdue conversations. I thought I heard the words "bad daughter" spoken from behind me. I glanced around and saw nothing out of the ordinary, so I returned to watching Terry. After a couple of minutes his face split open into a massive smile. I watched him transform from a serious man on a mission into a man full of childlike delight.

"I got them!" he yelled, "I got them both!" He laughed and started dancing in the field, half jumping, half jigging, and turning in a circle. I grinned while Daniel looked at Terry like he was nuts. Terry must have succumbed to a well-placed dip in the field because he fell hard halfway through the second turn of his dance. I thought that the fall might slow him down, but it didn't. He jumped back up without even using his hands, as if propelled in the same vertical motion as the longspurs, and jigged back around to face us, still smiling wide.

After netting the longspurs, our single line configuration wasn't necessary, and we split into different groups as we made our way across the fields toward some distant tree lines, with Terry calling which birds he heard and all of us watching for various species that were easy to see in the wide open spaces in which we were birding. I was excited to see Henslow's Sparrows in the fields and raptors gliding overhead. I was focused on a Wilson's Snipe when someone touched my elbow.

"I can't *believe* that you brought your mother on this trip!" Daniel said by way of greeting, "How could you do that to her? It is hard work to walk these fields. I am impressed that she is keeping up with everyone, but you were irresponsible to bring her here. You're a bad daughter!"

I realized that I had in fact heard those words uttered earlier; I had no idea that they had been intended for me. "My momma wanted to come on this trip and she's seen several new birds! And she's tough! Do you see her complaining? She looks happy to me. I think I'm a good daughter for bringing her out here!" Daniel huffed in response, rolled his eyes, and lumbered away.

We ended the afternoon looking and listening for Short-eared Owls. Although we were unsuccessful in this quest, when returning to the cars Terry heard a Lapland Longspur. He gleefully announced our longspur species trifecta to the group as the birders thanked him and Daniel for the day. I endured one more evil-eyed look from Daniel while I thought about birding by using sound first.

Sound is actually my favorite part of birding; without even realizing it, I listen to birdsong all the time. I first became aware of how listening was part of my everyday but unconscious habit when I stepped off a plane in Tucson, Arizona, in 2006. I wasn't even a serious birder then, but I noticed immediately that many of the bird songs I heard were a lot like a bird species I was familiar with at home, but not quite. And there were completely different sounds. I felt like I was in a different country in which the birds were speaking a different language because of it.

Birding by sound has several advantages; just like a particular bird might have several field marks that you can use for visual identification, a bird also has different songs. The average bird has six distinctive sounds; there are songs to attract mates, alarm notes, location pings, territorial chatter, and so on. Some birds, like the Blue Jay or Northern Mockingbird, have elaborate repertoires. Sound unveils an entirely new dimension for identifying birds, and because many species tend to hide, songs can be the easiest way to identify them. Although some songs can be tough to tell apart (I can't yet tell the difference between the songs of Bewick's Wren and Song Sparrow, for example), generally, they are distinctive. If you're not sure about one particular sound, keep listening, because the bird might switch to another sound that you're more familiar with. I have spent enough time stumped by a distinctive bird call before realizing that it was a common bird creating it that I created the maxim, "The unfamiliar song is usually a bird you know singing a song you don't." To my knowledge, I made that up myself, and I am unreasonably pleased with myself for doing so.

When I listen for birds, really listen by consciously opening my ears, it is amazing what I can hear. Not just the high pitched call of Cedar Waxwings, but the soft sound of the debris they pick from trees as it hits the ground. Not just the 80-millisecond-long thin chip note of a Savannah Sparrow, but the grass as it is caressed by the wind. The wings of an insect zipping by; the way that a falling leaf makes a series of flowing crashes as it hits other leaves on its downward drift; the loud chopping sounds of a mockingbird that always seem like joyful laughing; the high-pitched call of a Bald Eagle that sounds simultaneously cute to my ear and deathly to the birds around me.

When I listen in this vigilant manner, I am always shocked and frequently annoyed at how loud we humans really are. Airplanes, nicknamed "gas birds" by birders, can drown out every sound in the woods when they pass overhead. Whether I am birding in urban or rural environs, human-induced noise is almost constant. Traffic. Barking dogs. People talking. Construction zones. Four wheelers. Leaf blowers. Pumps. Generators. As I write this sentence, someone outside is pounding away with a hammer. Even the sound of my own feet can be too loud, especially in natural areas in which the roads are made of stone and gravel. I've become protective of my ears as I've gotten older because I've listened to too many birders wistfully talk about how they can no longer hear Cedar Waxwings; sometimes, I am the only birder in a group who can discern a distant call.

I often wonder whether the birds feel the same way as me about human noise pollution. Acoustic ecologist Gordon Hempton says that there are only about a dozen places in the United States free of human-induced noise for stretches of at least fifteen minutes at a time. Florence Williams noted that 83 percent of the continental United States lies within thirty-five hundred feet of a road and is thus subjected to the noise of vehicular traffic.[2] While I'm annoyed by human-induced noise that stops me from hearing every bird, at least it's not a matter of life and death. For the birds, not being able to hear the swoop of a Cooper's Hawk or the danger call of a protective parent could be fatal.[3] I'd hazard a guess that if birds could talk, they'd probably tell us to pipe down.

* * * * *

Another oft-cited reason for the love of birding is the sense of adventure—for example, finding birds that you've never seen before. For many years I birded without knowing the concept of a nemesis bird. I was happy to see whatever happened to be around when I went out into nature armed with binoculars. But as I spoke to other birders in the field, I realized that many times they were out trying to find a species that they'd never seen before. I think it was others' interest in so many different birds, and the challenge of chasing them, that began my own drive to see new species.

The first new bird I remember consciously wanting to see was a male Painted Bunting, considered by many to be the most colorful bird in North America. Luckily for me, Louisiana is one of only a few states in the country in which the Painted Bunting lives and breeds for part of the year. Harriett Pooler told me with confidence that she could get me one. On a day in early May 2004, Harriett took me, my mom, and several other birders up Whiskey Bay Road in the Atchafalaya NWR to see Painted Buntings as part of an Audubon tour. As soon as we pulled off the interstate at the base of the Whiskey Bay exit, we all got out of the vehicle and searched the short trees, hedges, and power lines for birds. And sitting right there on a power line singing its heart out was my first ever male Painted Bunting. Harriett had located that bird in the first fifteen minutes of a three-hour trip, and it wasn't the only one we saw that day.

Harriett was happy that my mom and I were so happy about seeing this bird for the first time; she shared that her nemesis bird was the Black-billed Cuckoo, which I had never heard of, much less seen. Seven years later, Lynn and I were birding in the Landry-LeBlanc tract, a forest of live oak and hackberry trees on Grand Isle, when we came upon a couple engrossed in watching a bird. I approached them slowly and quietly so as not to disturb their process or scare off the bird, and asked what they were seeing; observing other absorbed birders used to excite me to no end, but over time I realized that more often than not, people would be excited about a common species like a Prothonotary Warbler or Red-eyed Vireo, so I had learned to modulate both my speed of approach and my expectation. When the man said, "Black-billed Cuckoo" and pointed it out, I was simultaneously excited and thrilled; while I watched it, I wondered if Harriett had seen one yet. The next time I ran into her, I asked, and she still hadn't. Harriett finally got her Black-billed Cuckoo at Grosse Savanne, a remote lodge located between Sweet Lake and Calcasieu Lake in Cameron Parish, in the spring of 2013.

The Painted Bunting was my first nemesis bird, but it certainly was not the last. As I look back, I had not wanted to see it for long before I got it. Other nemesis birds, such as the Hooded Warbler, were quickly taken care of. Some are not short term, though—some can be downright painful.

The Northern Bobwhite has undergone a steep population decline in the past fifty years. Even so, its two-noted "bob white" or three-noted "bob bob white" song often rings through open fields across the eastern half of the United States. Due to its propensity to remain in tall grass or in ground cover, however, it is heard much more often than it is seen. I have gotten incredibly close to bobwhites without seeing them. In 2013, my father took me birding at Paynes Prairie Preserve State Park in Florida, where I saw a pack of wild horses and a Whooping Crane foraging with hundreds of Glossy Ibis and Little Blue Herons. I heard at least a dozen bobwhites on this trip. At one point, I approached a thicket about a foot high and approximately twelve feet in diameter and stood right at the edge while a bobwhite called incessantly within a few feet of me without ever showing an inch of its body.

On a field trip to Starr County during the Rio Grande Valley Birding Festival, we were birding a stretch of the Rio Grande River when our guide located a bobwhite in some tall grass adjacent to the river. "There's a bobwhite!" he said. The dozen taller folks in our group of twenty focused their binoculars and proceeded to ooh and ah while mom and I grumbled in frustration. The guide was at least six-foot-two, and the other birders were tall enough to see over the grass to the bird, which was stationary and about fifteen feet from us. I'm five-foot-one, and my mom is getting increasingly less close to five feet tall. Simple trigonometry meant that the lofty among us could see the bird while the rest of us couldn't.

I felt more prepared several years later, when during our big year adventure we took a summer trip to Fabacher Road in Calcasieu Parish, an area dominated by fields and roadside hedges with occasional tree lines great for raptors like the Crested Caracara. When we heard a bobwhite at the corner of Fabacher Road and Highway 108, Lynn parked our truck at the first pullout adjacent to the field from which the bird called, and we both stood in the truck bed with our binoculars. With the added height, I figured that we had it made—but alas, although we heard bobwhite calls from numerous places in the field, some close and some farther away, the grass was so tall that the three feet of added height was useless.

I was always buoyed by the bobwhite's beautiful call, but it started to become simultaneously frustrating because of my seeming inability to visually observe one. I began to get used to the idea that I might never, ever see a Northern Bobwhite.

One spring day, Lynn and I went to Muddy Creek Wetland Management Area in Theodore, Alabama, looking for a Prairie Warbler. Not even a minute after we pulled in to the empty parking lot, a turquoise pickup truck pulled in and parked right next to us. The truck sported tinted windows, so it was impossible to observe the person behind the wheel. The driver cracked the windows, cut the engine, and sat in the truck, despite the fact that it was hotter than a $2 pistol outside. Both our "creep alarms" went off—something just seemed off to Lynn and me. Why sit inside a truck and boil? Why park right next to us when there were a hundred other open spots?

I was frustrated, because the top of that trail was *birdy*. I could see flocks of Indigo Buntings and Blue Grosbeaks without even trying. We cautiously exited our vehicle, armed with our cell phones and vigilance, and birded the brushy habitat right around the parking lot, where we quickly added Common Yellowthroat and Eastern Towhee, but we didn't want to get too far away from our vehicle. It takes a decent amount of weirdness to make my creep alarm go off, and in this case it was a triple alarm. Although I am still not sure why it went off in this particular instance, I always heed my own alarm. After about ten minutes of hanging around the trailhead with the occupant of that truck sitting and sweltering, we left. Neither of us wanted to venture into the two-mile, desolate trail area, Prairie Warblers or not.

As an alternative, we headed to the Grand Bay Savanna Forever Wild Tract on Henderson Camp Road. This area features a parking lot and trail as soon as the road changes from asphalt to dirt; one side of the trail is a forest and the other side is meadow, bounded by barbed wire. As soon as Lynn parked, she announced, "I just heard a bobwhite."

"Are you kidding me?" I asked. Between the hot, humid weather and feeling pushed out of a perfectly good birding spot that boasts the Prairie Warbler, I was not in the mood to be kidded with.

"No, I mean it."

As she finished her utterance, one sounded off in the meadow's tall grass. We jumped out of the truck immediately and set about trying to locate this bobwhite. Recent rains had resulted in the trail being too wet to bird in our sandals and sneakers, and we hadn't brought our boots. After ten minutes of wandering the trailhead, including my climbing a three-foot wooden post and standing on top of it to peer into uncooperatively high grass, we decided to leave. We'd heard a bobwhite at three separate locations in the field, but the grass was at least ten times the height of the birds, so they once again proved impossible to see.

Back in the truck, I began my nemesis bird rant, which went something like this: "I've heard the bobwhite without seeing it in Ohio, Louisiana, Texas, Florida, and now Alabama—that's got to be some kind of sick record!" In response, Lynn stopped the truck on the side of road and whistled the bobwhite call through the open windows. One called back immediately, loud and strong, about fifteen feet from the truck.

I desisted in my monologue as Lynn turned off the truck and whistled again. The bird called back, and it continued to answer her whistles as I carefully exited the vehicle, picked my way down the roadside ditch, then up the ditch, then through a thicket of Virginia creeper, low trees, and something prickly to the edge of the barbed wire fence running the perimeter of the field. When I peered through the thicket, I saw a bobwhite in flight. I was able to note its brown body with thin, white spotting, its semicircular wings, and its somewhat labored

flight as it traveled away from me about six inches above the grass line before dipping below the grass about one hundred feet away.

Was it the best look? No—it wasn't the look Ed told us about, in which he observed a bobwhite with seven babies crossing the road in front of his car. It wasn't a great shot like you see in the bird books, where you're close up with a pair of them inside a grass thicket. But it was a look, and not a streak of a look either. I executed my own happy call, which pierced the air and was met with silence. All smiles, I then picked my way back through the creeper, the trees, the prickly plants, and the ditch to Lynn, who had once again whispered a bird for me. I didn't care that my legs were bleeding from the thickets. Lynn hadn't seen the bobwhite herself but was just as happy as I because she was now spared the "How many times am I going to hear this bird without seeing it before I actually *see* it?" rant.

My obsession with birds has actually drawn in a few other people—not that I try to convert people, but I guess that even as I attempt to edit myself, I talk enough about birds that eventually I wear down a person here or there. My friend Sarah Myers is one of those people. She and Linda Lee own a condo two doors down from us on Dauphin Island, and she watched me take off for the woods and listened to me prattle on about birding too many times to not get interested.

Nationally renowned birder Kenn Kaufman says that you need to let people bird the way that they want to—that the idea of there being a "proper" way to bird is silly. I have to keep that in mind with Sarah, because she birds by camera. She does not own a pair of binoculars and does not want a pair of binoculars. She has a 50X zoom on her camera and fresh young eyes to see the screen, and she's good with that—and I am too.

I took Sarah birding a few times in the winter and spring of 2013 and she slowly began to build a life list, consisting only of birds of which she's taken good pictures. One spring weekend, when she went to Dauphin Island and I didn't go, the spring Alabama Ornithological Society (AOS) meeting was being held there. Sarah connected with Tom Sheehan, one of her former high school teachers, who happens to be an avid birder and who attends every spring AOS meeting. Sarah ventured out with him and a group of other birders, armed with her camera and ready to tackle the bird world. When she called to tell me that she got a great picture of a Cape May Warbler, I about fell off my chair.

The Cape May Warbler had turned into my most difficult nemesis bird. Louisiana is toward the western edge of the spring migration route of this pretty warbler, and though they are possible to see in Louisiana and are not considered rare here, you can't dial one up at will. Joan has seen a Cape May three times on Grand Isle over the course of about twenty years, and at this point she spends almost the entire month of April birding there. The Cape May was the forty-fourth bird on Sarah's life list. At the time, I was sitting at 425 birds on my life list with no Cape May. I had forty-two of the fifty or so warbler species one can find in North America, but not the Cape May.

Sarah had also gotten fabulous pictures of a Black-billed Cuckoo and thought that this was the bird to get, because all her birder friends had fawned over the cuckoo, but no one was fawning over the Cape May, so she didn't think she had anything special. When I explained that it made sense that the birders would be more excited about the Black-billed Cuckoo than the Cape May Warbler, I had to explain why my reaction was the opposite and the concept of the nemesis bird.

The rest of the year was hell—there's just no other way to put it. Sarah Myers inserted that Cape May Warbler into just about every conversation I had with her, and the fact that she had seen it and I hadn't. For her, that teasing just never got old. I declared my intentions to see a Cape May in 2014 but had no real expectations—why should this year be different from the previous thirteen?

That April, Lynn and I were on Dauphin Island during the weekend of the AOS meeting. As with any group of birders, the AOS crew is a friendly lot. John and Jennie Stowers hold a potluck lunch at their house during every meeting, and Sarah always goes. Sarah is an extrovert. I had yet to attend the potluck, and although part of my staying away is the fact that I am less outgoing than Sarah, the bigger concern is that I'd waste a perfectly good hour of birding. I would much more easily consider a potluck if it were in the evening and the only things worth chasing were owls and nightjars, species that don't see much action on Dauphin Island.

Sarah, meanwhile, had managed to convince Linda Lee to get into birding. Linda Lee never does anything halfway; the first thing Linda did when she decided to try birding was to purchase a pair of Eagle Optics binoculars. She headed into the woods for the first time ever with me, Lynn, and Sarah during that AOS weekend. Dauphin Island in April usually sports great birding, even when there are not fallout conditions. We proceeded to the Indian Shell Mound and clicked off several species of warblers (Prothonotary, Hooded, Yellow-rumped) and vireos (White-eyed, Red-eyed), as well as the usual selection of buntings (Indigo and Painted) and tanagers (Summer and Scarlet)—it was a very colorful morning of birding. Sarah and Linda decided to take a break while Lynn and I continued. An hour later, they texted us that they were headed to John and Jennie's house for the AOS potluck lunch, and did we want to come? Let's see: birds in the woods versus fifty people in a closed space. We opted for the woods. Forty minutes later I received the following text:

Sarah: Have you seen the Cape May yet?

Me: NO! Why?

Sarah: Because I'm looking at one right now at John's house. No joke.

Me: Is it alive?

Sarah: Yes.

Me: Is it in his house?

Sarah: No.

Me: Are you really serious?

Sarah: Yes.

At this point, Lynn texted Sarah on my phone. Given Sarah's propensity for teasing me about the Cape May, we had to be sure.

Lynn: Sarah, you're sure you're not kidding?

Sarah: I'm not. Really. Come now.

We blew out of the bird banding area in the Dauphin Island Bird Sanctuary, jumped into the truck, and headed to the corner of Cadillac Avenue and Penacault Street. So many cars lined Cadillac that we had to find a place to park several blocks away and walk back toward the intersection. The first person we saw when we approached was Linda Lee.

"I got that bird!" she said excitedly. I mentally cringed—I understood her excitement, was excited for her, truly—but it was her first day of birding. I felt humbled on a karmic scale.

The bottlebrush trees adjacent to John and Jennie's yard were easily the most bodacious on the island—and in them, interspersed among dozens of Ruby-throated Hummingbirds and Orchard Orioles, with the occasional Prothonotary thrown in, was a male Cape May Warbler. The area in front of those bottlebrush trees was full of birders, the ones who had eaten lunch and were also treated to the Cape May. Where is it, I thought to myself? I tried not to be white knuckled while holding my binoculars and tried not to grind my teeth. The birders said that he only disappeared for short times and always came back out into clear view. I only had to wait about three minutes before one birder said, "There he is." With my heart beating strongly in my chest, I followed the birder's finger and found him with my naked eye. He was downright friendly and eating for all he was worth, at times hanging upside down on the pink bottlebrush flowers. I marveled at his large red cheek spot and the bright yellow collar around his neck. Lynn was able to take fabulous pictures, and I was able to stare at him a long time with and without binoculars. Lots of happy birders lined up in front of those trees—especially me.

Sarah found me in front of the trees, gave me a hug, and said, "You know, it was a really tough decision for me, to have to give up this one bird I have on you. Especially because you turned your nose up at the potluck. I made sure that Linda saw it first. And I made sure that my parents (who were not birders) saw it, too. And then I figured that I had to call you. And here you are—I got you the Cape May!"

A Gray Kingbird was camped out on a power line half a block down Cadillac Avenue, so Lynn and I joined Linda and Sarah to see that bird as well. A Gray Kingbird is a better bird than the Cape May any day of the week on Dauphin Island, but I didn't care. During a week's vacation three summers earlier in Key West, I had been treated to so many Gray Kingbirds on the wires that they almost felt like a yard bird. It was first time I had seen a Gray Kingbird on Dauphin Island, and I was happy for that, but it was the Cape May that had me elated.

After fourteen years of birding, I slept better that night. I finally, *finally* had the coveted Cape May Warbler, a male, on my life list. What a looker.

At the moment, I don't have an actively annoying nemesis bird on my list. The Chuck-will's-widow gave me fits for about five years, but I finally managed to locate one during an early May trip to Peveto woods, where I noticed a bump on a branch in one of the trees adjacent to the parking lot and realized that the bump was a sleeping "chuck." For all four of us present—me, Mom, Joan, and Harry Moran—it was a life bird. It is very satisfying to find a bird you've heard a hundred times without seeing, even with your momma crooning to everyone present about your birding prowess.

A pseudo nemesis that I am not actively chasing because the bird does not frequent Louisiana is the Clark's Nutcracker. This bird of the crow and jay family, and named after famous explorer William Clark (of Lewis and Clark), is common in western states. Several years ago, I was invited to speak at the Colorado School of Mines and I brought my mom with me so that I could show her the Rocky Mountains as well as some western bird species. We were driving out of Boulder and were headed for I-70 to look for a herd of wild buffalo known to frequent an area just west of the city. I took the scenic route out, which involved navigating a circuitous two-lane road cut into the side of a mountain. There was no shoulder and the area immediately adjacent to the road was snowy and lined with pine trees. I cranked down both windows and drove a little slower than the 25 mph speed limit with my head out the window so that I could listen Terry Davis style. About two-thirds of the way up this road, to where you could view the plateau at the top, I heard a Clark's Nutcracker in a pine tree right next to the road. No cars were behind me, so I stopped the car. Mom said, "Marybeth, we're in the middle of the road."

"I know, but there's nowhere to pull off and there's no one behind us. I just heard a Clark's Nutcracker."

"Oh," she responded, sounding unconvinced.

I could see that the bird was in the back of the tree—I saw branches moving and snow being tapped off them—but the bird remained hidden.

"Marybeth…" mom repeated nervously. I again looked in the rearview mirror—no cars anywhere.

"Just a minute," I said, exiting the car. If I could change my angle of view, perhaps I could get a look at the nutcracker. I got about fifteen feet from the car and looked again through my binoculars. The bird was still in the same place and I still didn't see it, but I could tell that my vantage point was getting better because I was starting to see around the side of the tree toward the back. Sneaky thing, I thought to myself.

"Marybeth, there's a car coming!" Mom was calling like a three-alarm fire. I looked and sure enough there was a car coming, but it was at least a mile down the road, and with the slow speed limit I still had a few more seconds to look.

"Just a second," I soothed, refocusing and looking again.

"Marybeth, get back in the car this instant!"

My body was moving toward the car before my brain actually picked up that my momma was bellowing—she had played the "obey me" card by shouting in the resonant frequency that my body knew and responded to immediately. If there's a better "snap to it" for me on this planet, I am not aware of it.

I silently cursed my bad luck as the nutcracker continued to play "bounce on the branch while out of sight," made my way back to the car, and drove off, still well ahead of the car behind me. We never got another chance at a nutcracker, and it remains on my heard-but-not-seen list. As much as I love bird sound, I admit that I'd rather hear and see a bird I've never seen before than just hear it. We neither heard nor saw the buffalo either.

My other "instant but accessed with difficulty" nemesis episode happened when Lynn and I hired dynamic bird guide Lascelle Tillet for a day of birding in Belize. While birding the entry area to the Philip S. W. Goldson International Airport, which included a tropical tree line and a number of wet fields that held Northern Jacana and Limpkin, Lascelle was naming birds that he heard before he saw them and pointing them out to us as they came into view. We were treated to looks at Grayish Saltator, Yellow-winged Tanager, and Blue-gray Tanager, among others. I heard a new chip note and Lascelle exclaimed, "That's a Keel-billed Toucan!" I was excited to see in real life the bird that graced the Froot Loops cereal box, but a split second after this utterance came an urgent edict: "Run for the van!"

Lascelle had been monitoring three men who were ambling toward us on the long airport entrance road; when we looked, we saw that they were sprinting toward us. The three of us ran quickly and piled into the van; Lascelle hit the "lock" button on the van literally a second before the first runner pulled the latch to get into the back of the van with us. I watched this man's eyes morph from hard and calculating to meek and guileless; he asked Lascelle if he and his friends could have a ride to the airport. Lascelle said no, turned our van around in a wide arc, and got out of there quickly. He explained that it was Boxing Day, a big celebration day in Belize that often involved a lot of drinking. Lascelle thought that the three men were drunk and up to no good.

From the airport, we moved on to Crooked Tree Wildlife Sanctuary, which was amazing. There I had my first ever sighting of a Laughing Falcon, a masked bird so majestic it took my breath away; ditto with the Bat Falcon, whose burnt-orange underparts were reminiscent of sunset. But throughout the rest of our day there was no Keel-billed Toucan. It remains in the same close encounter status of the Clark's Nutcracker; I wish I had seen it and will prioritize searching for it the next time I visit appropriate habitat, but until then there's no point in pining away for it.

* * * * *

Some people bird for the love of eating. Louisiana is famous for its food; most everyone knows about dining in New Orleans, but actually the entire state is a culinary playground. I divide people who bird for the love of eating into two categories: people who love to eat birds, and people who use birds to help them eat other things. Some may argue that the people in these categories are not actual birders, but I posit that people in these groups are as serious about birds as I am.

In Louisiana, lots of people love to eat birds. Louisiana is home to legions of hunters, and while duck hunting represents the marquis avian hunting event in the state, there are also seasons for doves (Mourning, White-winged, Eurasian Collared, Ringed Turtle), woodcocks, rails (Sora, Virginia, Clapper, King), gallinules, coots, geese (Snow, Canada, Greater White-fronted, Ross's), quail (Northern Bobwhite), and turkeys.

Joan holds an annual birding party at the camp during a spring weekend and invites all her birding friends, who spend the day birding Grand Isle during the height of migration. She and Joe cook out for everyone, and then everyone Cajun dances into the night. Joan's friend Skeeter begged her to let him host the party. Skeeter had a great camp, but a wicked sense of humor, and Joan wasn't sure if her friends would be able to handle him. After years of Skeeter's beseeching, Joan relented and brought ten of her birder friends to his place.

She relayed, "I had just finally relaxed because Skeeter was behaving, the wine was flowing, and everyone was laughing and having a good time. After a while, Skeeter finished grilling and put his concoction on everybody's plate. He served bacon-wrapped dove. As soon as the first birder asked what it was and Skeeter told him, everybody got real quiet. I mean, who would want to eat what they'd just been watching through binoculars? I'd like to have killed him for that!" That Grand Isle birding party remains the only one for which Skeeter was host.

I am a vegetarian and I don't hunt; I doubt I will ever shoot a gun. My background once made me distrust hunters, but this is no longer the case. While I'm still uncomfortable with the idea of killing creatures to eat them, I have come to the conclusion that hunters are conservationists. Hunters will take what they need and will use every part of an animal; almost every hunter I have met knows and follows the regulations that result in healthy, sustainable populations of ducks, birds, and animals. I also realized from talking with hunters that when they find a blue bill (Lesser Scaup) or a grey duck (Gadwall), or try to avoid a spoonbill (Northern Shoveler), they feel the same love for ducks while looking through their crosshairs that I feel while looking through my binoculars. We may have different ways of engaging with ducks and different purposes for them in mind, but our love of them binds us together. And for duck hunters, this love is a long-term affair. The truth is that if it weren't for duck hunters and their early conservation efforts,[4] today I would not have any wild places in Louisiana to look at ducks or other avian species. So, while I don't plan to hunt, I can say that I have come to appreciate hunters.

Fish are the other major "catch and eat" natural delicacy in the state, and while I don't fish either, Lynn partakes heavily. She is quick to tell me that I have the better deal because I can bird while she fishes, but she can't fish while I bird, unless it's on the water. Nevertheless, we have come to note the similarities between fishing and birding.

Observing a bird species depends strongly on the season; the same with the fish species you catch. For example, spring migration gets going and bird activity heats up in the woods at the same time that the saltwater inshore fish species Lynn loves move into the marsh. On days when fishing is productive, birding seems to be productive as well. You look for different fish in different water depths (bottom, middle of the water column, or at the surface) in a similar way to how you look for different kinds of birds at different heights (at ground level, eye level, mid-level heights, high in the trees, or in the sky, when looking straight up will give you "warbler neck"). You can sit on a pier or a bench in the woods and wait for the fish and birds, respectively, to come to you; or you can wade through water or walk trails to accelerate your pursuit. If you pay attention, there are all kinds of drama going on in layers above our heads in birding and below the surface in fishing.

If one travels out on a deep sea fishing charter, the charter captains chase flocks of diving Laughing Gulls. The gulls are diving for shrimp, and the presence of shrimp means that typically you'll have fish who like to eat shrimp in the vicinity as well. If you cast a line where gulls are diving for shrimp from above, you have a decent probability of hooking a fish that is feeding on shrimp from below. The same holds for Laughing Gulls fishing in the water close to shore; cast in here and you might locate a school of Redfish or Speckled Trout feeding from below. The phenomenon isn't confined to Laughing Gulls either. Some fishing guides swear by using Magnificent Frigatebirds. Because of the great eyesight of these black, dinosaur-looking seabirds, some guides say that the height a frigatebird flies above the water surface is equal to the depth of target fish like Tuna, Marlin, or Mahi Mahi in the water column.

There are limits to this strategy. Lynn was kayak fishing at Pointe-aux-Chenes when a Cajun man motored by in his boat, pointed at the Forster's Terns fishing around her, and said, "Dem little birds, dey lie." He meant that the small fish the Forster's Terns were eating didn't attract desired inshore fish species the way that larger baitfish chased by Laughing Gulls do. If you're trying to catch fish, watch for gulls, but pay no attention to terns. He was absolutely right.

* * * * *

Finally, some birders are fascinated with the love of learning and teaching. Louisiana is especially blessed on this account because of LSU's Museum of Natural Science in Baton Rouge, which boasts the third largest university-based bird collection in the world. Faculty and staff affiliated with the museum conduct research and share natural science with the public. The museum's ornithology program is among the best in the world, and its repository of bird DNA samples is unparalleled. Graduate students come from all points of the globe to study there, with opportunities to conduct field work in remote places that remain largely unexplored.

Steve and Donna have each worked for more than thirty years at the museum and have contributed to its international reputation. Professor and Curator of Birds Van Remsen created the bird classification committee for the birds of South America and even has a bird species named after him: *Doliornis remseni,* the Chestnut-bellied Cotinga. Van created LA-BIRD and is the state editor of eBird, a massive electronic database maintained by Cornell University that collects checklists submitted by birders from around the world to inform other birders and researchers about where and when birds are present. Volunteer editors like Van ensure the checklists are as accurate as possible, although even with this quality assurance check eBird still assumes that there is a 5 percent error rate. Van peruses checklists submitted in the state of Louisiana with the goal of reducing those errors. These birding paragons and others affiliated with the museum share their vast expertise and knowledge with the lay folk among us.

Although Baton Rouge is the epicenter for teaching and learning about birds, others carry this mantle at locations throughout the state. There's Casey Wright, a wildlife biologist who works for the Louisiana Department of Wildlife and Fisheries (LDWF) on Grand Isle and who will tour any birder through the best birding spots on Louisiana's only human-inhabited barrier island. Casey loves finding first of season (FOS) warblers in the local woods and currently holds the state record for the earliest Worm-eating Warbler (March 11).

Then there's retired wildlife biologist Marty Floyd from Alexandria. Marty never had a chance; he was destined to become a birder the way that Peyton Manning was destined to be an NFL quarterback. "My parents' first date was in Oklahoma during World War II. My dad drove my mom out to the country to see Scissor-tailed Flycatchers on the telephone wires." Marty's actual first name is Martin—he was named after the Purple Martin. So it's no surprise that he became a birder, a pursuit he has had in common with his parents since before he can remember, especially Christmas Bird Counts (CBCs). His dad started in 1938, and Marty has participated in almost two hundred CBCs since 1959. Marty shares his talents with birders by regularly leading bird trips during LOS meetings.

Erik Johnson from Lafayette is the Director of Bird Conservation of Audubon Louisiana. He runs research projects all over the state, from Prothonotary Warbler breeding in Bluebonnet Swamp in Baton Rouge to marsh bird monitoring at the Paul J. Rainey Wildlife Sanctuary in Vermilion Parish. After the BP oil spill, Erik created the Audubon Coastal Birding Survey throughout the central Gulf Coast to provide long-term monitoring of the populations of beach-dwelling species. According to researchers Haney, Geiger, and Short, the oil spill wiped out 32 percent of the resident Laughing Gull population, 14 percent of the Royal Terns, 12 percent of the Brown Pelicans, and 8 percent of the Northern Gannets.[5] Erik's program can help provide insight into the fate of these and other species in response to the spill and to other factors.

Jane Patterson of Ponchatoula is a computer scientist by training and a birder by hobby. Her adult leisure course on birding basics has given many citizens a start in their own avian adventures. Hundreds of Boy Scouts have earned their birding badges courtesy of Jane.

These folks and many others have built and sustained the birding community in Louisiana and remind us that there's always more to learn. One of my favorite things about birding is its standing invitation to partake in lifelong learning. I remember being thrilled when I received an email from Van after I submitted another of many eBird checklists from our kayak travels in Irish Bayou Lagoon and the south side of Lake Pontchartrain. "You have proven that the Nelson's Sparrow spends the winter south of the lake," he wrote. "Your next order of business is to figure out if they winter on the north side of the lake as well." It took years and a number of kayak trips to destinations like Big Branch Marsh NWR and Cane Bayou, when on a sunny afternoon in mid-February I located a single Nelson's Sparrow in the marsh adjacent to Cane Bayou and could say that yes, at least one Nelson's Sparrow was spending the winter north of the lake. I am still in the process of figuring out if that is true in more than one case.

I love to learn the canon of a particular aspect of birding and then the gray areas in which canon intersects with complexity. For example, mom and I participated in a RGVBF field trip to the Norias Unit of the King Ranch in Kingston, Texas. In addition to observing the trip's target, a Ferruginous Pygmy-Owl, whose face looked amazingly cat-like, we spent a significant chunk of time engaged with birds in a large area of fields and meadows. Barbara Rapstein, our tour guide, pointed out Western and Eastern Meadowlarks. I typically use the distinctive voices of these two species to determine which is which, but Barbara told us that in this particular field Eastern and Western Meadowlarks breed together side by side. As a result, Eastern Meadowlark babies heard and learned Western Meadowlark calls and vice versa. Thus, you couldn't use voice to distinguish the two species in this field; instead you had to use visual clues and the fact that Western Meadowlarks usually traveled in flocks, while Easterns tended to be more solitary. I was captivated by the fact that in this particular time and place, knowledge of the bird sounds of these species was not a reliable way for determining their identity.

Later this same morning we located some Sprague's Pipits. The twenty people in our birding group eventually tired of watching the pipits launch and fly in quarter mile long lazy ellipses reminiscent of the flight pattern of Smith's

Longspurs. Some birders continued looking at additional field species while others relaxed into conversation. My mother stayed trained on some pipits as they remained elevated for almost five minutes, turning in circles with binoculars raised to follow the trajectory of the birds. When they finally dove toward the earth, she jumped up and down in happiness. *"I got them!"* she roared. For a moment, every birder within a hundred yards looked at my mom, and then every birder smiled. Seeing a bird you've worked long and hard for can be a universal moment of triumph for everyone.

I also love having my assumptions challenged, an aspect of learning of which I never tire. I believe that being open-minded is a critical aspect to understanding any situation, especially one that is complex. If I can accurately identify multiple perspectives and not make assumptions that impede a solution to a complex problem, then I am a better researcher and engineer. For this reason, I make as few assumptions as possible and I have a justification for every assumption I make. Even with this effort, occasionally I make assumptions I shouldn't. Birds surprise me sometimes, like the Eastern and Western Meadowlarks learning each other's songs in the fields at the King Ranch. Sometimes people can surprise me too.

For example, I was birding Castor Plunge in Kisatchie National Forest, and while driving my car from one trailhead to another, the only other human I saw for miles was a young man fishing in a stream alongside the road. He was about twenty-five and clad in T-shirt, shorts, baseball hat, and flip flops, looking every bit the quintessential, summer-dressed Louisiana sportsman. The driver side door of his truck stood wide open and loud music was emanating from the vehicle. If I've painted this scene correctly, you are likely imagining country music blasting through the forest, and ninety-nine times out of a hundred, you would be right—but it wasn't country music. This observation had me shaking my head and smiling; you gotta love a sportsman who will blast classical music all by himself out in the sticks of Kisatchie.

Years ago, Lynn, Linda Lee, and I were sitting outside eating lunch at The Hollar, a restaurant in Madrid, New Mexico, an artists colony of about two hundred people. A table of seven bikers sat immediately in front of us, talking, drinking beer, and slipping table scraps to the two or three dogs who roamed the area. A baby bird was tucked into the crossbar support of the restaurant's wooden entry gate, and the bikers were paying it a lot of attention.

We heard them relay the story to two new bikers who arrived at the table. The bird had fallen out of its nest and was hopping along the ground when one of the dogs saw it, ran for the fledgling, and took it into his mouth. The bikers interceded and rescued the little bird, who scampered out of the dog's pried-open jaws and ran for the shelter of the gate. And there it perched, some three feet above the ground, calling for its parents.

A discussion about what to do ensued at the bikers' table, with some advocating for leaving the bird as is, but more leaning toward returning the bird to its nest. They made a decision, calling for their waiter to please do the honors, gently mind you, they insisted. The waiter, armed with an apron and a cigarette hanging out of his mouth, approached slowly, reached out his hands, and gingerly cupped the bird. It tried to squawk, but was so little that the sound came out a squeak, and vaulted out of his hands and onto the ground. From there it squared its tiny wings and got ready to run. The waiter bent down, still gentle but more confident, scooped up the bird, and held on despite its vocal objections. He strode to the nest, reached up, and placed the bird back home, while the nine bikers (and us) watched with baited breath. The bird jumped in the nest, turned in a circle, and flew to a bush ten feet away, not gracefully and not in a straight line, but flew nonetheless.

As soon as the bird took wing, a parent coasted in and landed next to the baby in the bush. A cheer went up from the bikers' table. They high fived and belly laughed, then paid the check and headed out. While I expect bikers to take a stand because taking stands is part of biker culture, I would not normally expect some sixteen hundred pounds worth of bikers to take a stand against one of evolution's tougher laws, and then use consensus decision-making to defy another to save 0.7 ounces of baby House Sparrow.

Examples like these teach me that boxing people into a monolith based on probability and assumptions is a mistake, that situations are often a lot more complex than they look initially, and that starting with what author Arlie Hochschild calls the "good angels" of our [human] nature is the best way forward to effectively address any complex issue.[6]

* * * * *

Whether for a love of sound or adventure, whether to catch a bird and eat it or to chase a bird to catch something else, whether to learn or to teach or for any other myriad factors, one thing is certain: Louisiana is a fantastic place in which to bird for love. One love, no matter who you are, no matter what your intention.

BIRDING FROM THE INSIDE OUT

In 2014, I decided to keep year lists in Alabama and Louisiana—my goal was to finish in the top fifty eBirders, in terms of the number of species, in each state. In the fall of 2013, Louisiana birder Kimberly Lanka had introduced me to a part of eBird called the "Top 100," where one can enter a country, region, state, or county, and the top one hundred list of eBirders would be displayed for that geographical location. I finished 2013 ranked sixtieth in Louisiana, tied with two other birders with 207 species, and fifty-ninth in Alabama with 118 species. I had only begun using eBird regularly in April, so I figured that the goal of finishing in the top fifty eBirders in both states was doable if I were to use eBird from the beginning of the year.

Lynn and I got off to a quick start on our Louisiana list. It was the coldest winter we'd had since moving to Louisiana, and fishing was incredibly slow. Lynn got tired of catching nothing, so she resorted to birding with me instead. The unseasonably cold temperatures remained with us into the spring. We weren't going all out on birding, but we hit the fields, woods, or water almost every weekend. Lynn told me at one point that if she had a nickel for every time I said, "I know we're not doing a big year, but . . ." she'd be able to go to lunch.

We planned to attend the LOS winter meeting in Lafayette at the end of January; I was excited to participate because I wanted to learn new places to bird in that area. A rare ice storm arrived the night before the Saturday morning field trips departed from Lafayette. We got up early with plenty of time to get to the departure point, but I-10 was closed between Baton Rouge and Lafayette. We jumped onto Highway 190, took "the old bridge" over the Mississippi River, and made it to Opelousas, where we turned south on I-49 to reach Lafayette. We then came to a standstill and sat for what felt like an eternity as minutes trickled away, and we knew we weren't going to make it on time. Finally, we got an opening into the passing lane and began to move in fits and starts, later realizing we had been stuck in a stationary line of trucks more than three miles long waiting to get access to I-10. We made it to the hotel launch point an hour late and then drove around to see if we could catch up with one of the guided groups. Unsuccessful, we headed to Lacassine NWR. Despite having no guides that day and losing about three hours in bad traffic that we would have spent birding, we still picked up forty-nine species, including eleven ducks. We had racked up 123 species in Louisiana by the end of January.

In early February, armed with the recently published *A Birder's Guide to Louisiana,* by Richard Gibbons, Roger Breedlove, and Charlie Lyon, we headed for the Fort Jackson area in southeast Louisiana. We were following the new birding guide spot for spot until we reached the place where someone had reported a Tropical or Couch's Kingbird on LA-BIRD the previous day. The person didn't specify which species because it's almost impossible to distinguish between them unless the bird calls, but either way, in Louisiana that's totally a bird worth chasing. If we found it, we could always observe it and use pishing or playback[1] to see if the bird would call.

We parked on the side of Highway 23 just south of Diamond, a tiny community near Port Sulphur, Louisiana, and notorious for two fatal chemical explosions at the adjacent Shell refinery plant and an ensuing battle in which residents successfully secured resources for relocating and for addressing health impacts.[2] The only other car stopped in the area belonged to Louisiana birder David Muth, who was also looking for the Tropical/Couch's Kingbird. The three of us birded the spot briefly and found a couple of Western Kingbirds but not the Tropical/Couch's. David was kind enough to drive us a quarter mile down Highway 23 to where he had seen a Grasshopper Sparrow on a chain-link fence just off the highway. He brought us to the appointed spot, and there among several Savannah Sparrows the Grasshopper sat unmoving, in plain sight, framed by the diamond-shaped opening of chain-link. It was the best view I'd ever had of the typically furtive species.

David was continuing his birding to the south toward Venice, an unincorporated community of about two hundred people aptly nicknamed "the end of the world"; it is the farthest south that one can drive along the Mississippi River. He pointed us in the general direction of where he'd seen a Scissor-tailed Flycatcher on roadside telephone wires in Diamond. We executed a U-turn on Highway 23 and found it within thirty minutes. Although a Scissor-tailed Flycatcher is much easier to get in the late spring or summer around Turf Grass Road, the Louisiana Highway 108 loop, or Lighthouse Road, our 2012 big year adventure had taught us a lesson—if you can get a bird now, get it now. So we did.

We spent most of the April weekends on Dauphin Island, hitting a couple of fallouts, one fairly close to spectacular and the other small but still fun. There's nothing better than looking up and watching birds in gorgeous breeding plumage drop out of the sky into the tops of trees. On April 19 we were at the Dauphin Island Bird Sanctuary's bird banding area, which is the best place in the 164-acre park to find passerines, when a flock of Indigo Buntings dropped into the woods. Collectively, they were so loud that they drowned out human voices—I had to raise mine higher than usual to talk to Lynn and she was standing right next to me. We were searching for recently sighted Blackpoll, Bay-breasted, and Cerulean Warblers among the throng of buntings, and it got tiring to see bunting after bunting when searching for something else. We did manage to find Blackpoll and Bay-breasted Warblers, but we struck out on the cerulean. A big rain puddle sported Louisiana and Northern Waterthrushes foraging together—it was wonderful to see both side-by-side for comparison. After getting fabulously long looks at both species, Lynn declared that telling one species apart from the other was not as hard as she'd thought.

In mid-April, I tallied up our species and we were ahead of our 2012 big year pace in Louisiana (208 birds in 2014 vs. 192 in 2012) with three weeks less birding and much less effort. This fact made me feel accomplished, but of course I had a much better grasp of "what was up" with birding in Louisiana than I had had two years before. I was now armed with a community of awesome birders, the LA-BIRD listserv, eBird's frequency histograms, and the new Louisiana birding book. There was not even a Pileated Woodpecker—an easy-to-find bird—on the list yet. During our initial big year attempt in 2012, we didn't have a House Wren until almost the end of the year; in 2014 we got it on March 30 in Bayou Sauvage NWR. We never saw a Wood Thrush in 2012, but there were quite a few in the Leblanc-Landry woods of Grand Isle on April 15, 2014. We actually had the same Louisiana rarity on both lists, the White-winged Scoter. In the winter of 2013–2014, almost all the Great Lakes had ice cover for the first time in decades. The ice cover drove White-winged Scoters south in droves, and they were almost common in south Louisiana in early 2014. One male hung out for weeks at the lake behind Pennington Biomedical Research Center. We spotted another male on Lake Pontchartrain while kayaking to South Point.

Lynn and I did a big day just for fun on May 3. We were hampered a second time by the interstate being closed—there had been a fatal traffic accident and I-10 was closed between Baton Rouge and Lafayette. We took Highway 190 to head for Cameron Parish, but on the way we also jaunted down Louisiana 975 to see if the fishing shirt I had left at the Little Alabama Road fishing bridge in the Atchafalaya NWR was still there. The answer was a resounding no, and we were also unsuccessful in locating Swallow-tailed Kites that often grace the road and sky along LA 975 at this time of year.

Back on Highway 190, we proceeded to Turf Grass Road, Pintail Loop at Cameron Prairie NWR, the Pool Unit at Lacassine NWR, what we nicknamed the "toxidation" pond in Cameron due to its unnatural blue-green color, the Cameron courthouse wetlands, and Peveto. We finished the day with 103 birds, including eleven new ones for our year list: Least Bittern, Purple Gallinule, Stilt Sandpiper, Black Tern, Yellow-bellied Flycatcher, Northern Rough-winged Swallow, Cliff Swallow, Gray-cheeked Thrush, Swainson's Thrush, Northern Waterthrush, and Scarlet Tanager.

At the beginning of May, I decided to add up the birds on my Alabama and Louisiana lists as if they were a single list in Louisiana, as if it were a pseudo mini big year—not that I was trying for a big year; I wasn't, truly. However, I was watching my cadence of birding and trying to gauge how much birding I needed to do to rack up species at a particular rate, while watching other eBirders in the state doing the same thing.

I knew that Alabama and Louisiana were not the same place, but I also knew that the more practice I had, the better off I'd be in the future. The Landry-Leblanc tract on Grand Isle is different than the Indian Shell Mound on Dauphin Island, but they're both coastal chenieres (or mottes, or whatever you want to call them), and perfecting how to find a Worm-eating Warbler or a Blue-winged Warbler is going to be a similar exercise in both places. It wasn't a 1:1 overlap; because Dauphin Island is two hundred miles to the east of Baton Rouge, some birds would be easier on Dauphin Island (Cape May Warbler, Black-throated Blue Warbler) whereas others would be more difficult (White-faced Ibis, Burrowing Owl), but still. If nothing else, I could use the fact that back in the day the panhandle ran all the way from Jacksonville to Baton Rouge and was once part of the same state. Okay, so it was Florida at that point. Whatever. It wasn't a big year. But it was an exercise, a really fun one.

In mid-May, I had a work-related meeting in Little Rock, Arkansas, and I managed to squeeze in a morning of birding at Holla Bend NWR—I added Bell's Vireo, Alder Flycatcher, Nashville Warbler, and Least Flycatcher to my overall year list. And again, Arkansas is not Louisiana—but the same principle applied. The latter two birds were fairly straightforward gets in Louisiana. Alder Flycatchers were not as easy, but at the tail end of August and in the first half of September, if you hold off deerflies successfully enough to spend some quality time in Peveto, or find fruiting rough-leaf dogwood at South Farm in Iberville Parish, you can find Alder Flycatchers. Bell's Vireos crept down into the northern reaches of Louisiana every year during the late spring and summer months, and if I could see the typical habitat in Arkansas and watch the bird's behavior in the bush there, I'd up my chances in Louisiana when the actual big year presented itself. Plus, I could always call Terry Davis and beg for help. I was sitting at 260 species combined in Louisiana, Alabama, and Arkansas on May 19—it was not a barnstorm birding kind of year, but totally respectable. And then the wheels came off the year 2014.

* * * * *

It was Memorial Day weekend and we had just retrieved our boat from the shop, where it had gotten a tune-up. We had friends visiting, and we were about to take a trip to West Point, the western tip of Dauphin Island that was cut off from civilization after Hurricane Katrina split the island in half.

Lynn and I both love West Point—Lynn thinks it's great because the waters around this tip feature a dramatic shoreline drop off from two to fifteen-plus feet, and big fish hang out in that deeper water. She had pulled countless Redfish, Speckled Trout, Spanish Mackerel, White Trout, and Flounder out of that deep bowl, and she had not had a chance to cast into it since the previous October. My favorite thing is the walk to what I think of as my own personal birding pond, which is about one and a quarter miles from West Point on the Mississippi Sound (north) side. You walk and walk and walk some more, past the sand bars of gulls and terns, past the small mudflats that hold plovers, even Piping and Snowy, and past old wooden structures that at some point served some purpose that I'm not even sure of, even past those. And then you reach the pond. It is surrounded by tall scrub—something that approaches trees, but isn't quite. The pond is about ten acres total in area—but in it and in the surrounding mudflats, you just never know what you're going to get. There are the common things you see almost every time, like Great Blue Herons, Great Egrets, and Red-winged Blackbirds. But there are also Clapper Rails that walk out in the open and hang out as conspicuously as the wading birds, probably because there are no people there. Gull-billed Terns might be fishing the pond, or a Red Knot or American Oystercatcher might be in the surrounding mudflats. There are baby Black-crowned and Yellow-crowned Night-Herons throughout the summer; studying them side-by-side in that pond led me to the realization that with the immature birds of these species, the ones with the mostly black bills are Yellow-crowned Night-Herons and the ones with the mostly yellow bills are the Black-crowned Night-Herons. So, the trip to West Point was one we were both excited about.

We drove our boat to the launch, backed it down into the water, and loaded it with our fishing, picnic, and birding gear. When Lynn tried to start the boat, the battery was dead. Linda Lee and I did a quick run to the Ship and Shore, the general store on Dauphin Island, to pick up a new one. After putting the forty-pound battery in Lynn's hands, I proceeded to the front of the boat to relax in the sun and listen to Royal and Caspian Terns singing as they swooped over the marsh. Normally I would have been handing Lynn tools as she swapped out the battery, but our friend Megan was with us and she loves fixing things, so she was in the back of the boat helping Lynn.

I was watching Lynn as she leaned over the battery compartment when I heard a muffled explosion. Lynn jumped up and immediately dove into the water, and Megan jumped overboard half a second later. A burning noise filled the air and drew my attention from Lynn and Megan to the battery compartment, which was filled with bright orange flames. A louder burning sound ensued and I actually heard the fire travel under the back of the boat from port to starboard. A symmetric opening on the starboard side of the boat provided a view of the four-foot-high flames that blasted out of that hole toward the front of the boat. It hadn't yet occurred to my brain to move from my vantage point on the bow. Instead, I panned back to the water that Lynn and Megan had leapt into. Megan was swimming for all she was worth, out into the channel, to put distance between herself and the boat. Lynn hadn't moved from the general vicinity in which she'd landed, about ten feet from the boat—her back was still to me and she was lolling in the water.

"Lynn!" I called, "Are you okay?"

"No, I am not okay," she said, without moving.

"Lynn!" I called again, "Are you okay?" I must not have liked what I heard the first time—I never repeat myself like that, but there's something about a critical moment that brings out one's reptilian brain.

"No, I am not okay."

As she answered, she turned toward me. I watched as her face and shoulders came into view, then her arms, and as she kept turning one of her legs came up slowly toward the water's surface. Attached to her leg was a long, wide, thin sheet of something grayish-beige. It took my brain a second to figure out that I was looking at a flap of skin close to the size of a piece of plywood board that stretched from Lynn's ankle to her thigh. I do not remember moving, but all of a sudden I was on the boat adjacent to ours, which was as close as I could get to Lynn without getting into the water. I put my arm down in the water, looked her straight in the eye, and urged, "Swim."

She looked at me for a moment and then started coming toward me, slowly, but making progress. I remember trying to figure out if I should jump into the water to help her up or stay where I had better leverage—I decided on leverage. Two others came up behind me to help. Meanwhile, a guy in another boat near us started yelling, "Your boat's on fire! Your boat's on fire!"

When Lynn finally got within arm's reach and put up her hand, I grabbed it, and she immediately let go of me and said, "Don't touch my hand."

As she pulled it away, I saw yellowish gobs of skin hanging off her palms and a very deep, dark red gash in one of her fingers. I grabbed her high on the arm and started pulling up. As the people behind me grabbed on too, I yelled, "Don't touch her hands!"

Within a few seconds we had Lynn out of the water and standing on the deck. Her clothes had almost burned off. Meanwhile, the squawking guy had changed his song from "Your boat's on fire," to "Cut it loose! It's gonna blow!"

Linda had astutely gone to fetch her truck, and with a person on each side of her for support, Lynn walked to the truck and lay flat in the back seat. Megan had made her way out of the water and we loaded her into the truck bed. Within a couple of minutes we were en route for medical care, though to where we didn't know. Quick calling on Sarah's part put us at the base of the Dauphin Island bridge, where local paramedics met us while an ambulance from Mobile was dispatched.

Lynn was calm, though quaking from shock. The local paramedics didn't have fluids with them, which are critical to burns because when you lose a lot of skin, you lose your ability to retain fluid. I was in the back seat with Lynn, pouring water down her throat. She kept opening her mouth for it and repeating, "Water." The paramedics were monitoring Lynn's blood pressure, and when one paramedic announced 60/60 to the other, they both looked worried; they estimated that Lynn was burned over approximately 50 percent of her body.

It felt like a long wait for the Mobile paramedics, but they arrived like the cavalry about twenty-five minutes after we reached the bridge. They quickly loaded Lynn, as well as Megan, who had burned both her legs from knee to ankle, and told me to get in the front seat. Lynn said later that one of the most painful parts of the entire ordeal was when she was moved out of the shade of the back of the truck into the bright sun as the gurney she was strapped to was wheeled from the truck to the ambulance. We took off like a bat out of hell for the University of South Alabama Medical Center, where there was a burn unit. I was as scared as I'd ever been in my life. Just like when flight attendants on an airplane look scared, when paramedics look scared, you know you're in trouble.

I no longer remember what the ambulance driver was saying to me while he was driving, but he was shooting the breeze with the calming spirit of a man who had done this many, many times, transported a critical patient in the back while comforting a loved one riding shotgun in the front. We jammed up Highway 193 with the siren on full blast on a sunny, gorgeous day. I didn't think about it at the time, but it was such a study in contrasts: our world was a hurricane, while around us it was placid and beautiful. We got about seven miles up the road with everyone getting well out of our way, and then we came up behind a car that didn't move over. Jeremy Hamby had to lay off the accelerator. He looked over at me, flashed me a thousand-watt smile, and said, "Look at this bozo. Watch this!"

He hit a button on the dashboard and all of a sudden the high-pitched, high-frequency siren had a companion. This second siren was lower in pitch and slower in frequency, and not nearly as loud as the first siren, but it literally created vibration. It reminded me of being at an intersection when a car with booming bass pulls up, and the way that the entire intersection vibrates when that happens. All of a sudden it was as if the ambulance was gently undulating up the road, adding an up and down motion to its forward motion, and it felt almost as if the ambulance had become the siren frequency itself, up, down, up, down, fast forward—and vibrating. The offending car moved off the road immediately, and the vibrating siren stopped.

Jeremy looked at me again, smiled, and said, "We call that the Jesus button. People who are deaf? They can feel the vibration on this thing! Every dog I pass howls at the moon when they hear this button. Notice that it only lasts for seven seconds—that's because if it stays on for twelve it can cause heart attacks with people who have atrial fibrillation; people with pacemakers could have them stop working! The good news is, no matter what, everyone gets out of the way."

Jeremy had to employ the Jesus button five or six times on his way to the hospital, and it worked like magic every time. He got up to 93 mph on I-10 and had us to the USA Medical Center in thirty-two minutes. I made this trip many times myself in the ensuing weeks, and the fastest I ever made it in was fifty.

Burn unit personnel determined that Lynn had been burned on 28 percent of her body; the burns started at the top of her arms and went all the way to her feet, mostly on the front. She had circumferential burning, which wraps around your entire body, on her lower legs and ankles. The doctors told me that with a burn on this amount of skin, chances were 100 percent that Lynn would develop at least one infection.

The first twenty-four hours after the boat accident were really tough. I thought that I was going to lose Lynn twice during this period, first due to low blood pressure, which the paramedics were able to start to address in the ambulance, and then due to a swelled airway. The body's natural response to burns is swelling, which is good from an immunity standpoint, but a swelled airway can be fatal. Thinking that you might lose someone close to you is a horrible feeling, like you're standing on the edge of a precipice—you haven't been forced to step over it, but you're not allowed to step back from the edge either. It's a terrible kind of slow motion limbo.

The situation was also devastating because although Lynn was the only one of us in the ICU burn unit, she wasn't the only one hospitalized. Megan was in the regular burn unit for her legs, and Sarah, who had been standing in front of the other open compartment in the back of the boat when the explosion occurred, had a small burn on her foot. Thankfully she had already exited the boat before the wall of fire came through that opening. Sarah was hospitalized in the regular burn unit for a day to make sure that there weren't infections in her wound. Megan had second-degree burns all over the front of her legs, and while the doctors were concerned that she might need skin grafts, she was able to avoid them and left the hospital after four days.

I wasn't allowed to stay with Lynn in the ICU, so I crashed on the guest sofa in Megan's room. Lynn was only about thirty feet away because Megan's room was just down the hall from the ICU, but it felt like I was a world apart. I slept pretty fitfully that first night; I woke up at 1 A.M. and 4 A.M. and both times I went to the nurse's station and asked them to call the ICU to check on her. Both times, the ICU nurses relayed that Lynn was resting comfortably and her vitals were okay.

After the first twenty-four hours, I felt much better about Lynn making it—the ICU burn nurses weren't looking scared and that was good—but it was still a turbulent flight. The phone calls to Lynn's family. A fever of 103F. An MRSA infection. (I knew that methicillin-resistant *Staphylococcus aureus* could kill, but when I said, "Oh my god!" in response to Sherri Raybon, the ICU burn nurse, she said, "Don't worry! We've got that totally under control, we have the antibiotic regimen set for that infection. It's *Vibrio* that we worry about in here, not MRSA. And she doesn't have *Vibrio!*")

Lynn also had a *Shewanella putrifaciens* infection. I have studied enough microbiology to know the names of typical microbes, but I'd never heard of that one—I'd never even heard of the genus *Shewanella*. Lynn was the rock star of the hospital's infectious diseases unit because that specific infection hadn't been seen in the hospital in twelve years. *Shewanella putrifaciens* naturally occurs in the environment and breaks down fish waste—if one ever sees a dead fish with pinkish bacterial colonies on it, the microbe contained in those colonies is *S. putrifaciens*. When Lynn dove into the water, she landed right next to a fish-cleaning station, so it made sense that she had this infection. I remained nervous through her two-hour skin graft surgery, during which 8 percent of Lynn's healthy skin was harvested to help heal the most burned parts of her body. After surgery I worried about "red man syndrome," an allergic reaction that Lynn developed in response to taking the antibiotic Vancomycin, which turned her unburned skin into a tapestry of angry reds and pinks.

Some moments were not turbulent, though. Some were downright funny. Lynn's sister, Eve, flew down from Ohio for moral support, and one evening the three of us were in near hysterics in the ICU. Lynn had managed to regain her typical sense of humor and was talking about drinking her margarita and sucking on her bong. The lemon-lime Gatorade that she was ordered to drink almost constantly resembled a margarita, and she had been given an incentive spirometer, a device that one blows into to help maintain lung capacity so that a patient won't develop pneumonia during an extended hospital stay. Lynn's exaggerated actions of drinking the Gatorade and blowing into the spirometer had Eve and me laughing like crazy. Days later, I was sitting next to Lynn in the ICU when Sherri came into the room looking uncharacteristically awkward. She stood at the foot of Lynn's bed, looking a little like a metronome as she rocked back and forth. Sherri said, "I am really sorry to tell you this, but it is the law in the state of Alabama and I have to follow it. Some of the medicines you're about to take would be harmful to a fetus. If you are under the age of sixty-five, you must have a pregnancy test." After a moment of stunned silence, Lynn and I simultaneously burst out laughing. Sherri relaxed, again looking like the confident nurse she was. She smiled and said, "Now, if that test comes back positive, I am not going to be the one walking in here to tell y'all—I will have the doctor do that."

* * * * *

The boat explosion was just a moment, slow and fast at the same time, and honestly, not a very dramatic one. When I conjure a mental image of "boat explosion," I think of what one usually sees in the movies, with fire forty feet high and debris spewing in every direction. The initial explosion sounded to me more like our boat burped and then proceeded to breathe fire like a dragon for several minutes. I had no idea that Lynn had caught on fire in the moment immediately following the explosion. She told me later that she dove before she was even thinking. "Hot" registered, and she was already diving. I didn't know that Megan was burned, or Sarah either.

This initially understated moment became a sharp demarcation point in my life. It's the kind of huge event that divides time "before event x and after event x," like before Hurricane Katrina and after Hurricane Katrina. For me, it was the first of that type since Katrina, except this moment hit closer to home. Instead of being a community-wide event that affected me and everyone around me, everyone around me was going on with their normal lives while I felt like I was standing there holding the bag and wondering what had happened.

I realized at some point that in the immediate aftermath of the explosion everyone communicated using words with two syllables or less—and that I didn't hear a Caspian or Royal Tern, or any other bird call, from the moment I heard the explosion. As events unfolded after the accident, I found myself in different rooms of an emotional house of sorts. First there was fear of loss, then survivor guilt, because Megan was burned instead of me. There were haunting thoughts about the cause of the accident—whose fault was it? That was Lynn's greatest fear, that the accident was her fault. There was the room where the rug was pulled out from under me as I tried to find a little routine in my days. Morning coffee was the hardest part of my day because I was used to brewing coffee for the two of us, and then we'd sit around, sip coffee, and shoot the breeze each morning before starting the day's activities. I wasn't allowed into the ICU until 8 A.M. (10 A.M. on Sundays), and I wasn't allowed to bring any food or drink. Further, Lynn wasn't allowed to drink coffee, so instead I sat at what I came to think of as my own hospital cafeteria table, with coffee brewed by someone else. This particular table had the best vantage point of the roof, where pigeons enjoyed hanging out within my line of sight. That was my new morning routine until I could enter the ICU. I often felt like I was in a safe room with my thoughts and feelings, a windowless room with soundproof walls and soft paneling. It was a comfortable place to be.

The boat accident felt like someone pressed a great big Jesus button on my life and on Lynn's. It shook up everything, and while it certainly wasn't a conscious decision, the accident made me examine every aspect of my life. After spending some time in the rooms of my emotional house, I realized that there was not a single thing I would change—and in that way, the experience was positive. I realized that life was hard at one hundred feet, and would be for the short term, but up at ten thousand feet things were really okay. Lynn would recover. We were lucky and blessed in so many ways: the burn unit was fairly close to the accident scene; when Lynn dove into the water just after the explosion, she didn't hit her head on the bottom; we had health and boat insurance; Lynn received superior medical care at the USA Medical Center burn unit; we had so many people, friends and family, who rallied around us; the leaky fuel tank that caused the accident was not our fault.

The hospital saga ended on June 4, when I drove Lynn to our house in Baton Rouge. The last thing medical personnel told Lynn as she left the hospital was that she was a super healer. They explained that a small percentage of the population has the ability to heal very quickly and that Lynn was among this select group; she made it out of the hospital twice as fast as expected. They explained that research on super healers was in its nascent stages but has shown that the structure of their cellular mitochondria is different from what the rest of us have. I always knew that Lynn was superhuman—now I knew that it had a cellular basis.

Lynn's getting well enough to leave the hospital was a big step, but just the first step, in a long recovery process. Going home was wonderful but also a challenge, because during our favorite season of the year Lynn was banished to the indoors except at night. She wasn't allowed to get into the water until her wounds completely closed up. And while being active was encouraged by the doctors, the injuries forced Lynn to move slowly and for short distances.

Lynn and I tend to have one speed: run. The accident caused us to stop, at least for a while, and then to ramp up a little at a time. Lynn couldn't go outside to fish or swim or see birds, so instead we birded from the inside out—literally in part, but also figuratively. For example, I'd never seen Brown Thrasher babies play. I watched out the window as one parachuted to the ground, where it face- and body-planted in the sand and remained there, unmoving. Is it dead, I thought to myself? Do I need to go check on the little thing? At that moment, a sibling followed the same vertical trajectory, landing feet first mere inches from the planted bird. In response, the planted bird jumped up and started playing with its sibling. The two ran long-legged and wide-eyed in figure eights around the yard. I'd never seen anything like it.

I watched Northern Cardinals feeding Brown-headed Cowbird babies at the neighbors' bird feeders. The immature cowbirds were almost as big as the adult cardinals. They were aggressive rascals with huge beaks and mouths and an attitude to go with it. They stalked the adult cardinals, demanding food, and the adults worked overtime to provide it. The baby cardinals were getting a little seed once in a while from their parents but had to do most of the work on their own. I had never noticed how pretty an immature cardinal is; the males are a patchwork of brownish-grays and bright reds.

The Red-bellied Woodpecker that our neighbors had nicknamed Woody frequented the feeders just like the cardinals, thrashers, cowbirds, and finches, but once in a while it would come to the eves and hang upside down to look at us on the porch. It actually seemed to check in to see how we were doing. One day, a White-winged Dove showed up—in all the years I'd been observing those feeders, I'd never seen one visit. Before the accident, we were content to listen to the neighbors regale us with stories about the birds that frequented the feeder, but we never sat to watch ourselves. But now watching the feeders from inside the house was the only thing we could do—and so we did it, with vigor.

The accident reminded me that at any time the unthinkable can happen and life can change dramatically. Of course I knew that, but when you live through a situation with a Jesus button, it adds an element of experience that changes your understanding of that intellectual concept forever. The accident scooped something out from under me that has never quite come back. At the same time, I gained something—I wouldn't call it confidence or even wisdom, but the knowledge that I can make it through a tough time okay.

The accident reminded me to live day-to-day and to connect with the things and people I love, because both helped me make the hard shifts necessary to navigate the situation. I love birds and love to run all over creation to see them, but I don't have to run to get joy from birds. It's still one love, even if circumstance prevents me from pursuing that one love in the way I like best. I can derive as much joy from watching pigeons perform a strut show on the hospital roof at the USA Medical Center as I can from executing a 60–0 deceleration at Four Magic Miles on Highway 82 in the hopes that I just spotted the rare but present Ferruginous Hawk instead of a Red-tailed, on a day where I rack up 250 miles on the truck. So: Dance in the fields of the Shreveport airport like Terry Davis. Decorate every plant and tree in your yard with red creamer caps to attract hummingbirds like Donna and Steve. Push to get into the eBird top one hundred in a completely different state, like Kimberly Lanka did when her father-in-law was sick and her family spent time in Illinois as his life wound toward completion. Or bond over watching Scissor-tailed Flycatchers on the wires, like Marty's parents.

* * * * *

Our first post-accident birding trip occurred during the evening of July 10. Lynn insisted on driving us the hour north to Cat Island NWR to look for Wood Storks. "Because that's what I do, I drive you to places to bird," she said.

Cat Island is open only part of the year because at times the Mississippi River floods it to the point that the road through the refuge is not navigable. (Before visiting there, one should always check that the Mississippi River water level datum in St. Francisville is under eighteen feet.) The Cypress-Tupelo swamp and bottomland hardwood forest habitats at Cat Island accommodate some good bird diversity. There's one main road in and out of the refuge, with a number of places to pull over or turn around; the entrance and exit are paved, but the road throughout the refuge is dirt and is slightly elevated compared to the surrounding swamp and trees, sort of like a mini-levee.

Years ago, on a visit to Cat Island, I birded and then parked myself in a chair next to our truck to read while Lynn and some of our friends were fishing for bass and bream in their kayaks. I'd gotten engrossed in my book and came out of it to realize that the water had flooded the banks and was beginning to cover the road. The water level had increased several inches in about twenty minutes and was lapping against the bottom of my chair. I yelled like a banshee to get everyone out of the kayaks, into the truck, and out of the refuge ASAP. As we made our way out of the refuge on the main road, crawfish were crossing the road by the thousands. We managed to avoid hitting them, although we would have been pulled over for suspected drunk driving had a police officer witnessed our weaving. We were all laughing because the crawfish were hysterical—each stood its ground as the truck rolled toward it, fearless with raised claws, each appearing to say to our truck in crawfish-speak, "Don't mess with me, I'll make you sorry!"

During our current trip, the only thing that Lynn could do was bird out the window. She was too weak to do more than that. She was still wrapped up in bandages from the top of her shoulders to her feet, and it was very hot and humid in the July heat, with a heat index of over 100 even though it was early evening. Still, she didn't complain—and I was reminded for the thousandth time that Lynn is quite a trouper. We entered the refuge, and at the first bend on the main road, standing in the mud at the water's edge, was a Solitary Sandpiper, doing its herky-jerky, "You're not going to come any closer to me, are you?" dance and sporting a bright white eye ring.

A tenth of a mile up the road, a warbler call cut through the din of egret and heron chucks and grunts, sending a chill up my spine. It was a call I knew, but I couldn't believe I was hearing it. I got out to scan the tops of the trees to follow the calls and realized after a minute or two that there were two birds, and they were singing back and forth. Lynn pulled up the Cerulean Warbler on her iPhone and we huddled together, quietly playing the bird's song inside the truck to see if my thoughts regarding the call were correct.[3] At that point my heart almost stopped, because the birds calling were exactly what I thought they were: two

Cerulean Warblers hurling songs back and forth between treetops about fifty feet apart. To my knowledge, the Cerulean Warbler had no business being in Cat Island NWR in the dead of a south Louisiana summer. So I waited. And I watched. And eventually one catapulted out of a tree, dipped down to about twenty feet off the ground, flew right over my head, then ascended again to land on the top of another tree across the road and across the muddy ditch—and I clearly saw cerulean blue when it dipped down toward me. Lynn was able to get a glimpse of the bird while hanging out the driver's side window with her binoculars. Two Cerulean Warblers. In July. Who knew?

A quarter mile up the road from the ceruleans, we spotted six Wood Storks camped out on the top of two cypress trees that almost grew together thirty feet off the ground. Between the Wood Stork's large, prehistoric looks and the shapes of the trees, I almost felt like I was in the African savannah. I put the scope on the storks to view them in spectacular detail as the sun lit up their features in the sweet light that occurs during the hour before sundown. Score! It was a good thing we got the Wood Storks then and there, because we didn't see any more during the trip, and when we turned around a few miles up the road and drove back out of the refuge, the storks had moved from their original location. At the turnaround point in the refuge, three male Painted Buntings were singing up a storm, painting the town blue, red, and green as they perched in the open, sounding a bit like they were rehearsing for the "knockout rounds" in the TV competition show *The Voice*. I exited the truck to better view them but was immediately attacked by large mosquitos, which reminded me of the Louisiana joke about the mosquito being the state bird.

Our short evening trip to Cat Island NWR was fabulous because now we had our wheels back under us. We even stopped in St. Francisville on the way home to have dinner at the Magnolia Café. It felt so good to start taking back normal, even if a little at a time.

At some point during those seemingly long summer days indoors, I remembered my top fifty eBird lists in Louisiana and Alabama. It felt like a long time since I'd visited them, but when I looked we were well within the top fifty for each state and in thirteenth and fourteenth place in the state of Alabama. I am not sure what took hold of me, but I decided that it might be fun to recalibrate. Could we shoot for a top ten eBird finish in Alabama? Lynn said sure, why not? This challenge gave me something to do, namely, to determine which trip(s) we could make within Alabama and when, to put our list over the top. I eventually settled on a late year trip to Wheeler NWR, in the northern reaches of the state, to give Lynn as much time as possible to recover.

We birded occasionally later in the summer and into the fall as Lynn continued to build her strength and endurance. A late August trip to Turf Grass Road was notable, not for the species diversity, but for the numbers of birds we saw: we had over twenty Scissor-tailed Flycatchers on the wires and in the grass, and a flock of ninety Buff-breasted Sandpipers out on one of the turfgrass fields. I'd never seen so many of either species at once. We added a species here and there in Alabama in the fall to keep our eBird rank in the low teens. For example, in late September a Merlin flew overhead while Lynn fished near the Bayou La Batre boat launch. Magnolia Warblers are easier to get on Dauphin Island in the fall than the spring, and we scored one in the Shell Mound in early October. We saw our first ever for Dauphin Island Scissor-tailed Flycatcher perched in tall grass at Fort Gaines on October 4.

On November 2, we headed out to the West End beach on Dauphin Island. Given the magnitude and direction of the winds we were experiencing that day, Lynn thought that if she fished on the Gulf of Mexico side of the beach, it would be the best fishing she could do on the island. She set up at a cut on the beach and proceeded to catch whiting after whiting. That particular fish species told her that winter was here. The day before, I'd observed a small flock of Yellow-rumped Warblers while walking—a sure a sign of winter for me.

After watching Lynn fish for a while, I headed for the large mudflat about three-quarters of a mile away from the West End beach parking lot. In the late summer, this flat teems with thousands of birds, but once you hit fall and winter the numbers are much reduced, though there is usually decent species variety. I wanted to see what was present. It was very quiet out on the West End beach that day; we were the only people, save for a lone fisherman sitting atop his cooler adjacent to the parking lot. There is something special about the beach in the wintertime—it's not austere, but very quiet. The 15–20 mph steady north wind did lend "noise" to what otherwise would have been absolute silence.

The beach was also very quiet with respect to birds—which led me to thinking that, as had been expressed on LA-BIRD, this fall was exceptionally slow as a season for migratory birds. I'd seen a couple of hawk kettles; there had been a redstart here, a Magnolia Warbler there, a nice Nashville Warbler on Lighthouse Road, a few Black-throated Green Warblers and Prairie Warblers, but nothing spectacular. As I was thinking this, a butterfly fluttered over my head and landed in some nearby beach grass. Unlike the fall birding migration, the butterfly migration had been, well, awesome. I am no lepidopterist, but I can appreciate butterflies, and they had been absolutely everywhere. And that's good. I actually uttered out loud the words "And that's good." That's probably weird (and the weird part is not a news flash to me), but out in the middle of nowhere, with no one around, it seems okay to say things out loud for emphasis once in a while, and I did.

I am not sure if it was in response to my utterance or my approaching footsteps, but all of a sudden the sound of wing flaps cut through the windblown beach grass. Up out of the sea grass, not fifteen feet away, rose a Short-eared Owl. I'd never seen a Short-eared Owl before, but I knew exactly what it was right away. It's the confidence that comes from wistfully studying a bird countless times with the hope that on some wonderful day you will actually see it. I saw its mottled brown wings as it took off, and its clock-like face; the bird changed direction a couple of times, showcasing beautiful shades of brown with cream-colored underwings. It was so long-winged for an owl that the bird reminded me of the bats in the animated children's movie *Hotel Transylvania*. I watched the owl until it landed, about a quarter mile up the beach, again in some beach grass.

I took off for Lynn, whose back was to me and who was oblivious of what felt like high drama for me. I was in permanent, fully developed goose bump thrill mode and maintaining a dead sprint, which felt fast to me. But when you're approaching fifty, feeling fast and actually being fast are two different things. I was screaming Lynn's name and realized that my mouth was starting to hurt—

and I realized that it was hurting because I was smiling ear to ear, as hard as I could, without even trying. Finally, on my fourth exalted yell, she turned around. "Short-eared Owl!" I bellowed.

Not many things will make Lynn Hathaway put down a fishing pole on a day when she can hook a Redfish, but the Short-eared Owl was one of them. She reeled in her line, stuck her pole in its holder, grabbed her binoculars, and followed me along the beach to where I thought I had seen the owl land. Just as I thought perhaps I was wrong and had misjudged the distance or location, the owl launched from the ground again and flew low at first, and then high into the sky, eventually joining a Caspian Tern and continuing on west: a two-minute show. I was like my mom on the Sprague's Pipits in the field at the King Ranch: *I got it!* I am absolutely enamored with that bird, number 470 on my life list.

On Friday evening, December 5, we departed Baton Rouge for Wheeler NWR. I was like a kid in a candy store; I had used eBird frequency histograms to figure out our probability of seeing birds that we needed to add to our Alabama list, and I'd determined that we could see as many as twenty-six birds, including two I'd never seen before, Lapland Longspur and Horned Lark. I also knew that eight new birds would break us into the top ten in Alabama, but that we ought to try to get as many as possible over that threshold because other birders were going to be birding the rest of the year to try to increase their year totals as well, and we wanted some cushion for this end-of-year rallying.

We reached Wheeler at mid-morning the next day. We parked at the visitor's center, and as soon as we got out of the car I immediately heard the high-pitched, three-note call of the Golden-crowned Kinglet. We quickly observed several of the small gray birds featuring a wide, yellow crown stripe in the trees in the parking lot. Score! We edged one species closer to the top ten.

The visitor's center sported a line of windows at the back of the building. A half dozen seed feeders were adorned with Purple and House Finches, and Blue Jays. The Purple Finches were new for the year, and the docents told us that occasionally Pine Siskins were being seen at the feeders. We waited a while for them to show up and kept checking back during the next couple of days, but we were never able to add them to our year list. After fully exploring the visitor's center, we headed out the back of the building and traversed a short, curvy, tree-lined path to the wildlife observation tower. A White-breasted Nuthatch was among the birds along the path, which made us plus three on our year list before we even reached the tower.

The tower was everything I'd read about and then some. It was a two-story building with floor-to-ceiling glass windows on both stories, mostly out the back of the building. The second floor sported glass across multiple walls that enabled us to see at least 120 degrees worth of a panorama. The observation tower was heated, and because heat rises, the second floor was downright cozy and a welcome break from the 50 degree and somewhat windy outdoor environs. Numerous speakers dotted the upper wall-to-ceiling boundary of the second floor, and through them a cacophony of bird sounds filled the room. When I stepped to the glass, I saw low rolling hills covered with grass and dirt, a couple of large ponds, and trees as a distant boundary around most of the area. I also saw birds everywhere—the ponds were loaded with ducks, and the land sported additional ducks, tons of geese, and more Sandhill Cranes than I'd ever seen at once. It was thrilling—plus there were new Alabama year list species out there. I just needed to locate them.

I was getting out my notebook to start my eBird counts when a woman walked up to me and introduced herself. "Hi, I'm Nicole Weaver," she said. "I'm here every day, and you're new." I told her that it was my first time visiting and that I was extremely impressed with the bird diversity and density. She proceeded to tell me everything about the place. I'm guessing that Nicole was somewhere in her eighties. She looked a little like a conductor as she talked about Wheeler while pointing and gesturing. I was impressed with the way that she did this while holding a pair of absolutely massive binoculars in her hands—she slung them around like a champ. When she took a breath after about ninety seconds of monologue, I couldn't help myself.

"What power are those?" I asked. "They're 10s," she said, and I was shocked at the size of them. She showed them to me and they were 10 x 50s,[4] which made a little more sense, but still—they were gargantuan. "I've had them since the '80s!" she said proudly. I decided that there was no point in telling her that optics are smaller and lighter now, I'm sure she's heard it a hundred times. People tell me the same thing about my 12 x 36s, but I plan to hold on to my relatively heavy binoculars until my hands can't take the weight anymore—I really like the extra magnification. I drifted back into Nicole's recital.

"I come here every day to check all the birds present. I was here in the year 2000, when the first Sandhill Crane showed up. He stayed all winter and then went out and told his friends how great Wheeler is and the next year we had ten, then fifty the year after that, then a thousand. Today, there are sixteen thousand cranes on this refuge! Look at that pond! American Wigeon, Mallards, look at that huge flock of Gadwall, and see the Northern Shovelers over there? There are all kinds of ducks out there!"

When you are lucky enough to encounter a birder as enthusiastic as Nicole, you roll out all your questions, so I began asking about birds we needed to add to our list that were good possibilities in Wheeler. I asked if there were any American Black Ducks in the area. "No," she said with concern, "They used to come here a lot, year round! They do nest here at the pond in the summertime, but I haven't seen any in a while."

"How about Wood Ducks?"

"No again, they're in the same situation as the American Black Duck," she answered. "I am worried about them because they don't seem to come around here anymore."

"Do you have any Greater White-fronted Geese out here?"

"Yes," she said triumphantly, pointing out a flock in the distance, "they're all hanging out right there." I observed over one hundred and mentally added another plus one to our year list.

"Do you know where I can get a Horned Lark in the refuge? I know that they hang out on agricultural fields and we drove by some as we pulled up to the visitor's center, but I don't know if those particular ag fields are a good spot to find them. I'm guessing that some ag fields are better than others—do you know?" Nicole looked at me like I had three eyes. "I'm not a *birder*!" she exclaimed. My confusion must have been evident, as she'd just given me species histories of numerous Wheeler birds. "I'm a *ponder*," she continued. "I just bird the *pond*. There are no Horned Larks at the pond, so I have no idea where to find them."

Nicole said her goodbyes, and Lynn and I proceeded to count all the bird species at the pond. We estimated three thousand Sandhill Cranes out the window, and like white needles in a gray haystack, we observed two Whooping Cranes in residence among the Sandhills. There were five duck species, and well over one hundred of several of them.

When we left the visitor's center and wildlife observation pond area, we had added eight birds to our year list. We were on the cusp of the top ten with much of the day to go, and the entire next day to bird as well. Later that day, as the sun set, we added American Pipit and Horned Lark to our year list on a dusty agricultural field at the Beaverdam Peninsula Tower. I'm sure that the name of this site has significance, but there was no beaver dam anywhere in eyeshot and the land didn't appear to be a peninsula in any way, shape, or form. However, I was elated—I ran around the elevated wooden structure with my arms in the air after observing fifteen Horned Larks playing with each other in the field. Their pale wings are notable, but were even more so in the setting sun.

All in all, we left the refuge with thirteen new species for the year, including the American Black Duck and Wood Duck, which we managed to locate in other parts of Wheeler. This bird total was enough to put us in eighth and ninth place in Alabama. During this two-day birding extravaganza, we hiked about six miles and put a good three hundred miles on the truck (Wheeler is a big place). Lynn hiked every step of the way and drove us every mile of the trip, because it's what she does, she takes me places to see birds, even if she's still wearing compression[5] on her legs and hand, even if she's not yet 100 percent recovered. This trip put me at 287 bird species for the year (Lynn was at 284) using the pseudo big year formula. When adding up birds in Louisiana and Alabama for both of us, and Arkansas for me, with that Wheeler trip we both eclipsed our 2012 big year total of 280 bird species. We still had three weeks to go to the end of the year, and with the accident, we had done much less birding than in 2012. We were clearly better birders than we'd been just two years before.

We returned to Dauphin Island for the holidays, and in the few days between

Christmas and New Year's we planned a couple more trips to points north to see if we could squeeze out a few more species. I was hovering in tenth place in Alabama, and Lynn was one species behind me in eleventh; a birder named Damien Simbeck was in the mix too, and the three of us were neck and neck. We ran up to the University of South Alabama campus in Mobile to see if we could get an Anhinga and a Barred Owl. We got the Anhinga at the wetlands in the back of the campus, but not the owl. We also visited Old St. Stephens Historical Park. Its tiny visitor's center featured a parking space right in front of the check-in shack that had a sign that read "LSU football parking." We thankfully knew better than to park in that spot, and the caretaker, who came out to greet us, said that his wife put the sign up so that she'd always have a proper spot to park in. He noted our Louisiana license plate and dared us to park in it, but we circled out of the lot and managed to add a Wild Turkey and a Fox Sparrow to our list as we hiked the trails in the park. On December 29, I had 243 bird species in Alabama and Lynn had 242. I just hoped that would be enough.

On December 31, I went running and decided to take a few trails at the Shell Mound to discover what there was to see and hear. I hadn't been birding in the Shell Mound for weeks because it just didn't have the targets we needed to continue to build our state list. As Lynn said, there hadn't been a Red-breasted Nuthatch or Brown Creeper spotted in the entire state in the last thirty days, and if those species were going to be spotted, likely it would be in the northern part of the state. So we'd been frequenting the golf course, looking for Scaly-breasted Munia instead. When I turned onto Iberville Street, I saw a single car parked in the Shell Mound parking lot. It had Mississippi plates and a hummingbird on the plate too—a birder. I wanted to find this person and tell them about the awesome birds I'd been seeing in case they wanted to go find them too. I ran through most of the trails in the mound before I found the lady at the oldest tree in the park.

"Good morning," I said, "what have you found in the Shell Mound today?"

"I've seen a kinglet," she declared with a huge smile.

"I'm a birder myself," I said, and "I've been on Dauphin Island for the past week. The Shell Mound is slow right now, but I can tell you about some of the awesome birds I've seen and where to see them, if you want to know."

"Sure," she said.

So I told her about the golf course—she knew exactly where to park on Hernando Street and how to access the dunes to reach its eastern border. I told her about the houses adjacent to the golf course and how at the second house, in the grassy area in the back, Scaly-breasted Munias had been seen by birders several times in the last couple of weeks. She smiled widely, "Oh, I've never seen one of those."

"Me either," I said, "and I keep striking out on finding them, but yesterday afternoon I was out there and I saw a Western Kingbird. If you go to flag six, there are three leafless trees adjacent to the green, and the kingbird was hanging out in those trees." Then I told her about west end beach and the three adult and three immature gannets I'd seen yesterday.

"They're so beautiful, aren't they?" she said.

"Indeed," I replied.

I started to describe other places when she said, "I haven't seen many ducks, do you know where I can see ducks?"

"Sure—keep going on the east end of the golf course and you'll run straight into a little pond. Yesterday the pond had Redheads, Mallard and Mottled Ducks, Ring-necked Ducks, and Lesser Scaup."

She nodded, then said, "My hip has been bothering me, I'm not sure why. I'm doing physical therapy and hoping that it will help. I've been doing what I can—I like to walk two to three miles a day and I like to get out and bird, but I just can't bird the way I'm used to. I don't think I can make it up that dune. I'm seventy-seven years old and I do what I can do."

"I am sorry," I said, and I really meant it. I felt like I could relate, given everything that had happened earlier in the year.

"Well, I'm taking turmeric, and that helps. That's a natural anti-inflammatory. I'm refusing to take the Mobic my silly doctor prescribed."

"I can understand that," I laughed, and then asked, "What's your name?"

"Mary Pickard. I'm Walter Anderson's daughter. I guess I have a famous pedigree."

"Wow!" I said, "My mom *loves* Walter's art and goes to the museum in Ocean Springs all the time."

"Well that's wonderful. What's your mom's name?"

"Kathleen Rogers," I replied proudly, "and I'm Marybeth Lima. It's very nice to meet you."

"You too," she said, and then asked, "You really think there's nothing to see in here?"

"Well, there's the usual: cardinals, Blue Jays, Carolina Wrens, and mockingbirds."

She looked me straight in the eye and said, "Well, what else could you ask for?"

I looked straight back at her and said, "You're absolutely right about that."

We said our goodbyes and she turned back along the trail near the old tree and kept birding. What a perfect bookend to 2014. I was reminded once again that it's so important to do what you love in whatever capacity you can do it. To troop on despite adversity. And to appreciate whatever flies across your path. What more can you ask for, truly.

* * * * *

I finished 2014 in ninth place on the Alabama bird list with 243 bird species, and Lynn finished in tenth place with 242 species. I had Lesser Yellowlegs, American Golden-Plover, and Black Tern that Lynn didn't, and in the spring she saw a Dickcissel and a Swainson's Warbler that I missed. Damien Simbeck came in at eleventh place with 238 species. Lynn and I finished tied for thirty-third place in the state of Louisiana, with the same 255 bird species.

Our boat needed two rounds of repairs before she was seaworthy, and the fiberglass on the inside storage cabin of the center console where the electronics blew out remains stippled and discolored. Lynn feels a kinship to the boat. "We both have scars to show from the accident," she says. The two of us took the boat for her first spin post-accident on March 25, 2016. We shared a look and a gulp as Lynn turned the key in the ignition while moored in the same slip in which the explosion occurred; we both relaxed when *Sweet Olive* started right up and vibrated strongly and comfortably as usual. Lynn drove us to West Point, where I observed migrating Eastern Kingbirds coming in from the Gulf and landing on tall grasses swaying in 10–15 mph north winds. *Sweet Olive* is still going strong today, as is Lynn, who made a 100 percent recovery from the burns.

Though Lynn says she has post-traumatic stress disorder every time she has to change a battery, she has had occasion to change car and boat batteries several times since and hasn't let fear stop her, though she does sniff the area to ensure that there is no leaking gasoline (a smart thing to do and highly recommended for anyone changing a battery).

Mary Pickard recovered from her hip injury and reports that she is "much more spry" now that she's in her eighties.

THE YEAR OF THE DAY TRIP

During the Thanksgiving holiday in 2015, Lynn and I drove to Steubenville, Ohio, and brought Lynn's mom, Mary, back to Louisiana to live with us. Mary's moving into our house was a decision we'd made some time before, though the conversation had been hypothetical because we didn't think that she would up-root from her lifetime home.

I'd like to be able to say that I had nothing but good thoughts in my heart about this momentous change in our lives, but I'd be lying. It's not that I was all gloom and doom either—but having someone, anyone, move into your house when you're not used to it is a hard adjustment. Mary is kind and an easy person to live with—but she also has congestive heart failure and debilitating arthritis, which translates into more chores. I work hard at my day job, but I usually felt "off" when I wasn't working. Now, I felt "on" during my "off" time in a way I wasn't used to—the responsibility to help care for someone felt like a second job had been added to my life.

It was in this context that I decided I wanted to try for three hundred bird species in Louisiana in 2016. It's not even that I decided—it almost felt decided for me. I finished the 2015 Christmas Bird Count season in Pine Prairie, in the middle of the state, on January 4, 2016. I rode around the Ville Platte area for the day with Marty Floyd. Marty explained that the Pine Prairie area represents the northern reach of coastal prairie and is a nice place to bird because it's at the northern edge of many south Louisiana species and at the southern edge of some north Louisiana birds. Because of this overlap, this particular CBC was a great way to observe wintering woodland birds. We ended the day with fifty-three species, including one notable bird, a Red-breasted Nuthatch that came in to add its bugle "go away" call to the cacophony of Carolina Chickadees, Blue Jays, Tufted Titmice, Hermit Thrushes, Brown-headed Nuthatches, and Yellow-rumped Warblers that mobbed an Eastern Screech-Owl call in the woods at the Crooked Creek Recreational Area. When Marty entered our checklist into eBird, we had a note from Van asking us for more information—it was the first Red-breasted Nuthatch reported in the state during the winter.

The Red-breasted Nuthatch is not a bird that occurs in Louisiana annually, only in irruptive[1] years. Somehow, that Red-breasted Nuthatch lodged itself in my brain and banged around, saying, "Hey, this is a pretty good bird if you're shooting for three hundred"—which was a *crazy* number; in addition to my full-time job, Lynn was in her first year as principal of her school. And we had Lynn's mom, who (we both decided, even if she hadn't yet) shouldn't be left alone for days at a time. We had more chores around the house, plus driving Mary to doctor's appointments, extra shopping, more paperwork, etc. And yet—in the face of all this (I suspect, because of all this)—the thought came, unbidden.

This thought was not at all about a big year—my understanding of what it meant to do a big year had evolved since 2012. To me, a big year is when you go for it and try to break the state record. The three hundred species goal was just a significant milestone to shoot for. I played with species and numbers—how many on the state bird list were straightforward gets, how many were gettable with work, and how many were sheer luck? Which species did I think we could observe, given our significant time constraints? My machinations led me to 292 bird species—only eight short of 300, but those last eight were all tough birds.

I was almost afraid to tell Lynn about the thoughts flying around in my head—truth be told, I was worried about her. Lynn carried the bulk of the responsibility for her mom. I was good to take out the garbage and recyclables, buy groceries, fix breakfast, and do small errands like the post office or returning clothes that didn't fit, but for the big things—doctor's visits, power of attorney, insurance, helping to manage Mary's checking account and drug regimen—for those, I was not involved. Lynn also carried a tremendous amount of stress in her job. In the twenty-three years I'd known her, I'd never seen her under so much stress, and the last thing I wanted to do was to add to that load. When I did confide, it went something like, "I'd love to go for 300, but I'm not sure that we can get beyond 292 or so." She thought about it for a minute and said, "Why not? We can at least get past our previous total."

And that was that. We were off to the races, though in a completely different way than before, now with much more knowledge and much less time. We also went with standard American Birding Association rules. Our year would begin January 1 and end December 31, and we would count "heard only" birds in addition to those we saw. We also had separate lists—we were both going for three hundred, but if one of us saw or heard a bird that the other did not, or went birding on her own, those species would be part of that person's list only.

To start the year, I figured that the best thing to do would be to try to "run the table" on ducks and sparrows and to chase rarities whenever possible. I thought that the rarities were really the make or break part of the venture. It's much easier to see a gettable bird than to chase something rare when you run out of steam and birds toward December. Although Louisiana is blessed with rarities at all times of the year, the best time to chase them, generally, is the wintertime.

A January pilgrimage to Cameron Parish and Pintail Loop in Cameron Prairie NWR was normal in any year, so there was no reason to change that tradition in 2016. The trip was productive—we saw eight dabbling duck species on Pintail Loop (American Wigeon, Blue-winged Teal, Green-winged Teal, Mottled Duck, Mallard, Northern Pintail, Gadwall, and Northern Shoveler), and we found several goose-filled fields along the way and were able to get three species of geese (Snow, Greater White-fronted, and Ross's) as well as Sandhill Cranes. But the best parts of the day involved hitting stakeout spots in which other birders had previously located rarities.

The Lapland Longspur is not particularly rare in Louisiana, but it doesn't come to the southern half of the state in droves. This year it had, in agricultural fields immediately adjacent to residences situated seemingly in the middle of nowhere, in an area northwest of Kaplan. According to LA-BIRD, playback brought in one hundred to two hundred longspurs for several birders, so we dialed in the GPS coordinates of this field (30.0765217,-92.3105621) and headed there to try our luck. I put my iPhone on the highest volume possible and played the longspur calls. (For some reason our Bluetooth speaker wouldn't connect and we couldn't deliver a sound with any kind of carry for the broad expanse of muddy crop rows which appeared to hold nothing but Killdeer.)

We slowly dragnetted the fields by driving the road adjacent to them in the truck, with me hanging out the passenger window and playing that call, to no avail. Finally, we stopped and I continued to play the call. Just when I thought that we needed to bag it and move on, a single Lapland Longspur answered the call, flying in and landing at the field edge, about ten feet away from us. He landed for a couple of seconds, long enough for a quick ID, then took off low and landed in some tall clover that formed the border between the field and the road, and he hid. Luckily for us, he thought he hid, but he only hid his front half. We had a chance to admire his rufous-orange back and wing pattern before he fully hopped into the clover and never came back out. But *bang*. Lapland Longspur! We were in business with a bird not often found in south Louisiana.

As the crow flies, the Couch's Kingbird stakeout spot was about twelve miles immediately to the south of the Lapland Longspur location, but country roads can't take you as the crow flies, so it took us forty-five minutes to navigate soft gravel and a nonlinear combination of roads to reach the kingbird spot. I was familiar with the place because I'd visited on a CBC the month before, where the cooperative Couch's Kingbird sang copiously and immediately in response to playback. The Couch's was somewhat similar to the longspur on this day in that it took a long time to locate it, and we finally did because I could hear it singing faintly, far back from the road. Once I heard its voice, it only took a few seconds to find the kingbird perched on a low, leafless tree rising up from a sea of cattails about 150 feet back from the road, singing straight at us with its yellow breast screaming "Notice me, I am beautiful!" Lynn and I both got great looks and swore only a little when we realized that the camera she brought had a dead battery.

Although we cut our day short, starting home at 2:30 P.M. instead of continuing into Cameron Parish because we didn't want to leave Mary alone for too long, I was satisfied. I wasn't counting total bird species, but instead just rarities and relative rarities, and as far as I was concerned we were plus two. (I was actually plus three with that Red-breasted Nuthatch and was hoping that we could get Lynn one at some point.) "This is the year of the day trip," Lynn said as she navigated back roads home. It was as good a slogan as any.

After we got home and as Lynn was preparing dinner for the three of us, Mary asked, "Were you successful in your trip?" I told her yes and brought *The Crossley ID Guide for Eastern Birds* to her bedroom to show her pictures of the longspur and the kingbird. Mary didn't have anything to say about the longspur, and I understood why, having gone through the "sparrows and related birds are boring" stage myself, but she got animated when she saw a picture of the Couch's Kingbird. "Wow, that's beautiful! I have never seen anything like that! We have goldfinches in the summer in Ohio that are kind of like that, but not exactly." Mary then regaled me with stories from her childhood in summertime Ohio until Lynn served dinner.

* * * * *

Charlie Lyon set the all-time Louisiana big year record in 2015 with 356 bird species. On January 1 of 2016, he took his boat out on Cross Lake, one of his favorite avian stomping grounds. While observing a flock of Ring-billed Gulls, a gull swooped right in front of his eyes and he immediately identified it as a Mew Gull. Charlie managed to get pictures of the bird and sent them to Van for confirmation, and sure enough it was a Mew Gull, the first ever record for the state of Louisiana. I am not sure if Charlie was frustrated that he got the Mew Gull on the first day of the new year instead of the day before, and thus missed adding it to his big year list, but I do know that once he saw it and reported it, he made it his personal mission to show it to others. When he offered boat rides, we jumped at the chance and set January 17 as the day we'd meet Charlie at the Shreveport Yacht Club to ride his boat to try for the Mew Gull.

When I asked what we should bring on this trip, Charlie said to dress warmly and bring as much popcorn as you could carry. You throw popcorn into the water because it brings in gulls to feed, and you can see your target birds better because they get close to you and your boat. I wasn't really thinking about how to secure a large volume of popcorn; if I had been thinking, I would have gone to a movie theater and ordered several large buckets. Instead we went to Costco, thinking that surely there would be large bags of popped popcorn available, since Costco sells large everything. There was no popcorn at Costco, and it was the evening before we needed to get up to drive four hours to meet Charlie.

"I know where to get it," Lynn said, "and you're not going to like it, but it is what it is."

"Where?" I asked with dread, already knowing the answer.

"Wallsmart." She knows to not even say the actual word to me, like somehow that might make it better.

I am not a stubborn person, but there are a few principles I have, primal principles, and on those I am staunch. I am a vegetarian and will not eat meat. I'm fine if people around me do, but I haven't eaten meat since 1988 and don't plan to start—ever. I became a vegetarian because I didn't like the idea of killing animals to live myself. Today, the fact that a plant-based diet contributes much less environmental impact and can help stave off climate change is important to me too.

The only other principle I stick to with that much fervor is Walmart. I hate Walmart. Suffice it to say that somewhere in the thicket of driving income inequality on a mass scale, a regressive social agenda, the killing of small town America, and an adeptness of playing strong to every evil imbedded in capitalism, I've decided that I will not, and I mean will not, shop at Walmart. For anything. But it was the night before a boat ride to see a once in a lifetime Mew Gull in the state of Louisiana.

"I'll go in and get it," Lynn said, "just don't think about it."

I muttered in the car while she went in to the Evil Empire. She came out ten minutes later and said, "Guess what? They didn't have it."

I smiled. Then she tossed a twenty-four-pack box of microwave popcorn in my lap.

"We're going to have to pop it instead." I didn't complain that we could have bought packaged popcorn at Target or any grocery store, or that this felt like fruit of the poisoned tree. I kept my mouth shut and when we got home I opened the box and started popping popcorn.

I popped twenty-four bags of popcorn consecutively, and I think that the microwave must have sensed my ire, because during the twentieth bag it quit mid-pop. I unplugged the thing, plugged it back in, and started again. The microwave seemed normal, but on the twenty-fourth bag it quit again. I unplugged it and left it alone for the night. When I plugged in the microwave the next morning, it turned on normally for two seconds, made a horrible noise, and quit entirely. The microwave never worked again. I thus managed to kill my microwave on Walmart popcorn. This state of affairs seemed fair in a karmic way.

Lynn and I left for the four-hour drive to Shreveport at 8:00 in the morning, after we had breakfast with Mary. With little traffic, we made it with plenty of time to bird the Shreveport area before meeting Charlie and his boat at 3:00 P.M. The gulls came in to roost at Cross Lake for the evening, so there was no use in searching for the gull earlier in the day. Charlie told us that if we left the dock at 3:00 we'd have plenty of time to bird parts of the lake for ducks and other Cross Lake species and then proceed to the target area in time for late afternoon gull action.

Lynn and I started our Shreveport birding adventure at Walter B. Jacobs Memorial Park, hopeful for north Louisiana targets that were not as frequent in the southern part of the state, including Purple Finch, Pine Siskin, and especially White-breasted Nuthatch, which we had never seen in Louisiana. I was happy because the park included a heated lodge and a huge picture window that overlooked a small water feature and a number of bird feeders. Although I'd rather hike a trail almost any day rather than wait around in front of a feeder, I am easily persuaded to bird by chair in warm environs when the temperatures outside are hovering around freezing. We camped out at the picture window for almost thirty minutes waiting for the Fox Sparrow and Purple Finches that the docent said were coming to the feeders occasionally.

After zero luck on both species, we proceeded to hike all the trails in the park. During this chilly venture we heard but did not see a White-breasted Nuthatch. Although the bird counted toward our year list, it would have been nice to *see* the little bugger, especially because in general White-breasted Nuthatches are not shy birds. This individual was calling from a tree far from the path, however, and it never came closer. We were successful in continuing to catch Lynn up on the list of CBC birds I had compiled with Marty, which I figured was going to be easy with the exception of that Red-breasted Nuthatch. We added Hairy and Red-bellied Woodpeckers, Tufted Titmouse, Carolina Wren, and American Goldfinch to Lynn's year list at Walter Jacobs, and upon proceeding to Cross Lake to bird the shoreline while we waited for the appointed hour with Charlie, we added Eastern Bluebird, Song Sparrow, and Pine Warbler to her list. The Brown Thrasher and House Finch were species pickups for both of us.

We met fellow Mew Gull searchers Suzanne and Kalem Laird at the entrance to the Shreveport Yacht Club. Just before Charlie pulled up to let us in, Lynn and I first heard and then saw a White-breasted Nuthatch sneaking up and down a wooden power pole adjacent to the road, only about thirty feet from us. We were both very happy as we high fived our first-ever Louisiana sighting. As we did so, Suzanne gave us a surprised, strange look and told us that the bird was common around here. Which was true—we just don't usually get them in south Louisiana. I was reminded for the thousandth time that when it comes to birds, it's often about location, location, location.

Charlie arrived, quickly loaded the group of gull searchers onto his boat, and started on a guided tour of Cross Lake in the beautiful late afternoon sunlight. Our first stop was the Western Grebe stakeout. In a matter of fact manner, he scanned the area, quickly located the grebe, and showed us exactly where to look. Although it was from a distance, the black and white, tall-necked bird looked cobra-like in the water. I was thrilled to see this life bird and a rarity for the state. We also saw Bufflehead, Lesser Scaup, Ruddy Duck, and Red-breasted Mergansers; although not rare, they were new ducks for the year. I was especially happy to observe a large flock of Canvasback near the Western Grebe; of all the common duck species in the state, I had come to the conclusion that, at least for me, Canvasback was the hardest to find.

Charlie proceeded to the gull spot, where we started to search for the Mew Gull needle in a haystack of Ring-billed Gulls. There were a few Herring Gulls mixed in, and several immature Lesser Black-backed Gulls—another species that is not the easiest to locate—but after searching for more than thirty minutes we had not located the Mew. "Well," Charlie said, "let's start chumming popcorn."

Lynn and I proceeded to throw handfuls of our "fruit of the poison tree" popcorn into the water, and it was promptly attacked by some five thousand Ring-billed Gulls. We continued looking in vain, and just as we were about to give up, here came the Mew Gull, which proved to be a class-A popcorn eater. Charlie expertly turned his boat this way and that, almost like the boat was a big phalarope itself, to give us beautiful close looks at the gull in the proper light for photos. As we watched the smallish, brown, immature Mew Gull, I found myself absolutely amazed that Charlie had seen it in the first place, and grateful and excited that he was willing to share it. Charlie finished the day by taking us to a back corner of the lake to see a Horned Grebe. As the sun set and he returned us to dock, he showed the group a pair of Great Blue Herons already setting up to nest.

We immediately transitioned from boat to truck and arrived in Baton Rouge at 10:30 P.M. It was a very long but very productive day trip that had netted us plus-two rarities. Mary was already asleep, and the two of us fell into bed as well. I ended the month of January with 127 birds on my list; Lynn had 111.

* * * * *

After Hurricane Katrina, parts of New Orleans never rebuilt, particularly in New Orleans East. You can drive past the old Six Flags amusement park and trace the spiral of weeds that have grown up the roller coasters, rusty behemoths that recall a better time.[2] Empty lots mark where houses used to be, and sometimes the only indication that humans were ever present is a set of brick steps that lead to nothing. New Orleans is a hub for Louisiana birders, in part because New Orleans is the largest city in the state, but also because the area has some wonderful places to bird. The overgrown spots that nature reclaimed after Katrina are favorite stomping grounds for birders.

During January and February, birders found a number of rarities in New Orleans East. I planned a visit to several of the identified locales in the most efficient order possible. It was the year of the day trip, and the shorter the trip, the better. The plan was to leave from Baton Rouge and make targeted stops in a long "out and back" loop. The first stop would be the abandoned Easthaven nursing home, where a Say's Phoebe had been staked out in the overgrown grounds. The second stop would be a little farther to the east in an area called Eastover; a pond at the end of a small, unmarked road there hosted a Tropical Kingbird. Recovery Road was a hop, skip, and jump from the pond, and along it an Ash-throated Flycatcher had been seen hanging out in the trees. Then, making a southwestern turn, we would end the day at the Chalmette Battlefield at Jean Lafitte National Historical Park, where two Groove-billed Anis and a Brown-crested Flycatcher were being reliably spotted. Our plan was to work all day Saturday to catch up on chores, depart Sunday morning at around 7:00, and to be back by 3:00 P.M., a round trip of approximately 150 miles. But on Saturday night Mary experienced respiratory distress and was admitted to the hospital. Trip canceled.

Rage is something I'm not typically in touch with—its currents flow like lava deep within the center of my psyche, and I don't often access that "brain stem" emotion. But a piece of the thing inside me that pushes me through difficult situations despite obstacles is a tiny, hard, coil of rage. Somewhere along the way, I felt the coil unfurl, just a little—with spending most weekends at home; with days at work and nights in the hospital; with running to the store to purchase an endless list of things I could never keep up with long enough to stay out of a store more than forty-eight hours; with walking an ever-present tightrope of ensuring that Mary had her needs and wants met while she did what she needed to stay alive with quality of life. Somewhere through all of that I realized, not in a moment of clarity but with something that felt more like slow osmosis, that I was feeling rage.

It wasn't directed at Mary, it was directed at the situation that was my life. I like to feel in control—or at least like I can exert some control—over situations in my life. I couldn't take control of congestive heart failure (CHF); the disease follows its own path, and I was just along for the ride. I tried to find pockets of peace and sometimes discovered them in everyday mundane moments, but I was having to search for peace and I wasn't used to that feeling.

Medically it was difficult too, because I often felt like we were flying blind. It seemed that no one wanted to give us a timetable. I understand that every case is unique, but even a sense of where Mary is on the continuum of CHF was not given. It seemed like each medical professional gave us a puzzle piece, but no full, larger picture in which to place it. The cardiologist liked to talk about the damaged mitral valve that Mary had as the result of surviving rheumatic fever when she was a teenager. Her CHF was the result of this valve damage, and he was considering whether operating on the mitral valve was feasible. The gerontologist was focused on trying to manage Mary's arthritic pain; we quickly realized that Mary's life centered around the time that she could take her next dose of hydrocodone. When she moved to Louisiana, she was already taking the maximum allowable dose, and it wasn't enough to control her pain. Every time I heard a story on National Public Radio about opioid addiction, I realized that it didn't hit close to home—it was at home.

I felt like we were walking a series of tightropes. For example, every person deserves as much control as they can exert over their life. Mary should be able to eat whatever she wants. But what if the sugar- and salt-filled foods Mary craves drive her in the wrong direction with CHF and diabetes? Who are we to say on the one hand? But on the other hand, if consuming those foods lands Mary in the hospital, and we are the ones who have to experience the grueling schedule of work every weekday and the hospital every night and on weekends, shouldn't we have a say? If Mary doesn't feel up to getting out of bed due to her arthritis pain, that is her choice. But if Mary stops moving, the CHF gets worse. And the worse it gets, the higher the chance that she'll land in the hospital. It was these tightropes that were so difficult to walk, for all of us. There is no right or wrong. There's just give and take. There are good days and bad days physically. There are up and down days mentally. And there are hard choices, and all of it in a sort of bubble with no clear road map.

Doctors at the hospital quickly got Mary's respiratory distress under control with more potent fluid-reducing drugs than she had been taking, and she was able to return home after just a few days. All seemed back to normal, but after several more days she was uncharacteristically sullen. Mary complained that none of her food tasted right, not even the beloved waffles with apple sauce that she ate every morning with a religiously consumed glass of orange juice. "Orange juice fixes me up every time," she said each morning at breakfast, "it makes my sugar right."

Lynn responded to Mary's complaints by making homemade chicken noodle soup, which was one of Mary's favorites. Despite being a pescatarian, Lynn made chicken soup from scratch, using a crock pot to let her homemade concoction simmer all day. Even I had to admit that the soup smelled really good. When Lynn served it to Mary, she took one bite and said it was terrible. "I about upchucked!" And she continued with disparaging comments about the chicken soup that she would normally never say about anything or anyone. Mary was a famous proponent of "If you can't say anything nice, don't say anything at all." I was shocked and almost humored, except for the fact that her behavior was so uncharacteristic, and because Lynn, despite putting on her best trouper face, was hurt. Lynn called our friend and neighbor Carol Lee to sample the soup; Carol Lee said that the soup tasted great, and Lynn gave her the entire pot. Upon hearing this, Mary was amazed. "She liked it? She could eat it? It didn't make her sick?"

Later that evening Mary became incoherent. She was speaking English and the words were clearly spoken, but they were just strung together in an order that made no sense. She was also weak and couldn't seem to get out of bed. We called the ambulance again.

Mary was diagnosed with a urinary tract infection (UTI). When we heard this news from the hospital doctor, we were shocked. "We had no idea!" Lynn exclaimed. The doctor explained that UTIs do not present in the elderly the way that they do in younger people. There tended not to be itching or burning, and often times no fever either, at least initially. What we had to watch for instead was confusion and mood changes. The doctors started Mary on antibiotics and she quickly came back to her typical sunny personality, but it took a few more days in the hospital to get her comorbidities under control. Mary was quick to tell people that she had CHF, coronary artery disease, A-fib, and diabetes. In the hospital, she dropped the fourth condition. Lynn thought that it might be because diabetes perhaps came with some shame on her mom's part. I just thought she was angling for better food.

When we were unpacking Mary's things in Louisiana, I was impressed to see that she had won the top student award in English in the state of Ohio in her senior year in high school; she came in 3rd, 5th, and 10th in her other high school years. I got to see Mary's rhetorical talents in action in the hospital. They'd go something like this:

Hospital employee: "Your blood sugar level is high."

Mary: "My sugar isn't usually high."

Hospital employee: "Well, it is now."

Mary: "That's because I'm in the hospital. I get a little stressed when I'm in the hospital. And that makes my sugar run high."

Hospital employee: "Oh." And then Mary would order whatever she wanted for meals.

Once we "got Mary back" from the grips of the UTI, she tackled in-hospital physical therapy while doctors fine-tuned her drug regimen. The doctors decided that she should start taking the blood thinner Coumadin because she was at high risk for a heart attack or stroke. Mary returned home with a home health order for physical therapy so that she could fully regain her strength, as well as for a health aide who could monitor her Coumadin level. Lynn and I resolved to watch extra carefully for mood changes and confusion so that we wouldn't have another hospital trip courtesy of things we didn't know.

At the end of February, Lynn and I had spent twelve days of the month in the hospital with Mary, twice as many days as we had gone birding. We had a total of thirteen new list birds for the entire month. I was plus five rarities (Lynn was plus four), but I was minus sixteen birds that I had identified as necessary to keep up with the winter list plan. It was time to double down on finding those must-get winter birds before spring hit in mid-March.

* * * * *

Mary was super happy to be home and settled in to a good rhythm. She enjoyed talking to her physical therapist, if not the actual activities that the therapist prescribed. Mary loved to spend time with our Catahoula hound dog, Hurricane; they'd pack up on the bed together and hang out all day long while Mary watched reruns of *The Golden Girls, The Andy Griffith Show, Reba,* and *Judge Judy.* Mary often declared, "Hurricane is my best friend!"

Although the workload of our respective jobs was intense for Lynn and me, life seemed a lot easier to manage with Mary out of the hospital. We squeezed in local trips, getting Rusty Blackbirds at Farr Park in Baton Rouge on March 5. Although neither of us needed the Red-shouldered Hawk we spotted just west of the park entrance, we were spellbound by a fine-looking individual that swooped down into wet grass and returned to an elevated perch with a two-foot garter snake in its talons. We watched the hawk eat the snake as the cooperating sun highlighted its orange breast. It was a National Geographic moment less than five miles from our house.

Once we got the next week under our belts to ensure that Mary was in fact back to normal, we headed for Cameron Parish with our typical stops along the way on March 12. From the standpoint of our year list, the day was epic. It was that time of year in Louisiana that didn't know if it was winter or spring, and so it compromised: we picked up species typical of both seasons.

Grass-piper-type shorebirds were out on the turf fields on both sides of Turf Grass Road in Jefferson Davis Parish and we picked up American Golden-Plover, Black-bellied Plover, and Pectoral Sandpiper as a result. We crushed out in happiness at a pair of Long-billed Curlews feeding in the grass fields only forty feet from the edge of the road. It was the first time we'd spotted this species, the largest shorebird in North America, at this location. We jammed over to the grain processing facility on Highway 397 near Lake Charles, which is usually good for Yellow-headed Blackbirds that mix in with huge flocks of Brown-headed Cowbirds in the spring, and we picked up a couple of females on the wires adjacent to the facility. We then zipped through Pintail Loop and were able to find the Glossy Ibis that had eluded us in January. Both species of whistling-ducks found in Louisiana (Black-bellied and Fulvous) were on my

spring "to get" list, but we happily took them on the loop. The Crested Caracara was a welcome addition too—this species is one I never tire of seeing.

We stopped at Four Magic Miles on our way to Peveto. It was our first crack at a beach in 2016, and shorebirds like the Sanderling, American Avocet, Piping Plover, and Ruddy Turnstone quickly made our day and year lists burgeon. We walked out onto the beach so I could scope a huge raft of Lesser Scaup out on the water; I spent almost forty-five minutes counting eight hundred Lesser Scaup while carefully checking the raft for Greater Scaup or scoters. My near nausea from the waves and length of time I fixated at 40X magnification paid off, as there were three Greater Scaup, and almost the last bird I counted was a Black Scoter. Lynn got views of these birds before we packed it in and headed for Peveto. While the woods themselves were not particularly birdy, we came away with three new species: White-winged Dove, Wilson's Warbler, and Great-tailed Grackle. Then we turned and headed home for Mary. We viewed our first Peregrine Falcon of the year sitting on the crossbar of a power line on Highway 82 at mile marker 24.5. We pit-stopped at the Hidden Ponds RV Park to look for the pair of Great Kiskadees that was being reliably spotted there, but didn't find them. Despite this miss, the day was fantastic. I added twenty-four birds to my year list, and Lynn added the same twenty-four plus one House Wren she needed to hers, and all of a sudden I started feeling much better about our prospects.

I realize that what I'm about to say is privileged, and I know it, *but*: one thing that seems cruel is despite the fact that Lynn and I are educators in large public school systems, our spring breaks almost never line up. We have, in all the years we've worked in education, had our breaks fully overlap one blissful time. Otherwise, they tend to stagger by a week. And 2016 was no different. Lynn's break came first, and due to the great flexibility of my job, I was able to squeeze out a day off on Monday, March 14. We went to Grand Isle, where Lynn did a little fishing on her kayak; we also added more shorebirds, like Wilson's Plover and Marbled Godwit, to our list. I was excited to see a Reddish Egret; although not rare, the Reddish Egret is not a bird you can dial up at will in Louisiana.

Lynn does not have the job flexibility that I do, and so a week later, at the kickoff of my spring break, I admit it: I cheated. I took my mom and headed for Grand Isle, where Joan was readying for her spring stint. Joan is a quintessential southern lady. She entertains friends and family with the best of them and will give you the shirt off her back, but she will not entertain nonbirders on Grand Isle between April 1 and 30. Period. Joan stays at the camp for the entire month; she walks from the camp to the store and the camp to the woods, and she's proud to say that's all she needs for the month. I keep telling her that she needs to extend her spring migration pilgrimage to May 15. She's gotten as far as May 7 before her Mississippi delta upbringing kicks in and she returns to Baton Rouge to support family and friends. I hope Joan stays until mid-May some year.

With the invitation from Joan wide open, we drove down Monday morning and spent the rest of the daylight hours Monday and Tuesday birding with Joan.

March 21 and 22 was really the onset of spring migration, so I wasn't expecting much. We were pleasantly surprised. During our two-day birding extravaganza we notched eleven species of warblers, including new-for-the-year Ovenbird, Louisiana Waterthrush, Black-and-white Warbler, Prothonotary Warbler, Hooded Warbler, Northern Parula Warbler, Black-throated Green Warbler, Yellow-throated Warbler, and Worm-eating Warbler. There weren't large numbers of these species (there were still plenty of Yellow-rumps), but the variety was better than I expected. I wound up with twenty new birds for my year list.

The most memorable bird was a Broad-winged Hawk. I heard it calling in the woods and told mom and Joan what it was. We crept into the woods and followed its copious calling and then found it. The hawk was a magnificent adult with an orange-flecked breast, and it sat there majestically for quite some time before flying away. We all got great looks at it, as well as wonderful views of a Solitary Sandpiper that spent lots of time working a large puddle in the Landry-Leblanc tract. Upon watching it at length, Joan remarked, "Why is it that some shorebirds always look like they're throwing up?"

We returned home Tuesday night, and on Wednesday my momma spent some quality time with Mary before she headed back to Mississippi. One great thing about our setup was our mothers having the chance to visit in person; because they'd always lived far away, they'd only met once in all the time Lynn and I had known each other. The two-hour drive between my mom's house and ours was conducive to their connecting. Although they had been raised in different generations despite only an eight-year age difference, they bonded around the love of their daughters—and each claimed both of us as daughters. My initial thoughts about Mary moving in with us were about the things that I'd be losing. As time went on, I began to realize that I was also gaining a great deal, much more than I anticipated.

Lynn was a good sport about my Grand Isle birding extravaganza and was chomping at the bit to catch up to me. I told her that it shouldn't be hard to do because I hadn't picked up any rarities, and it wasn't. On March 31 we executed almost the same Cameron Parish route that we had on March 12, picking up the Buff-breasted Sandpiper and Merlin on Turf Grass Road, Bronzed Cowbird at the grain processing facility on Highway 397 (which now hosted about fifty Yellow-headed Blackbirds), a Yellow-billed Cuckoo at Pintail Loop, and Indigo Bunting and Orchard Oriole at Peveto. During these stops, Lynn quickly began closing my Grand Isle bird list surge by adding warblers, vireos, and swallows that I had recorded earlier. We ended our day at Hidden Ponds RV Park.

It was the third time we had visited there to search for the kiskadees. We drove our truck back and forth in front of the park entrance and along a road that ran the east side of the property. Nothing. I apologized and told Lynn that I should have emailed someone to learn the exact location of the kiskadee nest, but I felt like Dan O'Malley's GPS coordinates had us pretty close. We idled in the middle of Ravia Road, almost at the park entrance, to consider our options. Dan's GPS coordinates appeared to be inside the park, but we didn't feel comfortable parking in someone's place to get out and poke around. As it was, five men were sitting on the porch of one of the RVs, drinking beer and watching us with half curiosity and half suspicion, which further tamped down our interest in entering the park to search. Playback was out of the question because the birds were nesting, and it would be a breach of birding ethics to play their calls in this situation. And so we sat mulling while the truck sat idling—what to do, what to do . . .

Then Lynn exclaimed, "*Look!*" I followed her gaze, and there, sitting silently on a power line twenty-five feet away, I saw the bright yellow breast and rufous wings of a Great Kiskadee.

"Get a picture," I said. We had forgotten the digital camera at home, so all we had were our crummy cell phone cameras.

As Lynn pulled the truck up close to use her cell, I couldn't figure out why she pulled slightly past the kiskadee. "Why would you hang out the window backwards to compose a shot?" I thought, and then I realized when she extended her phone out the window that she was actually focused on the top of a chain-link fence about ten feet in front of the bird on the power line. I followed *that* line of vision and watched her shoot a pic of the second kiskadee. I laughed and pointed out the kiskadee that I had seen. We'd each seen one and not the other. She took pictures of both and we left happy. It was our last new bird in the month of

March; the kiskadee was my 213th bird species of the year, and Lynn's 200th. We were another plus-one rarity!

* * * * *

"Those are for my mother-in-law," I said. "She loves lemon-flavored vitamin-water zero." I felt like a lesser person with a flimsy defense for saying it, but I just couldn't help it, even though it was true. My outburst was in response to the dirty look being thrown my way by a cashier as she scanned bottle after bottle of the stuff and packed it into bags.

Mary refused to drink plain old water—she wouldn't drink it out of the tap, or filtered from our refrigerator, or out of a bottle either. Mary drank two things: Diet Coke and lemon-flavored vitaminwater zero (LFVW0). If that's all a person drinks, and they drink a decent amount of fluid each day, then chances are that you're going to the store a lot. And I was. I'd gotten used to it—I had made peace with my inability to keep up with the dietary needs of three of us and resolved to go to the store when I needed to. But LFVW0 was not at every grocery store—and usually it was not sold in convenient six packs.

Costco had become my best friend for some things. I felt like a million bucks when I purchased a box of seventy-two Eggo waffles. Mary ate two Eggos for breakfast every morning, though I usually made three or four because Mary would fall asleep in the middle of eating and Hurricane would jump on the bed and eat the remainder of breakfast, which I'd have to remake after Mary woke up and was hungry. Seventy-two waffles provided at least eighteen days of reprieve from shopping for that particular item. Costco sold vitaminwater zero in packages of twenty, which would have been fabulous but for the fact that only eight of the twenty were lemon flavored, and Mary didn't like the orange and acai-blueberry-pomegranate bottles that comprised the rest of the pack.

So as far as LFVW0 was concerned, Costco was out and four area grocery stores were in—but only one of those stores sold six packs, and they weren't always stocked. So I generally bought bottles singly. I bought out the shelf in each grocery store on a rotating basis an average of two times each week, to give each store a chance to restock before I visited again. Most times, the cashiers didn't say anything, or if they did, they joked about how much I must love it. But every once in a while I'd get dirty looks—and for some reason I wasn't able to handle them without retort.

I entered April feeling pretty good about our three hundred species adventure and about life in general. Jay Huner sent me an email and asked if I was "going for it," meaning going for a big year, when he saw me pass the two hundred mark. I told him that Lynn and I were trying for three hundred, and he replied that we were progressing at a decent clip for it. Jay would know; he's the one eBirder in Louisiana who had crossed the three hundred plateau seven years in a row and was in the midst of working on his eighth. He told me that if we had 265 birds by mid-May we should be in pretty good shape. I filed that tidbit away for later. In the meantime, the plan for this prime month of spring migration was to get out as much as humanly possible.

Lynn and I got our first bird of April in dramatic fashion at 4:32 A.M. on April Fools' Day. I mentally peeled myself off the ceiling at Hurricane's intense, nonstop howling. There was only one thing in the world she bayed at that vigorously. Both of us jumped out of bed and cranked open the French doors leading to our backyard to better hear a migrant Chuck-will's-widow repeating its name incessantly somewhere at the back of our property. Hurricane hurtled out the door to get close to the Chuck and return the call with her loudest bark. It took some doing to get her back into the house. Lynn and I sleepily high fived and returned to bed, hoping that Hurricane had not woken the neighbors.

We headed for Cameron the next day, especially because a strong north wind was blowing. We didn't have huge numbers, no fallout, but warblers characteristic of mid-migration like the Blue-winged Warbler and American Redstart graced us with their presence. We also added our first Swainson's Thrush and Philadelphia Vireo of the year.

The next weekend was off limits for birding, but for good reason. My playground team had been working with a group from Leadership Ascension, a yearlong program for citizens in neighboring Ascension Parish run by the parish chamber of commerce. The program's purpose was to teach leadership skills while citizens worked in teams to address a need in the parish. I had been asked to collaborate with one of the teams, whose dream was to bring a playground to an area of Donaldsonville, Louisiana, that had none. My engineering team had worked with neighborhood children to develop a community-based design, while the leadership team fundraised over $100,000 in actual and in-kind donations. Our playground build was set for April 9 and 10, when my playground research and design team would work with about one hundred volunteers, including many from Leadership Ascension, to construct the playground.

On that Saturday, I organized volunteers, hauled concrete, assembled equipment, and spread soft surfacing material under a climber. I came home tired, and while Lynn made us dinner I explained details of the build to Mary and showed her pictures, because she asked me to tell her all about it. The local TV news had done a story, and Mary told me how excited she was to watch me on television, but she wanted more in-depth information than was on TV. When my head hit the pillow at 9:30 that night, it was with the knowledge that I'd sleep really well due to all that physical labor.

At 11:00 P.M. I started awake. I listened hard into the darkness and after a minute I heard a thump down the hall. It wasn't loud. I thought it was Mary dropping a bottle of LFVW0. She did that sometimes, as the arthritis in her hands made it tough for her to grasp things, an issue that was happening with increasing frequency. My muscles were sore, and for a fraction of a second I considered not getting up, but then I thought that if I were Mary, I'd want that drink at my bedside. She needed it to take her middle-of-the-night dose of hydrocodone, if nothing else. I got up and padded down the hall, and blanched when I hit the threshold of Mary's bedroom. Mary was on the floor and was not moving.

"Lynn!" I screamed. Lynn was kneeling at my side so fast it almost seemed like she beamed there. "Mom, can you hear me?" The only response was a guttural, fluid-filled, rattling groan. I wasn't sure whether Mary was trying to talk or trying to breathe. "Call 911," Lynn said urgently. I ran for my phone as Lynn began speaking calmly and clearly to Mary, telling her where she was, that we were with her, and that help was on the way.

The ambulance was at our house in less than five minutes. I had just enough time to move my car out of the street so that the ambulance would have unfettered access to our front door. I met the paramedics and directed them to Mary's room, and they had Mary in a sling and out the door within three minutes. Their speed was impressive. Lynn jumped into the back of the ambulance and rode to the hospital with Mary while I executed "the home drill," which consisted of collecting Mary's purse with all her medical information and the plastic bag containing her eleven prescription drug bottles so that medical personnel would know what she was taking, grabbing a change of clothes for her and a snack for us, and driving to the emergency room.

Lynn texted me that they were stationed in the hallway within the ER and that Mary was doing better. When I reached the hospital some fifteen minutes later, I couldn't believe my eyes. Mary seemed completely back to normal! "The paramedics figured out that it was low blood sugar," Lynn told me, "they gave her a shot of glucose and she came right back. When they first tested her blood sugar level, it was undetectable."

The ER was hopping and full. Every room was taken, and Mary was one of five occupants on stretchers camped out in the hallway. All were awaiting a room. After a couple of hours Mary was given a room inside the ER. We were informed that the doctors wanted to admit her because they weren't sure why her blood sugar dropped, but at the moment no rooms were available in the hospital. Mary would stay in the ER room until a regular one opened up.

Lynn sent me home at 4:30 A.M.; my plan was to sleep until 6:00 and then return to the second day of my playground build at 6:30. "I got this," Lynn offered, "go finish your playground." I crashed into dreamless sleep. When the alarm went off at 6:00, I got up, made myself a cup of coffee, and took stock of the situation. I texted Lynn and she said that they were still in the ER, no regular room was available yet. Mary's blood sugar had dropped precipitously several times during the night, and they'd had to give her successive shots of glucose to fix it. The doctors weren't sure what was going on.

Should I finish the playground or should I go to the hospital? The answer was clear. I felt amazingly rested, all things considered, but Lynn had been up all night. I hated to miss the playground build, but I knew that Scot Givens, the professional installer who ensured that our volunteers assembled the playground equipment correctly, didn't need me. Jackie Tisdell, the Leadership Ascension team leader, had been on top of every aspect of the project and could finish without me. Grant Gonzalez, the senior leader of my playground research and design team, could take care of student volunteers without me. I texted all three, and each gave me the same answer: "No problem, we've got this. Stay with your family. It's more important."

I returned to the hospital and encouraged Lynn to go home to sleep after the all-nighter she had just pulled, but she insisted on staying until Mary was admitted into a regular room, which finally happened at 10:00 A.M. I stayed with Mary through the afternoon; she rested comfortably while Grant and Jackie sent me pictures of the build in action, and Scot texted to let me know when they'd finished successfully at midafternoon. It was a great reminder that there is no "I" in team. If you build a good team, the members will get it done.

Lynn took off the first two days of the work week, and I juggled classes and meetings and was able to be at the hospital most of the time. Sometimes the two of us tag-teamed it so that the other could get a break. I don't know how single caregivers do it—the two of us were a united front and it still took everything we had.

For the life of them, the doctors could not figure out how to control Mary's blood sugar—for days. It was a crazy thing to witness, the correlation between her blood sugar and the speed of her talking. When her blood sugar was high, 300 mg/dl or higher, Mary could talk a mile a minute about anything and everything. When it got significantly below 100 mg/dl, her speech would slow to the point that Mary would half fall asleep, half pass out in the middle of a sentence. When glucose was injected into her bloodstream, her head would snap up and she'd commence talking a mile a minute.

Although not being able to control her blood sugar was scary, Mary seemed to enjoy this hospital stay more than previous ones, likely because she was being given high-sugar foods. The fact that she always ate waffles with apple sauce instead of syrup was Mary's compromise with respect to her blood sugar. Now she was being encouraged to eat waffles with syrup, and she was happy with that.

Lynn told me that a hospital doctor had taken her aside and said, "If you can't keep your mother out of the hospital, then you should consider skilled care. I mean, I wouldn't do that to *my* mother, but I'm a doctor."

On Tuesday afternoon, Mary's fourth day on the blood sugar roller coaster, a nurse came in to check her vital signs. She initiated a conversation with me and Lynn while Mary was napping.

"So, they're having trouble with her blood sugar, huh?"

"Yes, they can't figure out what's causing it," said Lynn. "The doctors initially thought it was dehydration, but they've ruled that out."

"I wonder if it's a drug interaction," the nurse said.

"Well, they've checked all the meds she's on and they don't think it's that," Lynn responded.

"Have there been any recent changes to her drug regimen?"

"Well, she started getting symptoms of a UTI last week, so her physician called in an antibiotic." At this, the nurse stood up straighter and looked pointedly at Lynn.

"Which antibiotic was it?" she asked.

"Clindamycin."

"And is she on Glipizide to control her blood sugar?"

"Yes!"

"It's a drug interaction between Clindamycin and Glipizide," the nurse said confidently. "I've seen it before. The antibiotic enhances the efficacy of Glipizide. It'll tank your blood sugar. I know I'm right, but let me check real quick." She stepped to a computer inside the room and after a few keystrokes she nodded and said, "Yup. Drug interaction."

The nurse left to communicate her information to the doctors, and within two hours Mary was taken off the antibiotic. Her blood sugar stabilized immediately and she was released from the hospital the next day. Lynn told me that the doctor who talked to her about putting Mary into skilled care was nicer after she stabilized. He didn't apologize and never admitted that it was a drug interaction, one that in my opinion he should have caught; he continued to insist that it might have been dehydration.

I left this episode with several truths. First, that generally medical personnel are competent and professional, and that often they never get any real thanks because the situation is unfolding so quickly, like those paramedics who recognized that Mary's blood sugar was critically low and immediately addressed it. Mary would have died if they hadn't recognized her condition quickly. And the nurse, who was kind enough to strike up a conversation with us and pay attention to it, as well as to possess enough knowledge to figure out what the issue was. Second, even though most medical personnel are competent and professional, once in a while you can run into a jerk—or maybe just someone having a bad day. If you encounter such a person, keep their message in perspective. They might know more than you about medicine, but they don't know more than you about your situation or the people in it, which means that they don't necessarily know what's best for your situation. Third, try as I might, after April 9, I could not sleep as well as I had been able to before. Every bump in the night woke me up and had me running down the hall to check that everything was okay. I was so thankful that I heard the bump that started the entire ordeal and that I'd acted on it. If I had ignored it, we would have found Mary dead on the floor in the morning. And that would have been devastating. And fourth, even with your best efforts, and with trying to keep on top of taking care of someone, sometimes even then, there are things that you just don't know. It doesn't mean you aren't doing your best—you just cannot anticipate everything.

We didn't know that symptoms of a UTI present differently in the elderly, and thus missed the first UTI that sent Mary to the hospital. We were on top of it the next time. Earlier that fateful week, Mary had gotten confused and spoke words that were strung together in a way that made no sense. Mary shook her head, laughed, and said "Oh, what was I talking about?" This time we knew what was happening. We called the doctor, who called home health; home health collected a urine sample and delivered it to the doctor's office, where it was cultured. An infection was confirmed and a prescription was called in, which we picked up and Mary started taking. Less than forty-eight hours later she was in the hospital. We didn't think to check any sort of database for drug interactions when her regimen was changed. We didn't know. So far, it had been fool us once—now we knew to watch for confusion or mood changes with Mary for UTIs *and* to double check with her pharmacist regarding possible interactions on any new drug she was prescribed. But in advance, we didn't know. We were doing our best, but we didn't know.

* * * * *

We stayed close to home to bird through the middle of the month while Mary built back her strength, and we picked up typical spring migrants like Summer and Scarlet Tanagers on Whiskey Bay Road. On April 23 we missed the spring LOS meeting in Cameron for the second year in a row. The Tiger 12 is the highest honor an LSU senior can earn at the university, and for two years running one of the members of my playground research and design team was selected for this elite class. For the second year in a row, the award ceremony was on the same afternoon as the LOS spring meeting. The ceremony consisted of each student's mentor giving a brief speech about their student, and each member of the class giving a brief speech about their LSU experience. As the mentor of my students, neither wild horses nor wild birds would have stopped me from being there to make those speeches. As proud as I was of my students, though, LOS was an admittedly painful meeting to miss with so many migrants on the line.

Lynn and I headed for Cameron early the next day, armed with news of what had been spotted the day before. We did a full birding day without guilt because Mary was feeling good and shooed us out the door. We quickly birded Turf Grass Road on the way and picked up Upland Sandpiper and Bank Swallow. Several miles west of there, we pit-stopped at a State Highway 165 overpass where a number of Cave Swallows had built nests and added that "used to be rare in Louisiana" bird to our list. We found a Common Tern in a small mixed flock of gulls and terns on the beach at Four Magic Miles. But the premier destination was Peveto, and our premier target was the Golden-winged Warbler that had been spotted the previous day.

There were lots of birders in the woods and thankfully lots of bird varieties as well. It took us a little more than two and half hours to explore every trail of those woods, and we picked up thirteen warbler species in the process, including four species we needed for our list: Cerulean, Blackburnian, Magnolia, and Chestnut-sided. No Golden-winged, but we added a number of non-warbler species to the list as well, including Veery, Baltimore Oriole, Painted Bunting, and Blue and Rose-breasted Grosbeaks.

We checked in with Mary and she was doing well, so we decided to try our luck at Lighthouse Road, where a male Black-throated Blue Warbler had been spotted the previous day. I was elated at finding several more species for our year list, including Scissor-tailed Flycatcher, Prairie Warbler, and Bobolink, but I was upset to see evidence of new industrial activity on the remote, gated road. Cheniere Energy owned this land and was expanding their natural gas processing facility; the pristine habitat along Lighthouse Road was being compromised as a result—already there were more roads, fewer trees, and less marsh grass. Birders had been lamenting that the company might close off access to this area permanently due to the expansion. I hoped that this wouldn't be my last-ever trip to the area.

We struck out on the Black-throated Blue and decided to give Peveto one more shot. Two hours had passed, and at the height of spring migration in Cameron Parish such a time interval could mean that some birds had continued their trek north and left the woods while others had come in from the Gulf. And who knew— maybe the elusive Golden-winged would cooperate.

When we pulled into the parking lot we saw that most of the birders had left. Only two birders were present and both were new to us. Jim Delahoussaye and Brad Moon reported that they had been in the woods for several hours. I asked about what they had seen, and their day list sounded similar to ours, except they had seen the Golden-winged Warbler. When I asked where, they reported two places—the scrubby area near the water drip, and right where they were standing, at the entry to Peveto. The two of them were done hiking the area and were just camped out waiting for the Golden-winged to show itself again.

We joined the pair, and the four of us birded at what felt like 100 mph, where you raise your binoculars to your eyes ten times a minute because there is so much to see. The trees and brush at the entry to the woods held a number of

Chestnut-sided and Black-and-white Warblers, mixed in with American Redstarts, Blackburnian Warblers, and Magnolia Warblers. Constant movement of birds gave us lots to look at, but we kept seeing the same species over and over, with no Golden-winged. After twenty minutes of birding silently, we began to talk—friendly conversation doesn't happen much at Peveto, at least not with me, because generally I'd rather bird than converse. But we were the only birders in the entire place and we weren't disturbing anyone, plus we could bird and talk at the same time.

Jim was clearly proud of his colleague, Brad, who was a biology professor at the University of Louisiana at Lafayette; Jim told us about the snake research that Brad published and how it was the most famous research that had ever come out of the university, about the strike speed of nonvenomous snakes being as fast venomous ones. His research had been written about in the *New York Times* and had been covered on national news. Jim then confided that Brad's true passion was dragonflies.

"I like birds," Brad chimed in, "but dragonflies are *awesome*." Brad got downright animated talking about them; he dug out his phone and said, "Look at this!" It was an amazing picture of a green, brown, and yellow dragonfly with bright blue eyes called a Southern Snaketail. Brad went on to tell me that there are 145 species of dragonflies in Louisiana. "He's on a mission to get pictures of them!" Jim bragged, "He's already seen about 90 percent of all the species in the state and has photographed most." I was amazed by the 145 species. To this point, I had noticed maybe six different species of dragonfly. I suppose that the average nonbirder has probably noticed about six different species of birds, so that made sense. Brad scrolled through a number of other dragonfly pictures on his phone, and all of a sudden I felt like I was immersed in a parallel natural universe that had been unknown to me before.

We'd been standing in the same place for forty-five minutes, seeing the same bird species and having a great conversation, but with no Golden-winged Warbler. We needed to start home soon and the scrubby area near the water drip was calling, so we told them that we were going there to look for the golden-winged and to call us if they happened to see one. The only notable thing that happened near the water drip was that Lynn saw a Bay-breasted Warbler, and try as I might, I could not find it, even as she provided detailed instructions on where to look. About thirty minutes later we were birding a stand of oak trees on the other end of the grove from the entry when I heard Brad's voice carrying over the wind: "We got one!"

Lynn and I set off for the entrance immediately at an awkward half-walking, half-running clip and made it back to them in a couple of minutes. "Well, it *was* here just a few minutes ago," said Brad, "We had to call you several times before you heard us." I uttered a silent *ugh* inside my head as Brad pointed out the last spot he'd seen it. We began the golden-winged search again. Ten minutes later Brad announced, "Found it!"

He oriented us to the leafy area twenty feet away, above the first branch of the closest tree and below the third branch of the tree behind it, and for two precious seconds the black triangular throat and golden cap came into clear focus before the busy Golden-winged headed toward the next row of leaves. I broke into gooseflesh as I said, "I got it!" Five seconds later and from a slightly different vantage point Lynn sounded, "Me too!" We got one more furtive look at the thing and then it was gone, but hallelujah, we had the bird. We immediately headed for home but not before profusely thanking Brad and Jim for yelling across Peveto, hugging them, and taking a victory pic with our phone. Although not exactly rare, the Golden-winged Warbler was not a bird that I'd identified as one of the 292 I thought we could see.

At this juncture I had stopped counting rarities. I was instead using the "target species" feature in eBird; using this feature, a birder can track, in ranked order of historical probability, a list of the birds needed in a region for their list of choice (life, year, month, etc.). I had begun to enjoy knocking the number one bird off my year list in Louisiana as we continued our adventure. I'd removed Eastern Kingbird, Great Crested Flycatcher, Black-crowned Night-Heron, and Painted Bunting successively, and then picked off Inca Dove and Yellow Warbler as the spring wore on. Once I got to Rufous Hummingbird, I knew it was going to be the number one needed bird for a while. Although I was not worried about finding it and the Black-chinned Hummingbird (almost guaranteed in late fall at Donna and Steve's house), also in my top ten of needed birds, not being able to remove the number one bird until toward the end of the year was slightly annoying. Still, the target species list was immensely useful, because I used it to plan trips to find birds on that list.

Although we weren't able to bird as many times as we'd hoped in April, the trips we were able to make were well-timed to pick up early to mid- and then late migrating species. We completed one more Peveto trip in the first week of May and added seven new birds to the list: Black Tern, Least Flycatcher, Warbling Vireo, Gray-cheeked Thrush, Tennessee Warbler, Nashville Warbler, and Blackpoll Warbler. I also picked up the Bay-breasted Warbler that Lynn had scored without me. One common bird that Lynn missed all spring was the Louisiana Waterthrush; it was the only bird from my Grand Isle spring break trip that she missed.

I was lucky enough to notch a day of birding with Steve and Donna in late April, courtesy of the Shorebird Extravaganza festival that they co-organized. It was held in the middle of the week, and Lynn couldn't miss work. The best bird by far was the Hudsonian Godwit, a bird for which Steve and Donna used the local nickname ring-tailed marlin, ring-tailed for the white band around its tail and marlin for its long beak. The next weekend, I directed Lynn to the same location in Vermilion Parish where we had observed the flock of forty godwits lift up from green rice fields and fly around us in large circles a couple of times before landing again out of sight among the rice stalks, but we were unable to locate them.

My mom came to visit in early May, and I took her and Joan birding in Cameron Parish. We notched a respectable 114 bird species for the day. This count would likely have been higher, but the ferry across the Calcasieu Ship Channel was out of service and it took us almost ninety minutes to drive up and around the channel to the west side of Cameron Parish. The jaunt across the channel typically takes twenty minutes, fifteen of which is waiting for the ferry to come. I picked up a new-for-the-year Western Kingbird on Lighthouse Road, and back home our moms once again had a great chance to connect and converse.

Lynn and I coasted into mid-May with me focused on finishing the school year and Lynn leading her school toward the same place. On the 15th, I had 266 bird species on my year list. Lynn had 260. We were both in the 265 mid-May range that Jay Huner had mentioned as being on pace to reach 300 species by the end of the year. I was cautiously optimistic that we were going to make it.

THE QUEST FOR THREE HUNDRED

THE MARATHON

The first and second halves of a marathon can be very different experiences; there are "bad miles" during the second half, those that I have to slog through to make it. They've come to me in almost every one of the marathons I've run, as early as mile thirteen and as late as mile twenty-four. I'm physically exhausted and I have to push through the urge to stop; getting through is a mental and spiritual game that I play with myself. During a bad mile, I think of a person I love and conjure up poignant memories involving that person. When I reach the next mile marker I change to another loved one, and continue to do so until I work my way through the bad miles.

Birding in the dead of summer in Louisiana reminds me a little of the bad miles during a marathon. South Louisiana typically experiences heat indexes that reach 100 degrees or higher. Even when birding inside the truck with the AC running full blast, it's hot. Although we had already seen most birds possible for the season, there were still about a dozen we could chase.

Mary was stable and enjoying time with us and with Hurricane, so we walked the tightrope between chasing birds and being home as much as possible. For the summer season, I planned four trips: (1) to the west central part of Louisiana for the Greater Roadrunner; (2) to Shreveport for the Bell's Vireo and Willow Flycatcher; (3) to Peveto in late August for migrating flycatchers; and (4) out into the Gulf of Mexico for whatever pelagic goodies might be there.

We also planned short chase trips for needed birds. For example, when Janine Robin posted about baby screech-owls she was observing daily in a Wood Duck nest box in her backyard, I contacted her immediately to see if we could yard crash.[1] She assented, and on June 1 we rode over to the tiny village of Folsom after Lynn got out of work. Janine came out to greet us as we pulled in her driveway and took us to her backyard, which consisted of three acres of birding paradise. Feeders were everywhere, with lots of colorful gardens, open expanses of grass, and a tall tree line that surrounded the back of her property. Janine led us to where the ground level dipped toward a swampy low area that didn't quite look like a ditch but could become one during a good rain. The nest box was located in this low area and close to a small pond. Janine positioned us at the edge of high land, just before the dip and about thirty feet away from the nest box opening.

"Let's just watch the hole," Janine said, "they show themselves every so often. I haven't seen them yet today, but it's getting toward evening and this is a good time to see them."

We stood together scrutinizing the hole. Although there was no action, the birds in the tangle of brush and short trees in the immediate vicinity provided plenty of ancillary entertainment. Janine ticked off several bird species while we waited, including Yellow-billed Cuckoo, Hooded Warbler, and Summer Tanager. When the whistled song that ends with what sounds to me like "here, here, pitch it here" rang from the floor of the pseudo ditch, I smiled broadly and declared, "Swainson's Warbler."

"Yep," Janine agreed.

"*Yes!*" said Lynn. We happily added plus one to Lynn's year list.

A few minutes later I saw movement in the nest box hole. I immediately lifted my binoculars, and when I focused them I got the briefest glimpse of gray feather down and a yellow eye. "Owl!" By the time Janine and Lynn trained their binoculars on the hole, the edge of owlet face I'd seen had withdrawn. We stayed focused on the hole for the next ten minutes with no action whatsoever. Just as Lynn started joking that I must have hallucinated, a tiny head reappeared. All three of us chuckled as the owlet stuck its face even farther out of the box, and we collectively took in breath as a second face appeared behind the first. Four eyes looked to the south, in the same direction in which we'd heard the Swainson's Warbler. We were as quiet and unmoving as they were, just watching them as daylight continued its leisurely summertime baton pass toward evening.

The first owlet retreated and the second remained, beginning to move its neck around to consider its surroundings. A second head reappeared, and Janine said, "Hey, that one is more red than the other two. I think it might be a third! I knew I had two owlets in there, I didn't realize that I might actually have three!"

Lynn and I left a few minutes later to take "the long way home." Normally we'd return the way we came, on I-12, which runs east-west just north of Lake Pontchartrain. We elected instead to drive south across the Causeway Bridge to I-10. The reason? An unexplained phenomenon that started in 2015—decent numbers of pelagic birds known as Brown Boobies had decided to spend the summer in the vicinity of the Causeway in Lake Pontchartrain. For all we know, they could be spread across the lake, but most were spotted by birders as they drove across the twenty-six-mile road that connected the New Orleans suburb of Metairie to the small city of Mandeville. For the past several years, boobies had been spotted on the length of the Causeway, but especially around mile marker 16, which was close to the middle of the lake toward the Mandeville side. Boat trips to this area produced sightings of fifteen to thirty-five boobies; they seemed to like the concrete bridge structure at this juncture, where their perching locations were not visible from the bridge but were fully visible from a boat. Even so, many flew around the area and were visible to vehicular traffic. We took a jaunt over the Causeway and kept our eyes peeled, especially between miles 17 and 16, but no Brown Booby.

On Friday, June 3, we commenced operation "find roadrunner" at 1:00 in the afternoon. I was thankful for the extra flexibility of Lynn's summer work schedule, which enabled her to leave at noon on Fridays during the month of June as long as she'd worked forty hours that week. Our idea was to drive what I dubbed "The Matt Pontiff Roadrunner Loop." It isn't really a loop; it's a U-shaped route with Highway 190 as the fourth side, or "loop" connector. According to Matt Pontiff, who is the expert on where to find roadrunners in the state, the other three roads include rich habitat for the roadrunner.

The Matt Pontiff Roadrunner Loop was some five miles west of DeRidder, Louisiana, which is almost fifty miles north of Lake Charles, so it's in that "slouching toward Texas" part of the state, but in the central part of the state as well. I am more familiar with the southwestern edge of the state, where Louisiana has a coastal, scrubby feel. I was interested to see what this west-central section of Louisiana was like because I had never birded it. According to MapQuest, the start of the loop was a 2 hour and 49 minute drive from our house. The plan was to bird the route, hopefully locate a roadrunner in the process, and then head home with a stop at Turf Grass Road on the way back.

Andre Moncrieff and other LSU ornithology graduate students did a big day on April 22, 2016. They fell only one species short of tying the Louisiana big day record of 221 species, and Andre wrote about it in a blog post that I read with interest.[2] In the post he mentioned finding a Barn Owl in a known stakeout location. I contacted Andre and asked where to get a Barn Owl, and he reported that Turf Grass Road, just after dusk, was a great spot for them. He said that if you played their call, they immediately called back, and that if you go at night with a spotlight you can find them on top of power poles. He also said that while unconfirmed as a roost site, one reliable spot was in the barn on the northwest corner of Cormier Village Road and Landfill Road.

Although we traveled efficiently, the GPS lied and it took almost four hours to reach the intersection of Highway 190 and Seth Cole Road, where the Matt Pontiff Roadrunner Loop started. Some of the slowdown was Friday afternoon traffic. I-10W was amazingly full of cars, even west of Lafayette, where traffic usually thins out considerably. Once we hit DeRidder, traffic was even more frustrating because in smaller towns there are smaller roads, and even though there's less traffic, the infrastructure creates frustratingly long parades of cars. It almost seemed like we were getting farther away even as our destination grew closer. We finally made it through, and then west of DeRidder, with mutterings about crappy traffic and inaccurate timing with GPS. At 4:53 P.M., we turned south onto Seth Cole Road from Highway 190 West and at last began our search for the roadrunner.

We rolled down the windows on the truck so that we could listen. Almost immediately we heard the single "bob" call of a Northern Bobwhite. Lynn stopped the truck right away. She scanned the fields to the east while I did the same for the grassy area to the west. Almost right in front of me was a ten-foot-high pile of branches and sticks that someone had stacked up, and almost at the top of that pile, 100 percent visible and only twenty feet away, perched a male Northern Bobwhite. My one-time nemesis bird that I finally saw in Alabama had since presented itself to me visually two more times, once in Arkansas—a fast but excellent look—and fleetingly in Louisiana. I had never, to this point in my birding travels, seen a bobwhite perch off the ground and in the open.

"*There it is!*" I half shouted to Lynn, and she followed my pointed finger and said, "*Wow.*"

We watched the male for at least two minutes. He didn't move, just sat, seemingly content to show off his chestnut cap and white eyebrow, calling occasionally, before flying south toward the cornfields.

We headed past the cornfields while birding the terrain and power lines on either side of the road, happy to note several Scissor-tailed Flycatchers. After a couple of miles we turned onto Pershing Loftin Road. Of the three legs of the Matt Pontiff Roadrunner Loop, this was clearly the star leg.

I usually try to compare the terrain I'm birding to other places I've been or terrains with which I am familiar, but Pershing Loftin Road defied comparison. The recent flooding in east Texas was also evident here, as parts of the road were covered in one to two inches of rain in a couple low spots. The small, steeply triangular-shaped ditches on both sides of the road held water, and barbed wire fence set back a couple of feet from the ditches was buffeted by a low tree line on the north side of the road and cattle fields to the south side. There was a short grass strip on both sides of the road, located between the road and the ditch, which appeared to be bone dry, yellow, and dead. The strips looked desert-like, even as the rest of the scene was lush, green, and wet. It seemed a strange hodgepodge of habitats quilted together in a uniquely patterned way.

We slowly drove Pershing Loftin Road, making note of the birds we saw throughout, including Blue Grosbeak, Turkey Vulture, Eastern Kingbird, and Cattle Egret. About a half mile down the road, Lynn stopped the truck to look at a distant bird standing on the border between the road and dry grass. "Mockingbird," she said disappointedly, and then, a few seconds later, "*I got one!*"

She had scanned the dry grass road edge from the faraway mocker to closer and closer to the truck, and had located a roadrunner partially hidden in the dry grass near the edge of the road. She quickly directed me to the roadrunner, whose head, upper back, and long tail were visible about 150 feet in front of us. I experienced a happy shiver down my spine as it crouched, unmoving at first, and then tentatively but fluidly walked onto Pershing Loftin Road, leisurely making its way across the road and entering the dry grass on the other side. Lynn crept the truck forward, and after we advanced on the bird fifty feet, it jumped across the water in the ditch and made its way through the barbed wire fence to the tree line and scrub immediately on the other side. When we pulled even with where the bird had entered the fence, we saw that it was still there, peering out at us. We watched as it walked parallel to the fence line in the same direction that we were driving in its long-legged, bicycle-peddling-esque strut. It walked about one hundred feet before turning north and disappearing into the scrub. We high fived and kept exploring, feeling great with our plus-two birds for the day, the Northern Bobwhite and the big score, a Greater Roadrunner.

Matt had told us that there was a road off Pershing Loftin that ran to the south, and to check that as well for roadrunners and for Wild Turkeys—so when Bubba Loftin Road presented itself, we drove south and kept birding. Although we missed the turkeys on this road and in other places in the loop where Matt had seen them previously, we felt elated to have traveled so far and been successful in our target. We continued adding birds we already had but were still great to see: Eastern Meadowlark, Common Yellowthroat, Pileated Woodpecker, Painted Bunting.

When we completed the loop, Lynn said that we still had time to run the loop again to check for the turkey before heading for Turf Grass for dusk. Since I never say no, we did. Pershing Loftin was even better to us on the second try, because we observed two roadrunners at once. One may have been the same individual from before, because it was in essentially the same place even though forty-five minutes had elapsed since our first pass. But on the other side of the road, clearly visible and about two hundred feet from the first, was roadrunner number two. The only thing better than one roadrunner is two. With the bobwhite and the roadrunner, I had 271 birds on my year list; Lynn was at 264.

There were only a couple of residences, both set back from the asphalt, on Pershing Loftin Road. Lynn put the truck in park in front of the biggest one, which sported a large front lawn, some mature trees, and a meadow across the street. There were tons of power lines at this juncture, and I wanted to check every line, every fence post, and every inch of the ground, because we were still looking for another potential but low-probability addition to the year list, the Lark Sparrow.

I had done research on about fifty bird species that were possible to add to our year lists, assuming that the birds we needed to get to three hundred would be contained in these fifty possibilities. For forty-nine of these fifty birds, I had a plan that included at least two places and appropriate times of year to maximize our chances of locating each species. The one bird that I had no plan to find, other than by sheer luck, was the Common Ground-Dove.

It is only a slight tangent to say that it drives me crazy when the word "common" is in the name of a bird that isn't common at all. I'm sure that it is or was common somewhere at some point—but not in my neck of the woods. Common Yellowthroat? Yes, very appropriate. Common Sandpiper? Common Merganser? No such luck.

On my day of birding with Steve and Donna at the Shorebird Extravaganza festival in late April, I had asked if they had any good intel on where and when to get a Common Ground-Dove, and they said, "No, it isn't that kind of bird." That confirmed my suspicions, because for all the years I had birded in Louisiana, I'd seen a Common Ground-Dove exactly once, in 2012, by following Ed Wallace's directions to the tee and finding one mixed in with some Mourning Doves at a grain processing facility in Convent, within a day of his reporting them on LA-BIRD.

Because I had no plan for finding a Common Ground-Dove, I had almost written it off as one we would get on our journey to three hundred. So it was with utter elation that, with the truck stopped and us carefully scanning each and every bird (mostly Mourning Doves and a couple of Eurasian Collared-Doves), a Common Ground-Dove flew up from the ground right in front of the truck. We could see the short, dark tail, the small dove shape and stature, and the uniform light gray/beige upperparts. So, no Lark Sparrow, but a single, very welcome addition to our year list. We left this approximately eight-mile-long birding paradise in the best of moods with a bird list hat trick[3] and headed for home via Turf Grass Road.

Lynn and I reached our destination about twenty minutes before sunset and rolled the windows down to listen and bird for whatever was present. I was impressed that at this hour birds were still calling before bedding down for the night. The most amazing sight was Crested Caracaras—we counted ten along a short stretch of Turf Grass Road. Most were gathered on the tops of power poles, and they all flew east and low over the turf fields and meadows as dusk fell, still visible in the "afterburn" of sunset.

We made our way to the intersection of Cormier Village Road and Landfill Road and waited a few minutes for dark to set in. Lynn played the Barn Owl call several times and got nothing in response, and then decided to drive down Landfill Road to see if we could find an owl perched on a power pole. We saw nothing but a couple of Great Egrets in the ditch in front of the landfill. We returned to the corner. It was now fully dark, with deep purple hints of the beautiful sunset left in the western sky. Lynn played the call again and listened carefully. Nothing.

It had been a long day, first with work and then with an epic drive and a very successful birding quest. We decided to start home via Turf Grass Road to Frontage Road to the interstate; we were still some 120 miles from home. We kept the windows down, and where there were trees and power lines we stopped a couple of times to play the Barn Owl call and listen. Still nothing.

We were approaching the bend in Turf Grass Road, near its intersection with Cormier Village Road, where there was a large house with a number of tall trees in the lot. It looked like a promising spot. Lynn played the Barn Owl call from her side of the truck toward the homestead, and we heard an immediate call back. Success! We whooped a little in the truck and tried to figure out if we could angle the truck and its headlights in case we could see anything, since we were not armed with a spotlight. Our effort was helped by an outdoor light that came on at the homestead, and by the owls' continued yelling. Between the illumination provided by our headlights and the nearby light, I saw two Barn Owls and Lynn saw three. They were on the ground and had their wings spread as they jumped around before packing up together in formation. One even flapped from the ground to a nearby tree and then vaulted back immediately. I watched as another stomped from one foot to the other, almost like a Weeble wobbling, but on short legs and with outstretched wings. The Barn Owls looked like mini marauding soldiers, with their half yell, half screech: "Hey! Who are you? Where's the other owl? We're all here, right?" We had stopped playing the call immediately, but once the Barn Owls got started, they kept going. Their response was raucous and loud and wonderful and nonstop.

I was smiling from ear to ear when Lynn said, "Oh boy, we've got company." I followed her gaze, and in the road in front of us a truck finished backing out of the driveway of the residence we were watching. It crept toward us on the road, first with no headlights, and then, as it got closer to us, the headlights blazed on high beam and the truck drove down the center of the somewhat narrow road, so that even if we wanted to pass the vehicle, we would be unable to do so. The truck pulled off the edge of the road and drew even with Lynn's open window. The man inside put his window down and said sternly, "What are y'all doing?" His grin was almost immediate when he glimpsed the binoculars.

"We were watching your owls, sir," Lynn said. His pseudo-menacing look entirely gone, he relaxed into conversation. "Oh, my screech-owls," he said. And no, we didn't bother to tell him that they weren't Eastern Screech-Owls, any more than you'd tell a local that a crane is a Great Egret or a yellow swamp canary is a Prothonotary Warbler—because people who live and work the land have their own language for the birds they live with, and that's fine by me.

"Once they get started like they're going now, it's hard to get them to shut up. I have four—and some nights they keep me awake all night. You're welcome to turn into my driveway to see them better if you'd like."

We thanked the man for his offer, but we really needed to get home to Mary. We said our goodbyes, and as we headed down the last stretch of Turf Grass Road for home, Lynn turned to me and said, "I think that guy had a shotgun on his lap, just in case we were trespassing."

* * * * *

As the dog days of summer settled in and I moved fully into the most creative part of my work year, I had more flexible time to spend with Mary and more mental space to reflect on where things stood. I had managed to become more at peace with uncertainty, even as the puzzle that no one talked about in totality seemed to be coming together more clearly. I was aided by helpful information I found on WebMD; for example, I learned that half of the people diagnosed with CHF were still alive five years after their diagnosis. Mary was a little more than four years into hers.

When she arrived at our house in November, Mary fixed all her own meals and helped clean the kitchen every day. Lynn and I laughed about the unspoken war we had on dishes—Mary was compelled to put away clean dishes, while we were happy to keep them in the dishwashing rack and use them as needed. Lynn and I frequently played WWMD, or "What Would Mary Do?" when looking for a particular pan or plate. After her first hospital stay, Mary worked to regain her strength and topped out at being able to get most of her meals and helping to clean the kitchen most days. After the second hospital stay, Lynn or I got her breakfast, she got her lunch, we got her dinner, and Mary cleaned up the kitchen occasionally. After the third (and fourth), we got most of her meals and cleaned up the kitchen.

Mary fell a lot. Usually she was able to stand up herself, but her balance became increasingly unsteady. Lynn was strong enough to pull her momma upright when she couldn't rise herself, but Lynn confided that she was afraid that at some point she might not be able to. And even though Mary ate pretty regularly, she lost weight. Although Mary's mood was consistently happy except when she had a UTI, it seemed like she was getting less vital, a little at a time. Each hospital stay set her back, and although she recuperated each time she returned home, it was never to the previous level she'd enjoyed before. While it was impossible to know, I felt like I was figuring out slowly that Mary probably didn't have a lot of time left.

Part of this realization came after Mary had follow-up visits with her cardiologist and gerontologist in the aftermath of her April hospital stay. The cardiologist decided against the mitral valve operation that could address some of the CHF issues because he thought it too risky. The gerontologist made the decision to take Mary off Glipizide; home health could monitor Mary's blood sugar level, and as long as it was not sky high she was not worried about diabetes. The real risk was stroke or heart attack. Plus with this approach if Mary got another UTI the antibiotic that effectively treated it before could be used without any worry of a drug interaction.

Although no one came out and said it, when the Glipizide was unprescribed, it seemed to me that maybe the gerontologist was doing what Atul Gawande mentioned in his immensely helpful book *Being Mortal: Medicine and What Matters in the End*—moving from providing medical care that prolongs life to medical care that enhances quality of life. I changed my outlook a little as well. Before, I'd encourage Mary to eat fresh bananas. Now, instead of trying to ensure that all bananas were eaten before they got too ripe, I used leftover bananas to make banana bread. Mary *loved* banana bread a hundred times more than she liked regular bananas. As long as her sugar was not too high, why not? She'd eat banana bread, she'd enjoy it immensely, and maybe she'd maintain her weight better. Mary was a huge fan of pie of all kinds, and her favorite was cherry, the same as mine. I dug out my pastry cloth and put it to work all summer long making cherry pies, apple pies, and even a key lime pie with fruit from the tree we keep in a large pot on our pool deck.

Mary had once again settled into a pretty decent place health-wise. She didn't complain about dips in her health or her lessening ability to provide for herself. She was very thankful to us for bringing her food and drink and for meals and conversation. At the same time, she pushed us out the door. "Go find your birds!" she encouraged. Mary had taken care of three people at the end of their lives, including one who had used guilt as a weapon. Those experiences, I believe, influenced her to be as supportive of us and our crazy adventure as possible. She never tried to guilt us once. Instead, she reveled in every colorful bird we saw when we showed her pictures we took or illustrations from our birding guides.

I almost felt like I was flying in an airplane through thunderstorms in which the pilot has found a pocket of clear air—you can look out the window and see clouds above you and clouds below, but where you are at the moment is smooth traveling. And you know that you can't cruise like this forever—eventually the clouds might creep into your pocket or you'll need to land, and the only way to get to your final destination is down through those clouds. But until then, I was reminded time and time again of how important it is to seize the day. Mary's supportive words and actions reinforced that maxim. And so we continued.

* * * * *

In early June, Joan and Joe invited us to Grand Isle to take a boat trip to find American Oystercatchers. We arranged with Mary to have Sydney Fletcher, a friend of ours with medical training, stay overnight so that we could go. Lynn was excited because she could do some fishing while looking at whatever birding highlights Joan and I found and pointed out. We executed another summer birding hat trick, picking up the Magnificent Frigatebird and Gull-billed Tern on the beach, and a pair of oystercatchers feeding together on a shell bed several miles offshore. Lynn's bonuses were catching Speckled Trout from Joe and Joan's boat and locating a Least Bittern tucked into some marsh grass on Queen Bess Island. Mine was watching Seaside Sparrows on an uninhabited island; several vaulted straight up into the air and executed aerial tricks that involved full flips before dropping straight down into marsh grass. The oystercatcher was bird number 277 for me in 2016. It had been the 280th bird Lynn and I observed in our initial big year adventure. Despite being at almost the same rank in species number, we got the oystercatcher in June and not December, and we'd only been at our quest five and a half months instead of twelve. Joe and Joan told us they were thrilled that they'd been able to contribute to our year list. I was thrilled too, with Joan and Joe's continuing generosity and with the opportunity for Lynn to regenerate a little through fishing.

In mid-June we took a quick trip after work to the Rigolets for Lynn to kayak fish. On the way, we pit-stopped at New Orleans' City Park, where we zoned in on Tad Gormley Stadium to see if we could locate year-round resident Monk Parakeets. We heard them calling as soon as we pulled up, and within one minute we observed one of the big green tropical birds. The parakeets had constructed their condo homes in almost every light fixture in the stadium. We stayed about five minutes, counting several, then proceeded to the Rigolets Marina in Slidell. We launched our kayaks and paddled toward the Geaughan Canal, where Lynn caught Speckled Trout. There likely would have been more fish in the box, but an impending summer thunderstorm cut our trip short.

We started home by traveling north up Highway 11. Lynn stopped at a pull off across the street from the Irish Bayou Truck Stop. A man of indeterminate age and ethnicity was sitting on an ancient lawn chair, the kind popular in the 1970s, with brown and yellow webbing. He greeted us when we pulled up, and Lynn, upon seeing the fishing pole in his hand, uttered the standard Louisiana fishing greeting: "Doin' any good?" The man said no, stroked his long beard once, and popped his cork (bobber) in frustration. Lynn got out her pole to fish the grassy water edges for Redfish, as it appeared to be picture perfect habitat for them. She fished for twenty minutes with no bites, and bearded guy hadn't gotten any either. Lynn announced, "Time to get home to mom," so we packed it in, but when Lynn turned the key, the truck didn't start. Lynn thought it was a dead battery and cursed when she realized that our set of jumper cables was not in the truck; we asked the guy if he had jumper cables and he said sorry, he didn't. I called AAA and told Lynn that she may as well keep fishing while we waited.

Soon after, a sedan pulled up to the bearded fisherman, likely to discuss the day's fishing report. Within thirty seconds the sedan moved on to us, and the man inside rolled down his window and said, "Heard y'all need jumper cables." When Lynn said we did, he replied that he had some, angled his car in front of our truck, and exited to begin setting up the cables.

All of a sudden, the bearded fisherman started yelling. At first I couldn't tell what he was saying, and I wasn't sure if he was yelling in general or yelling so that we could hear him, but he pointed out over the water. As I followed his finger, what he was saying registered. "Hey, that's a caiman! Caiman!"

I saw what looked to me like an alligator about five feet long that was swimming toward Lynn's bright orange cork. I removed the fishing pole from the holder in which Lynn had left it before tending to the truck and reeled it in quickly. The last thing you want is a gator on your hook; Lynn had once hooked a small alligator that attacked her cork and it had taken quite a bit of finesse and opening and closing of the bail[4] to get the gator detached safely. We still have that cork, replete with a row of teeth marks to prove it.

Thwarted in his hunt, the large reptile swam close to shore and turned 90 degrees in the shallows about fifteen feet from the water's edge and right in front of me, close enough that I could observe luminous brown eyes that seemed bigger and lighter than those on the alligators I was used to seeing. The animal's snout seemed to have a little higher ridge than that of a typical gator too. It almost seemed like the creature was looking right at me. It wasn't shy at all.

After regarding me in statue mode for a couple of minutes, the caiman headed toward bearded guy's cork. This action produced a monologue of muttering from bearded guy; I couldn't hear all of it, but it was something about caiman aggression and who let this thing go, and no wonder there weren't any fish around. Bearded man reeled in as the caiman closed in on his cork. It stopped about a dozen feet away from bearded man, right in front of the vintage lawn chair.

The muttering continued as caiman and human seemed locked in a stationary stalemate. The man wasn't moving from his chair, and the caiman appeared to be waiting for a cork (or a fish in the form of a cork). It sure was close—I'd never seen a large reptile cruise so close to a human and square off. It almost reminded me of barracuda and the way that they square off with you when you're snorkeling. They don't attack you, but they don't retreat either; they just look at you head to head, and they'll maneuver with you to keep that head-to-head configuration.

Meanwhile, Lynn and the guy in the sedan, who introduced himself as Louis, had finished connecting the cables. "Crank it," he said to Lynn, and our truck started up right away, like a dream. We had to let it run for a while, but instead of leaving, Louis stayed, and he and Lynn started into a fishing conversation that I understood only part of. Even though I didn't follow all the technical terms, I understood that they were trading love the same way that I do when talking birds with a fellow birder: fluorocarbon or monofilament; bait caster or spinning reel; silver or gold spoons; Carolina or Texas rigs; nuances in bouncing jigheads off the bottom; the location of favorite fishing holes.

"I used to fish every day after work," Louis said, "and then I got promoted. I needed the extra money and it's been great for me and my family, but it takes away time from fishing. I haven't fished in forever, but I still stop by on my way home from work to see what other people are catching. And it's nice to be able to help out a fellow fisherperson in need."

We tried to buy Louis a six-pack from across the street, but he was having none of it, so we shook hands and said our goodbyes, including to bearded man, who waved perfunctorily while still staring down the caiman. As we headed home via the Causeway, I canceled our AAA call and looked up the term *caiman*. I was shocked to see, upon looking at pictures, that the bearded fisherman was correct. I had never heard of a caiman, much less seen one in the state. Caimans are in the same family as alligators and crocodiles but are in a different genus— smaller, thinner, and often more aggressive than alligators. They are not native to Louisiana, but people keep them as pets. I wondered if the bearded man's mutterings were true, that someone had released a caiman that had grown too large to be a pet and it was now patrolling the waterways gorging on popping corks and native fish.

Brown Booby try across the Causeway: Brown Pelican, yes! Brown Booby, no.

* * * * *

I had called Terry Davis to beg for help in finding the Willow Flycatcher and Bell's Vireo; he responded by offering to guide us through the Yates Tract inside the Bayou Pierre Unit of Red River NWR, a location some twenty miles south-east of Shreveport where it was possible to find both species. Lynn and I left the house at 3:20 A.M. on June 18 to meet him at Yates by 7:30. Despite outstanding, detailed directions, we still missed the overgrown entrance to the unit located exactly 1.09 miles north of parish road 401. We were texting updates to Terry, and he came out onto the road to direct us into the almost secret entrance after we U-turned to try again. He locked the gate behind us and gathered the caravan of people he had invited.

Jay Huner, Ronnie Maum, Dot Rambin, Larry Raymond, and the rest of us rolled down our windows and watched and listened with Terry as the thick summer air quickly heated up. The short, scrubby trees and medium-length green grass smattered with yellow wildflowers reminded me of the Arkansas countryside. We were the only vehicles in the place; Terry was in the lead truck and stopped every quarter of a mile to survey birds. He located a cooperative Bell's Vireo at the very first stop; I wasn't sure about Lynn, but I was pretty excited that our 3:20 A.M. departure time wasn't in vain. It took us almost four hours to bird the narrow road that wound through the pretty habitat, which sported more Yellow-breasted Chats and Dickcissel than I'd ever seen in my life; we also had numerous looks at Bell's Vireos. About two-thirds of the way through the unit, at a 90-degree turn in the road, Terry cocked his head and stated, "I just heard a Willow Flycatcher!" We piled out and looked for it, and though it took a while to spot, the willow cooperated enough for all of us to see it and for Ronnie to get a fantastic picture.

When we circled back to the entry gate, Terry and others in the party planned to bird more of Bayou Pierre for shorebirds; Lynn and I had another couple of area targets to chase, so we said our goodbyes to the group. I asked Terry if he knew of any foolproof spots for the Western Kingbird. "Sure!" he said, "Go to the intersection of US-71 and Caplis Sligo Road; there's a gas station on that corner and the road in front of it leads off to the west and runs into a marina back there. There are some power poles and lots of electrical lines at this intersection, and there are a couple of Western Kingbirds nesting in this area—look anywhere between the lines and the marina."

We headed north and navigated straight for the intersection while munching on homemade "wish sandwiches," so named by our fishing guide friend Theo Atkinson because "it has two slices of bread and wish it had some meat on it." We found the intersection, pulled into the parking lot of the gas station, and searched the power poles and lines. I was immediately rewarded with two Scissor-tailed Flycatchers and a Loggerhead Shrike. Within two minutes we located a Western Kingbird. Lynn was stoked—it was another "catch up" bird and the last time we would see this species in 2016.

We checked in with Mary, who was excited to hear that we had been successful in our trip and encouraged us to take our time and explore some more if we wanted to. I had perused *A Birder's Guide to Louisiana* in anticipation of this trip, and in the northernmost reaches of the state, another twenty-five miles north of where we idled at the gas station, the book stated that there were nesting Grasshopper Sparrows in the summertime in the meadows on Old River Road. We'd be taking on at least one more hour of driving, out and back, to return to our current location.

"Wanna go for it?" I asked?

"Well, we're this far, what's a few more miles?" Lynn the ultimate trouper pointed our truck north and continued, "You need to review for me. Show me a picture of the bird and play me its call."

I complied as we encountered increasingly rural terrain. The last sign we saw before wholesale countryside took hold announced that we were in Plain Dealing, Louisiana. I had never heard of the town, approximate population 970. It was so far north that some of the town's residents could spit and hit the Arkansas state line.

Lynn navigated LA-537 to Old River Road, but when we tried to turn left onto this road to access the meadows, we were crushed—the road entrance was blocked with a metal cattle gate and chained shut. We had traveled twenty-five miles farther from home for a road that was off limits. I exited the truck at the intersection; even though we were stopped in the middle of a state highway, absolutely no one was present, so it was fine to stand there. Heedless of the heat index that was also north, north of 100 degrees, I listened hard into the heavy, shimmering, sweltering air for the high-pitched call of the Grasshopper Sparrow, which true to its name sounds reminiscent of a grasshopper. Nothing.

"Well, we better start home," Lynn said. It seemed a reasonable suggestion, so I sighed and got back into the truck. After traveling about a mile south on LA-537, I yelled for Lynn to stop the truck.

"Look at that! A Scissor-tailed Flycatcher nest!" I said excitedly. Sure enough, the pair of adult scissor-tails was very devoted, feeding bugs to the three babies craning their necks up from the nest toward their parents' offerings. Lynn got out to take pictures of our first ever scissor-tail nest, which was wedged between the center shaft and top cross member of a wooden power post. While happily watching the scissor-tails I heard a sound that rippled goose bumps across my arms despite the intense heat.

"Lark Sparrow!" I cried. All of a sudden, the extra twenty-five miles north seemed fully worth it. We were both all smiles as we began the long ride home. When we left I-49 and headed east on US Highway 190, I told Lynn that we were going to ride right by a spot on US-71 where Jay Huner had reported seeing Wood Storks several days earlier. It had been a long day and we were tired, but if we could get the stork now, we wouldn't have to drive all the way out here to see it later. Lynn turned north onto US-71 and I began looking out the windows at the wetlands on both sides of the road. She only had to travel three miles before we found a bunch gathered in some shallow water on the east side of the road.

We made it home in the early evening; Mary was amazed at the size of Wood Storks and the way that they looked so prehistoric. I was amazed that we had pulled off a hat trick's worth of hat trick (or hat trick plus) summer bird trips.

* * * * *

The first bird of 2016 to take on nemesis status was the Wild Turkey. If you're laughing right now, you should be, because for several reasons there aren't many birds easier to see than the Wild Turkey. If you look at the species bird map on eBird, the Wild Turkey inhabits almost the entire United States—they're just about everywhere. I-10, what Van Remsen calls "that great biogeographical divide," is a boundary of sorts for the Wild Turkey—it is scarce south of I-10 in Louisiana, where I live. Okay, so I reside in one of the few areas in the country where the turkey does not regularly occur. Even with that, it's not far away—a thirty-mile trip puts me in its territory.

Besides being widespread, turkeys are so big that even nonbirders recognize them. With a head to tail length of three to four feet for adults, they cannot be missed. Add to that the fact that many times turkeys hang out in the open, and I would venture to guess that the probability of finding 282 birds in the state of Louisiana without the Wild Turkey among them would be extremely low. And yet, the bird proved very difficult to find. I actually saw a turkey in the spring, but it *so* didn't count. I was driving on I-10 and came up behind a battered pickup with a caged turkey in the truck bed. I felt bad for the bird and at the same time almost laughed at its comical look; it seemed to stare at me quizzically for miles.

Our friend Chantal Correll observed Wild Turkeys several times along a small levee immediately south of the I-12 exit in Livingston Parish during the spring. Lynn and I rode by this exit regularly, and every time we did we took a pass through the area for turkeys. Six consecutive trips through the late spring and summer months yielded nothing. Two trips down LA-975 right through the heart of Sherburne and the Atchafalaya were equally unsuccessful. And of course, we missed the turkeys on the Matt Pontiff Roadrunner Loop.

When Janine Robin posted on LA-BIRD about seeing a pack of thirteen turkeys in late July, including adult and sub-adult birds, we went in pursuit of them the very next day, making the sixty-eight-mile drive northeast of Baton Rouge on a Sunday. We marveled at the pretty assortment of houses, followed by horse farms mixed in with woods and fields, as we traveled the length of Damiano Road, several miles north of Folsom. We observed typical summer species like Blue Grosbeak and Mississippi Kite, but no turkeys. The only living soul at the end of the road was an old fisherman sporting Cajun waders[5] and a cane pole. We asked if he came here often and he said yes, he'd been coming here a long time, even before all this stuff built up—he gestured toward the horse farm in the distance. Had he ever seen turkeys here?

"No, but they're definitely around. If you want to see them, you gotta come first thing in the morning or at dusk. I don't have one no more, but I used to in my backyard. They liked to eat the acorns from my live oak tree. What you need to do is figure out where they cross around here, and then wait for them until they come by."

"Doin' any good?" asked Lynn.

"No, not today," he replied wistfully.

On a whim, we drove about ten miles north to Bogue Chitto State Park, where the attendant at the entrance informed us that Wild Turkeys were all over the park. Despite our coverage of every road in the park and hiking some promising looking trails, as well as observing habitat that looked like turkey heaven, we were not graced with the presence of one. We did see a Bachman's Sparrow, so at least Lynn got another catch-up bird.

We tried Damiano Road on the way back to Baton Rouge—nada. Ditto with Chantal's Livingston exit. Naturally, Janine Robin saw two turkeys in the same spot the very next day at 11:30 in the morning (we'd visited at noon the previous day and at about 4:00 when coming back through). Ten tries. No turkey. Even though it was July, the turkey was already our nemesis bird of the year.

July 24 jaunt across the Causeway in search of the Brown Booby: Strike out!

* * * * *

During a normal summer, I spend a decent amount of time writing journal articles and working with my playground research and design team on playground designs and proposals for funding. This summer wasn't normal; I was still writing and working but not with as much vigor or mental energy as I usually mustered. I was also doing things that were atypical. I was playing gravity-defying games of Jenga with the recyclable bin in the pantry. I could stack the enhanced volume of recyclables produced by our household amazingly high before I finally bothered to empty the bin into the recycling can outside. I was gaining weight, courtesy of helping myself to the plethora of baked goods I created that were intended for Mary. And I was slowing down. I have been a faculty member for twenty years, and for every single year of my career I felt like I drank out of a fire hose in my quest to get things done. My fixation with my to-do list had been the consistent driving force in my professional life, and my ability to accomplish things had not diminished one iota in all that time. Until now. This slowdown was intentional on my part, though something I came to in small steps.

Initially, I experienced a lot of mental teeth-grinding when working with Mary to accomplish what were simple, fast things for me, like putting on a pair of socks or a shirt, or calling someone on the telephone. Doing such things were so important to Mary, and she did them at the speed she was comfortably able. My "yoga breathing" strategies to assist her by matching my speed to hers in an effort to be the most helpful eventually morphed into an appreciation for not having to go full speed all the time.

It was a lesson I thought I had learned with Lynn after the burn, but I had to learn again with her mom. "Repetition compulsion" is what my friend and colleague Lilly Allen calls it, those lessons that you have to learn over and over. Some things I've only needed to learn once. Slowing down was not one of them. Over time, I became willing to stop what I was doing to have an honest conversation when Mary asked me a question. Even farther down the road, I stopped working early to go into her room to initiate such conversations on topics like Mary's hopes and dreams for her grandchildren, her legacy of advocacy for school children, and the importance she placed in faith, family, and community.

Then an atypical experience came knocking—or flowing, as it were: the great flood. You'd think that living twenty years in Louisiana would make one well aware of natural disasters. And yet, somehow, we missed this one until it was already upon us. It started raining on August 12 and didn't stop all day; when Lynn got home from school and checked the ditch that ran in the back of our property, the five-foot-deep crevice was almost full, so full that for the first time ever we could kayak the two hundred yards down our ditch into adjacent Dawson Creek.

"Wanna go for it?" Lynn asked. I'm a sucker for an adventure just about any day, and our success in finding birds early in the summer meant that we had nothing to chase until the end of the month. I'd been missing our birding adventures, so I jumped at this chance. I was hopeful that once we reached Dawson Creek perhaps we'd be able to observe large numbers of Mississippi Kites in the thick tree lines that hugged both sides of the creek bed.

The water level in Dawson Creek was so high that we were thwarted in a long paddle, first to the south and then to the north, because we could not pass under road bridges at Kenilworth Park and Perkins Road. We returned to our house, put away the kayaks, and made dinner for Mary. Long rainstorms are not uncommon in Louisiana, so I was used to and comforted by the muted sound of raindrops hitting the roof; the sound was our constant companion all evening, and I fell asleep to the showering music.

I woke up at 3:00 in the morning to the rushing sound of flowing water under our house from the front yard to the back, something I had never heard before. Looking out the bedroom window, I couldn't see anything in the darkness. I woke Lynn, and together we went to our front door and walked out onto the covered porch. Lynn flipped on the porch light and we could see that water was standing in our front yard and had reached the first step to our front door. It was still raining. Lynn was concerned about our vehicles, so she threw on her raincoat and moved them to the highest point in the area, in front of Carol Lee's house.

We returned to fitful sleep and conducted a brief reconnaissance with coffee cups in hand several hours later. It was still raining and the standing water in our front yard had come up to the second step of our house. Out back, only the top foot of the four-foot-high wooden picket fence that Lynn had built by hand was visible. What had seemed like a fun kayak ride yesterday seemed incredibly stupid this morning, because all the items under our carport that we hadn't thought to move were flooded, and water was lapping against the carport door.

As the water continued to rise, Lynn and I had the shocking realization that we might have to evacuate, and if we did so, there would be no easy way to get Mary out of the house. She would be unable to use her walker or wheelchair in the deep water. We figured that if it came to it, we'd load Mary into a kayak and pull it to our vehicles, which remained amazingly unflooded; the water level only reached halfway up the tires. We told Mary of our plan, and she was opposed to leaving. "Well hopefully it won't come to that," said Lynn, "but if it does, we want you to know that we have a plan."

Thankfully, it didn't come to that. The rain stopped later that morning. The water continued to rise and made it just past the fourth step, one step short of the entryway that was our trigger level for evacuation. Then it slowly receded.

Lynn and I each contacted our respective workplaces through well-established natural disaster networks. Lynn's school had flooded, and as principal of the school she was the point person for subsequent clean up. Many of her students had lost their homes in the flood, as had many of mine. I worked to assist recovery efforts through the LSU Center for Community Engagement, Learning, and Leadership. We both channeled our efforts outward in service to our communities, and inward as we worked to reclaim our pool and repair our flooded carport.

We squeezed in a couple of quick birding trips even so. We tried for the Alder Flycatcher at South Farm and we might have had it, but because the bird we saw did not call and it was a fast look, the ID went down as *Empidonax sp.*[6] I am the kind of birder who needs a *really good look* to make a call on a silent Alder Flycatcher. And a photo if possible. And I still might need consultation with an expert even after that. This trip would have been frustrating for the miss, but we hiked a new trail in the huge area, our target still the Alder Flycatcher. Instead we came away with a Wild Turkey when we weren't even looking for one. We finally got you, sucker!

Ditto on the Brown Booby. The fourth try was the charm! There was much whooping and cheering in the truck at mile marker 6.6 on August 23 when we saw one gliding near the Causeway on the western side of the road.

Mary shooed us out the door for a day trip to Peveto at the end of August to try for migrating flycatchers. We managed to find an Alder and an Olive-sided Flycatcher in the woods, and I was thrilled to score a Canada Warbler flitting in thick cover on the western side of the sanctuary. On the way home we birded Four Magic Miles for gulls, terns, and shorebirds and located a single Snowy Plover, the bird I had come to regard as my personal "saved from riptide" talisman, on this stretch of beach.

As August hands off to September, wet heat transitions to dry, and the skies seem bluer with the lower humidity. My friend Moonjung Choi translated a statement from her native Korean to describe this phenomenon: the sky gets higher in September. As the drier air blew and hummingbird migration reached high tide, I felt our lives shift to an ever-slightly harder gear. Mary had good days and bad days, but the tough ones slowly started to outpace the good ones. She was still in high spirits but was often exhausted.

I functioned on a type of autopilot: Get up, make coffee and breakfast, relax while drinking coffee with Lynn; make breakfast for Mary after Lynn leaves for work; work in my home office; make Mary breakfast again if the dog gets it; work some more; check in with Mary, bring her a stash of food and LFVWo for the day in case she isn't up to visiting the kitchen while we are at work. Go to work. Stop at the store on the way home, or volunteer with flood clean-up and then go home. Eat dinner, let the TV watch me for a couple of hours, and go to sleep with one ear open for clunks on the floor. Get up some nights because I hear a clunk, always thankful that the clunk is a dropped glass and not my collapsed mother-in-law; refill the glass, make sure all is okay, go back to bed. Repeat. I began once again to feel like I was walking a tightrope, this time between taking care of business and taking care of myself.

I watched Lynn function on the same type of autopilot but with extras, like doctor visits and picking up prescriptions. The national opioid crisis had resulted in increased barriers to securing Mary's hydrocodone: the maximum number of days per prescription was decreased from twenty-eight to twenty-one. Each time the prescription needed to be renewed, Lynn had to call it in to the doctor's office, even as other medications Mary took were renewed automatically. Lynn then had to pick up the prescription from the doctor's office in person and deliver it to the pharmacy, and only she could retrieve it when filled.

I wasn't sure if we'd be able to take our trip to Venice, Louisiana, to see pelagic birds, but we went ahead and lined up Sydney to stay with Mary and figured that we could always cancel if Mary was having a bad time. I had helped to organize this trip, which put me in touch with a number of birders I hadn't met before. I hired Captain John Coulon, a fishing charter guide who was familiar with pelagic birds, and I worked with Van to recruit people to fill the boat; with 20 slots available, the price per person was a reasonable $150.

I had chosen September 10 because it was the only Saturday that Captain John had available other than the one before Labor Day, and I thought I'd have a hard time recruiting people for that date. September 10 is the statistical center of the height of hurricane season. Few people outside this area realize that there's a "high hurricane season" within hurricane season. Regular hurricane season runs from June 1 to December 1, corresponding roughly to the time that ocean waters in the Gulf reach 80 degrees or higher and remain there. Although the season seems kind of long, it is really the season within the season that gets most of the action. High hurricane season runs from August 15 to October 15. If you look at the big hurricanes that have hit Louisiana and the Gulf Coast, most have struck within that window. So it wasn't only Mary's health that I was watching; I had my fingers crossed and my eyes glued to the National Hurricane Center forecast for two weeks leading up to the trip.

The pelagic trip was in a way a form of cheating, for a couple of reasons. First, because people who try for three hundred species typically get there with land birds only and don't resort to plumbing their state's offshore waters[7] for extra bird species. Two, I had no experience with pelagic birds, minus a trip to the Dry Tortugas National Park and a fishing charter off the coast of Key West. I was happy with my Brown Noddy, Sooty Tern, Masked Booby, and Band-rumped Storm-Petrel, but I had the assistance of people with expertise for these identifications. It felt a little like cheating to go on a trip in which you have to rely on other birders to make the calls for you. I knew I could study my birding guides and get some of the birds, but I also knew I couldn't identify them all myself.

Friday, September 9, came and I was excited and nervous both. I was super excited about the trip, which was a go. There were no storms in the Gulf, and the prospect of seeing pelagic anything had me giddy. Even better, Mary had been feeling good, so good that we were able to take her to the mall, where she got her favorite watch resized and we ate a meal together at the food court. Lynn and I were elated because we hadn't been able to get Mary out of the house for anything other than a doctor's appointment for months. I was nervous because I was holding all $3,000 for the trip. I felt responsible—and while I feel perfectly comfortable being responsible for myself, I was now aware that if I broke down on the side of the road and didn't make it, no one would be able to get on the boat without that money.

Lynn and I planned to leave Baton Rouge at around noon, with me picking up Lynn from school, heading for Venice, and making a strategic stop en route to bird either at Couturie Forest, a sixty-acre bird magnet located in City Park in New Orleans, or at Fort Jackson in Port Sulphur. Fall migration was on, and while we were likely too late to score Lynn a Louisiana Waterthrush, we both still needed the Northern Waterthrush and they were a dime a dozen all September long in south Louisiana. I was grinding my teeth from seeing all the reports of such birds on my daily list of needs that eBird emailed me courtesy of the target species function. I could handle all the Rufous Hummingbird reports because I would get to that bird, and I could handle the Yellow-bellied Flycatcher reports because that's a tough bird to get, but the Northern Waterthrush sightings bothered me. It's like they were screaming, "Hey, I am the one easy bird that you should have by now and you don't. What are you going to do about it?" Well, I was going to do something about it on the afternoon of September 9.

And then life happened, like it does sometimes. Lynn needed the full day to work just to stay almost even with all the crazy extras that happen anytime you live through the aftermath of a natural disaster. Four of Lynn's teachers had been reassigned to other schools to follow their displaced pupils, and Lynn picked up a bunch of students from Ascension Parish who were doing virtual education (she ran the parish program for that) from the myriad, distant places to which they had evacuated. When you add the extras of these activities to your regular workload, you fall behind even working full time. Truth be told, I was really glad that she needed the full day to work; although I quit work at noon, I needed the extra hours to clean house, visit with a good friend who had just lost her husband, and pack for the trip. Lynn came home from school, and I figured that since we were leaving at 4:15 we'd still have time to stop in Couturie Forest to search for the waterthrush.

As in post-Katrina, post-flood traffic was terrible. I'm not even sure why. It likely had something to do with extra people, but sometimes I think that per-turbations in one sphere lead to ripple effects—more tightropes, if you will. Add Friday afternoon onto swelled post-flood traffic levels, and I admit that I was heavily frustrated. It took us one hour to travel five miles, including the two from the house to the interstate. Things usually sped up at least marginally once hitting the interstate, but not this day. We crawled along for another half hour before learning the source of the problem: A tow truck with two cars on it had broken down in the middle lane on the interstate. Beautiful, I thought cynically, and a metaphor of sorts: even the institutions that were created to help are in need of help themselves.

After we passed the stalled tow truck, traffic was still heavy, and we hit major slowdowns in New Orleans. I crossed Couturie and a crack at the waterthrush off the list as we passed the exit with a mere twenty minutes of daylight left. Traffic was thick all the way through Belle Chasse but thinned once we got onto Highway 23, and we both started to wind down and look forward to the impend-ing night we were going to spend at the Le Matidora Inn, a unique converted house in Buras that sported an eclectic mix of tropical, Cajun, Americana, and hunting décor.

It seemed that the farther south we traveled, the more remote the land became—we usually drove this stretch during daylight, not at night. The occa-sional lights of oil and gas facilities lit our way, as did the occasional boat on the Mississippi River. Highway 23 meanders with the river along the west-side levee. Because the river was higher than the road, we could see the lighted tops of the tall boats floating on the river, far higher than our car as we rode along.

My phone rang at 8:00 on the nose, when our GPS said we had 5.3 miles to go to make it to the inn.

"Is this Mary?" said the voice.

"Marybeth," I said, "yes, it is."

"Can you tell me when you're going to be here?" I realized that I was speaking with the woman who had taken my reservation at the inn several weeks previously.

"Yes, our GPS says that we're five miles away."

"Okay, I'm going to wait for you, then."

Living in the south has had an amazing influence in calming me down, but it's also made me more sensitive to being an annoyance to someone else. The caretaker of the inn was ready to go home at 8:00, and even five miles away, I felt bad that she had to wait. We missed the turn onto Highway 11 from Highway 23 and had to backtrack about a half mile. When we turned on to Highway 11, the darkness was total. We turned on our high beams and followed the GPS. I figured that we were good—we kind of, sort of remembered the place, but we had last been there three years ago in daylight. Still, how lost can you get when you're on the same road as the inn? Our GPS piped up after a mile and said, "You have arrived at your destination. Ending route guidance."

We looked around. Fields were on both sides of the road. I've heard people my age talk about how "kids today" have no navigational skills because they rely on GPS. I've always been a fan of human ingenuity and the ways in which your skill sets are highly adaptable to your situation. Kids today aren't dumber than people my age. In fact, ask a kid how they feel about the technology skills of a person my age and you'll likely hear about dumb old people. I wonder what would happen if instead of judging others who grew up in different generations, we instead admired their uniquely adapted skill sets. Young people may not have had to navigate with a paper map or compass or by looking at the position of the sun in the sky, but they still need to know how to navigate for those times in which the GPS says that you have arrived and you have not. I mean, you're close, it gets you in the vicinity—but you're not quite *there*. My daddy always says that "almost" only counts in horseshoes and hand grenades. It doesn't count in GPS. And the lady was waiting.

With only minor cursing, we continued up the road, attempting to make out the numbers etched on mailboxes set back from the road and thus not within the light stream emitted by our headlights. It was about as easy as trying to read the band numbers[8] on a Piping Plover. After another mile or so we saw the inn, but we couldn't quite remember if the driveway leading to it was before or after the building itself. The driveway didn't line up with the inn, we remembered that much. Lynn stopped at the driveway before it, began the turn, and when it didn't look promising, put the car in reverse. Just as she reset herself on the road and began inching forward, the phone rang again. The lady. I picked it up and heard the words, "You're here, that's it. Just come up a few more feet and turn in!"

Lynn pulled up, and I jumped out of the car, ready to be yelled at for being twelve minutes late, but the lady was all smiles, warm and welcoming. She told me to come into the office with her, and I followed her and stepped in front of a tiny counter while she got my license and credit card and rang me up for $85.

"We are full up tonight!" she said, "well, mostly full up. I always need to leave the one room open just in case the owner ever wants to stay here at the last minute, and I have another room that's got a bunch of stuff in it, bunches of linens and things you need to run the place, but that room is never available.

"I'm looking forward to going home tonight. It's going to be good because if people call me at 2:00 or 3:00 in the morning, I can tell them that we're full, and I don't need to get up in the middle of the night to check them in. People do that, you know—it's because they know that if they get past 2:00, the rate drops from $85 to $65, because it's only a partial night. It's couples that wait, you see. They want to use the room for you know what. And they want to spend less money—and they still complain to me, saying, 'Hey, why do we have to pay $65 for just a few hours?' And I tell them, 'Well, the rate is what it is and if you want to go somewhere else, go on ahead.' And they don't, know why? 'Cause all the rest of the places around here are $100 a night. They know it and I know it, and still they complain."

The lady's blonde hair was well kept but frizzy in some places, as if static electricity had visited in random spots. Her face exuded friendliness and her eyes sparkled intelligence—this woman was made for the hospitality business. She was warm and outgoing, even with her last straggling travelers of the night. After checking me in, she walked me outside and around the corner of the inn to show me where our room was. We were standing in the middle of the main driveway.

"Now, normally you'd be able to pull around and into the back here," she continued, "but you see how I have this wrapped with caution tape? It's because I just pressure washed it, see how nice it looks? It's because we have a wedding tomorrow, they're gonna get married right here on this slab. But the owner? He done drove his nasty, dirty truck up on this thing yesterday, after I had pressure washed it the first time, and messed it up. I had to pressure wash it again, and this time I was smart. I wrapped this thing with caution tape, and I told him, 'You are not gonna be driving your nasty truck on this driveway!' Anyway, you're all checked in. Enjoy your night!"

Lynn and I hauled our stuff up to the room, which was painted a bright yellowish green reminiscent of the color of a female Painted Bunting, and which sported a psychedelic painting of Jimmy Hendrix over the bed. An old-time desk phone with punch buttons was on one of the nightstands. I picked it up, shocked that it was still there, but when I held it to my ear it had no dial tone—apparently the phone was just for show. We enjoyed the balcony view for a minute before heading downstairs to the pool area.

I was excited to find the beer-filled vending machines we had encountered on our last stay, but alas, the beer had been replaced with cold drinks.[9] We then located an ice machine on the property because we needed to refill our cooler with ice for our food and drinks to take onto the boat. I was happy to see that while the beer may have vacated the vending machines, it certainly hadn't left the premises. Upon opening the ice maker I found a twelve-pack of beer, a single coke, and the ice. We left the beverages alone (they hadn't been offered), got our small cooler iced and organized, and went to bed.

I had a fitful night of sleep because there was no alarm clock in the room and no wake-up call. We had to rely on our iPhone alarms, and I wasn't 100 percent certain that they worked 100 percent of the time. We set both of them and had Chantal, right across the hall, text us when she got up as well. I woke up at 1:10, 2:30, and 4:00 A.M. just to check the phone—was it time yet? Our alarms sounded off in synchronicity at 4:30 A.M., and Chantal had texted us ten minutes before to make sure that we were up.

I was running on adrenaline—we were off to the races! I noticed that despite my nerves, my body was in perfect shape because the mattress we slept on was outstanding—I had started to notice these things in middle age. As we clunked outside with bags and cooler, a rooster was calling nonstop in the darkness. I hoped it was a good omen.

We fired up the GPS, which didn't work for the first three miles of the thirty-one we needed to travel to reach our destination, backtracked our way to Highway 23 in the darkness, and set out full speed for the Venice Marina. We got there with just enough time to run upstairs to grab a cup of coffee and breakfast (both of which were served at the inn but not at 4:30 A.M.) and meet the other birders. I finally relaxed. I had the money, and I was here.

David Muth is the director of the Gulf Restoration Program for the National Wildlife Federation. He is also the state's pelagic guru, having taken some forty trips into the Gulf of Mexico from Venice over the course of thirty years. David provided an orientation before we got on board; the twenty of us spanned the spectrum from beginning birder to world-class ornithologist. The first piece of advice from David was to not expect a single pelagic bird. "The northern Gulf of Mexico just doesn't have the pelagic bird density that you'll see off the coast of California or in the warm Gulf Stream off North Carolina," he explained. "I've been on many trips where we didn't see a single pelagic bird. So enjoy what you do see, even if it isn't pelagic."

I thought this was a good piece of advice. I'd been on this exact same boat three years before. We had spotted a Brown Booby on the Mississippi River, and it seemed like a good sign. But once we got out into the Gulf we couldn't find the clear, blue water necessary for pelagics and we didn't see a single other pelagic species. Although I enjoyed the hundreds of frigatebirds we saw that day, it wasn't the lifer list boost I was hoping for at the time.

Van was in charge of bird checklists for our trip and explained that he was doing it the old-fashioned way, with pen and paper, and that he would start over every hour with a new checklist and was tracking our progress with GPS. Boat occupants were welcome to add their sightings as we traversed the boat channel into the Mississippi, proceeded downriver, and then emerged into the Gulf. He told us to count carefully and make sure we didn't double-count birds, and that he was not going to count the laughing gulls until we hit the Gulf because there were just too many to keep up with.

Ed Wallace was on board, and the three of us stood side by side as we took off down a channel called Red Pass and headed for the Mississippi River. We checked off White Ibis, Boat-tailed Grackles, and Roseate Spoonbills as the boat picked up speed moving out of the channel. "Least Bittern!" Lynn yelled as the bird flew toward our boat, turned out over the water, and flew back into the marsh in a wide, perfectly semicircular arc. I knew that Lynn was excited to see the bittern; though she'd seen one earlier, she hadn't had a truly good look all year long. Others were calling out a plethora of wading bird species and Gull-billed and Caspian Terns as we made the turn from the channel onto the Mississippi River.

It's twenty miles by river from Venice to the Gulf of Mexico, and though this last stretch of the Mississippi before it empties into the Gulf isn't a place where you typically see pelagic birds, it is part of the trip that I love. The river seems big and mighty where it winds through Baton Rouge, at about a half mile wide and fifty feet deep, and is even bigger in New Orleans, where it is two hundred feet deep and you can observe the great power and speed of the current. By the time you hit Venice, the river seems less constrained and more placid. Part of that might be because there is no longer any human habitation, with the exception of Pilottown, permanent population zero.

Without buildings and roads for perspective, the scrubby trees and tall grass known as roseau cane that line the river were more noticeable than usual. Water and vegetation shared the river's edges similar to the way that great friends stand closer together than strangers do, and the way that they share space makes clear that their bond is a palpable, friendly force. Pilottown brought two welcome birds: a Bald Eagle perched on a nest platform intended for an Osprey, and a Brown Booby flying north up the river.

A couple of miles past Pilottown, we reached the Head of Passes, also known as the mouth of the Mississippi River. Here, the river splits into three parts, or passes, out to the Gulf: Southwest Pass (to the west), South Pass (the center), and Pass a Loutre, to the east. This part of the river is appropriately named "Bird's Foot Delta." Captain John had done his homework to determine the best pass to traverse to get to blue water the fastest. Other fishing boat captains had shared that heading toward the southeast was productive, so Captain John selected the South Pass.

I was looking starboard when David Muth called American Bittern from the port side of the boat. My brain lit up like a Christmas tree: *Bird I need!* I scrambled in my best "bottom feeder" manner, ducking under other birders' shoulders, to get into position to try to spot it.

"You see the second and third power poles?" David asked while pointing, "It's heading away from us, between those two poles, just over the cane line."

I looked and saw nothing. Although David and Mac Myers were the only two birders on the boat to see the bittern, I felt the crush of missed opportunity that seemed heavier as I edged closer to the magic three hundred mark. The American Bittern is not the easiest bird to find—most people who frequently bird Louisiana in fall and winter find them, but it's not like you can dial one up at will. I was counting on getting one in the Cameron Courthouse wetlands during the fall LOS meeting, but I hated to start the trip with a miss.

The river seemed even smaller and the vegetation looked increasingly saltwater tolerant as we chugged closer and closer to the Gulf. I noticed a number of open wooden platforms fifteen to twenty feet high, stationed at the river's edge and tall enough to stand above the roseau cane, replete with primitive ladders and enough open space to hold eight people with ease. I guessed that they were hunting platforms and asked David Muth what they were. He said that they were old survey markers installed by the Army Corps of Engineers before GPS technology was available. Because the ground-level survey markers were frequently buried by the river's sediment, the Corps decided to "take the high road" while installing these "permanent" survey stations, no longer needed thanks to technology.

We spotted frequent, small flocks of White Ibis and assorted tern species, including Black Terns, as we continued our southern course. Soon we passed Port Eads, a tiny enclave on the southern border of South Pass that consists of a small lighthouse, two lodges, and a marina. The place is rented out to people who want quick access the Gulf for deep sea fishing. No one was there to greet us as we motored past, but that didn't dampen the excitement of the group as we saw the rock jetties that marked the end of the pass and our entry into the Gulf. The twenty of us put up a small cheer as we crossed the threshold. We were sprung!

For me, crossing into the Gulf was like crossing from birding well-known territory to birding the largely unknown. There were few enough trips like this one to make our checklists research-worthy. Although I was an underprepared and amateur observer, I was excited that the pros were on board and hopeful for what we might find on our high seas adventure.

Few birds were visible at the confluence of river and ocean as Captain John hit wide-open throttle and we picked up speed, just an occasional Royal Tern and Magnificent Frigatebird. The water was muddy, but was mixed with clearer, bluer eddies. A few minutes later, the clearer, bluer water had taken hold. David said, almost to himself, "I don't want to jinx our trip, but I've never seen blue water this close to the Mississippi River before. It's a good sign."

Flying fish launched out of the water as we approached them, charting straight-line, low trajectories away from the boat and across the water for up to twelve seconds at a time while we watched them with our bare eyes or with binoculars. David was amazed that we were seeing flying fish so close to the river; they usually frequented blue water at least twenty miles offshore, and we were less than five miles into the Gulf. "The water is looking really good really fast," he reinforced.

We didn't have to wait long for the hopeful tone in David's voice to be rewarded. "Great Shearwater!" called Van. All twenty of us came to attention at once, and the whir of multiple camera shutters commenced as the bird glided right past the boat, providing spectacular looks for everyone. Van was excited and told us that this sighting was one of only a few state records of this species. Our trip was already made and it wasn't even 9:30 yet.

As we continued our beeline in a southeasterly direction, a couple things quickly became apparent. First, LSU ornithology graduate students Oscar Johnson and Andre Moncrieff were fantastic spotters. The mere mortals among us could find birds in the immediate vicinity, while the two of them located distant birds and were often able to identify them from afar. And second, this trip was definitely going to be pelagic; we were seeing frigatebirds and Black Terns like last time, but a few miles farther out into the Gulf we spotted our first Cory's Shearwater. This was the one bird I knew from study based on the bird's shape and yellow beak; almost immediately, Oscar and Van began a conversation about whether it was a Scopoli's or *borealis* subspecies, quickly eclipsing my knowledge base. A second Cory's was called, and the onboard experts ascertained that we had one of each subspecies.

As I observed the birds gathering in this area, I noticed sargassum grass, which is actually a floating algae, on the water's surface. I knew from Lynn that boat captains were always excited about the presence of sargassum because it held a lot of marine life, including pelagic fish species like Mahi Mahi. Fishing boat captains like to find "a grass line" of sargassum and follow it to fish; such trails were typically anywhere from one to thirty feet wide and could curve along for miles, sort of like a country lane in the middle of the ocean. Captain John had parked along the semblance of a grass line; perched on a tiny piece of flotsam within it was our first Bridled Tern of the day. The twenty of us were quite the merry band of birders as we were entertained by the aerial acrobatics of the Cory's, with a few Royal and Black Terns hanging out, and several frigatebirds bearing witness from above like silent sentries.

"Jaeger!" someone called out. All of a sudden, the drama level among our small flock of birds picked up as the dark-brown torpedo zoomed into the mix. A second jaeger appeared within several minutes. We watched the birds zig, zag, and chase each other over who would lay claim to a couple of small fish. One jaeger was identified as a Pomarine, but even the experts weren't sure about the other one. Van urged the photographers on the boat to get as many pictures as possible. A third jaeger was spotted in the distance.

Lynn and I both wore what felt like permanently full blown smiles. The Great Shearwater, Cory's Shearwater, Bridled Tern, and Pomarine Jaeger were not just new year birds, but also lifers. Our luck for the trip continued to hold as we ventured ever farther out into the Gulf. We were treated to close looks at three Great Shearwaters sitting together on the water surface; all told, we saw an amazing twenty-three Cory's Shearwaters. When Captain John chummed popcorn soaked in fish oil after locating another small bird flock, a single, immature Brown Booby joined the melee. The booby seemed almost clownlike with its short bursts of low flight and energetic if not graceful dives into the water for food. I welcomed its presence and laughed at all the unsuccessful sprees across Lake Pontchartrain we had taken to find this species.

Around lunchtime we observed a line of storms off to the south, and Captain John abandoned our southeasterly course and started a run due west to avoid them. We were eventually hit with a little rain, but it didn't dampen the spirits of the birders one bit. Most piled into the boat's covered area to ride out the storm, though several adventurous souls braved the elements to continue birding. The sky turned white and reflected off the water, so that there were places in our 360 degree panorama of vision in which the sky ran into the water and there was no contrast between them. It is an amazing thing to see an erased horizon.

Although we didn't see another pelagic bird once we turned west, we viewed hundreds of frigatebirds and Black Terns. I was used to watching Laughing Gulls and Brown Pelicans pile onto the rigging of shrimp boats that troll the coastal waters. Far out here, the cargo boats were bigger than the shrimp boats, and the bigger frigatebirds sat on their rigging the same way that the smaller birds did closer to shore.

In midafternoon, Captain John started heading back toward Venice so that he could get us to dock by dark. As we traveled up the river and wetland habitat reestablished itself, I was paying quite a bit of attention to see if another American Bittern might be around. There wasn't. However, as we all stood on the bow of the boat, once again calling out the names of a plethora of wading birds and

gull and tern species, someone yelled "passerine!" I watched the single bird in the twilight as it flew from starboard, out in front of the boat, to port, and disappeared into the vegetation on the west side of Red Pass. I could tell that it was indeed a brown passerine—what kind, I could not say.

"Northern Waterthrush," stated Oscar with confidence.

"Really?" Van asked.

"Yup," he responded.

And that was that. Lynn and I looked at each other in disbelief. Before this trip, Lynn had said that getting one new bird would be good, two would be great, three would be fantastic, four would be unbelievably incredible, and five would be impossible. With the waterthrush, we had nabbed our fifth bird of the day for the year list. All five, especially the waterthrush, were "cheap" in my book, but I would take them. We reached the dock just as the night sky bloomed into full darkness; in order to get back to Mary as soon as possible, we turned down two dinner invitations that I would have loved to say yes to, and we drove home feeling awesome.

Van collected everyone's jaeger photos and shared them with one of the nation's experts on this species. He followed up with everyone several days later to tell us that one of the jaegers we watched at length was a juvenile Long-tailed Jaeger. It was only the fourth record of this bird in the state.[10] The distant jaeger we saw went down as unidentified. I was reminded for the umpteenth time that being an expert doesn't mean you identify every single bird you see. You do your utter best and use every tool at your disposal, but if you don't have enough information, the best you can do is a "spuh" call (sp., species only).

Due to the multiple ornithologists onboard and off, Lynn and I exceeded the impossible according to her rubric, with six birds for the day. I was sitting at 293 species and Lynn was at 290. Even with the missed bittern, I felt very confident that we would both reach 300.

And then I forgot about birds.

6

SWAN SONG

Less than forty-eight hours after we returned from Venice, Mary experienced a massive headache. She responded by doing the same thing she did when having a flare-up with rheumatoid arthritis: she took four Advils every four hours in addition to her hydrocodone. She managed to get through the day but told each of us in turn when we got home from work, "Wow, this headache is as painful as childbirth."

After that headache, Mary was not the same. The occasional unexplained arm tremors that her doctors had been monitoring were suddenly worse, and she was very, very fatigued, to the point that she asked for a bedside commode. We were hit for the third time with "we just didn't know" dread when, upon looking online, we learned that a terrible headache is a symptom of a person having a stroke. We were relieved that Mary had a previously scheduled appointment to see her gerontologist, a routine visit that had been delayed when the great flood impacted the medical office. When we contacted Terry Sanders to see if we should bring Mary in sooner, she immediately sent a home health aide to draw blood for tests.

Lynn discussed the results with me two days later while we sat in the relative privacy of the back porch. I knew from her somber expression and timbre that bad news was coming. "Her blood cell counts are way off, indicating internal bleeding. They could try to scope her, but they don't think she can take a scope. Even if she could and they could figure out where the bleeding is coming from, they likely can't stop it anyway. Her liver enzymes are way off, indicating that her liver is failing. Terry says that her shortness of breath and super fatigue are not surprising given her blood levels. The results are matching what

Mom has been saying for the past two days: she is dying. Terry has suggested hospice."

We talked to Mary together, with Lynn explaining the situation. I wasn't sure if this conversation would be emotional, but it wasn't. Mary took the news in stride and said, "If they are half as good to me as they were to my husband, then I'll be great. Yes."

Transitioning to hospice is an acknowledgment that a person has six months or less to live. Enhancing a patient's quality of life is the entire focus of hospice; prolonging it is not. The hospice team takes over all medical needs, so for Mary there would be no more trips to the gerontologist or cardiologist or neurologist. From this point on, all medical needs would be met through the hospice team, and they made house calls.

Lynn phoned the hospice agency immediately after our conversation, and the intake person visited within twenty-four hours. Emily met with Mary alone, with Lynn and me together, and then with all three of us, explaining everything about hospice and their particular agency, and answering any questions we had. Lynn confided to Emily her concern that we were putting Mary in hospice too soon. Emily replied, "I don't think you're putting her in too soon—at all."

The one thing I was excited about, if it is possible to be excited about anything with hospice, was pain control. Morphine is the gold standard of pain relief, and finally Mary would have enough morphine to block the constant pain that hydrocodone could not. Emily explained to us that Mary would be required to sleep in a hospital bed instead of using the queen mattress in her room. Mary listened to the entire explanation of why the bed was necessary, and when Emily asked if a hospital bed was okay, Mary smiled and said, "I'll take three, one for me and one for each of them." She still had her sense of humor.

The transition into hospice happened quickly, as the hospital bed was delivered to our house the same day as the intake. Lynn and I quickly tore down the old bed to make way for the new one. That hospital bed was a tough physical reminder about the change we were undergoing. It is one thing to start hospice and to feel the emotional part of that shift; it is another to have a physical manifestation of this finality as well.

The bed was wonderful because with the touch of a button Mary could achieve the perfect position to sit up or lie down at will, and the height of the bed could be adjusted so that she could exit easily. But the bed was also difficult because it was a single and not a queen. Hurricane couldn't cuddle up with Mary anymore. Despite all kinds of trying, our sixty-pound Catahoula couldn't find a single configuration that would comfortably accommodate both of them. Hurricane settled for sitting right under Mary's hand at her bedside for pats and scraps, but she was not happy about this turn of events, and neither was Mary, who stated several times that she missed Hurricane being in bed with her. We missed being able to sit on the side of Mary's bed too, as we often visited with her like this, so we positioned a chair on each side of her bed so that we could sit with her as close as possible to the way that we did before.

The first few days were mostly smooth sailing. The switch from hydrocodone to morphine was a little rough initially because the morphine dose wasn't high enough; when the prescribing doctor doubled it, Mary's pain was controlled for the first time in years. The large white van that brought all of Mary's medicines to our house was a welcome change. Lynn would not need to endure another pesky trip to the doctor's office to pick up a hydrocodone prescription.

Donya, the hospice nurse, visited regularly and put all of us at ease with her peaceful spirit and competence. Ashley, the aide, quickly earned the nickname "my hospice angel" from Mary. Ashley visited three times a week to bathe Mary; she took her time and talked to Mary while giving her the full spa treatment. "She makes me feel like a million bucks every time," Mary said. Once when I thanked Ashley for the five-star care she was providing, she said, "I treat my clients the way that I'd want to be treated. And I want to be pampered when I get to that point in my life."

The transition to hospice made me feel simultaneously peaceful and sad; peaceful because Mary seemed in good spirits and accepted her life as it was without any illusions, and sad because everything seemed to be moving so fast toward her final breath. It is hard to know "where you are" in the process while it is happening. I felt like if this hadn't been my first experience, I would have understood it better, but Donya said that every death is different. "Most of us need help coming into the world," she said, "and most of us need a little help leaving it too." I was very comforted by this statement and repeated it to myself often.

I took mini-breaks on our covered back porch, where I watched the peak of the Ruby-throated Hummingbird migration. I noticed how full of life and drama it was, and was struck by the contrast with what was happening twenty feet away as Mary slowly faded. Simultaneously, I found myself more aware of life than usual; mundane actions seemed more noteworthy and colors seemed brighter. I almost felt more alive while bearing witness to Mary starting to leave the earth and being at peace with it.

Four days after entering hospice, we woke up to Mary being completely out of her head. She didn't understand a word we were saying and her sentences made little sense, though she communicated that her late husband, Russ, was in the room with us. Hospice staff responded immediately, confirmed the recurring UTI, and called in an antibiotic, which was delivered immediately by the medicine van.

Mary came back cognitively after a couple of days, but she brought what seemed to be additional realities with her. Mary had visitors in the form of her favorite TV show characters. To me and Lynn, they were imaginary, but to Mary, Opie from *The Andy Griffith Show* and Reba from her own sitcom sat in the chairs next to her bed or, in the case of Opie, played nearby on the floor. She didn't see these characters every moment of every day, only sometimes, almost like there were holes punched in reality through which they entered our world.

The one thing Mary was not able to bring with her after this UTI was her strength—she needed help getting from the bed to the commode two feet away. I wasn't strong enough to help Mary with this transition, and Lynn was at the limit of her strength, especially because Mary's balance continued to deteriorate. Lynn helped Mary make one final lumbering, treacherous transition from commode to bed and that was it. Catheter time.

Mary agreed to have one and was okay with it when she was cognitively present. But she became increasingly less present. She was still sunny Mary when she was with us—other times she was conscious, but not really herself. It wasn't the UTI universe and it wasn't a fugue state, but it was a semiconscious, alternative-reality space, almost like Mary was suspended somewhere between this three-dimensional world and a fourth dimension beyond.

This was the point when I came face to face with my naivety about hospice. I thought that life would be generally better for Mary, and though it was in some ways, it wasn't in two other notable ones. Once again, I just didn't know. First was the catheter. I quickly came to hate that device because its presence tormented her so. Mary was a lady and simply not comfortable with a catheter and a Depend in case of leaks. The catheter was necessary, and we all knew it, but conversations tended to gravitate toward removing it or having to go to the bathroom even though the catheter was already doing the job. Or wanting to wear underwear but not being able to do so.

A typical conversation with Mary in the 3.5 dimension would be:

Mary: "Do you have underwear on?"

Lynn: "Yes."

Mary: "I want underwear on!"

Lynn: "You're wearing a Depend, mom."

Mary: "I don't want a Depend! I want underwear!"

One day when it was just the two of us, Mary told me she wanted to wear underwear so many times that I thought to myself, "Fine, let's put on her underwear, over the Depend." I accomplished this action with much pulling on my part and maneuvering on hers. I experienced two minutes of blissful silence, and I hope that Mary experienced two minutes of peace. Then she said, "Can you help me take my underwear off? I have to go to the bathroom." I removed them—and that was it with underwear.

Second, I really believed that once we got the morphine dose to the proper level, all would be right with the world as far as pain control. And while that was mostly true, it was also true that Mary was allergic to morphine. Morphine caused intense, nonstop itchiness, and the strongest prescription anti-itching medication didn't fully quell her symptoms. The hospice doctor didn't want to remove her from morphine because he said it was truly the best painkiller. He suggested giving Mary some Benadryl midway between doses of the anti-itch medication. That regimen worked for the most part—not fully, but for the most part.

We initially tried skipping a Benadryl dose in the middle of the night because we hated to wake Mary when she was sleeping soundly. We quickly realized that skipping wasn't worth it. Mary would ask us to "scratch her wings" (where her arms met her back) constantly if we missed a single dose, and it took a few doses to get those symptoms back under control.

We went on a rigid three-hour cycle and took turns getting up in the middle of the night to keep the itchiness under control. We also used fast-acting liquid morphine for "break through pain," which occurred despite all the morphine Mary was taking. Donya counseled us to write down the time and description of every medication we administered; it was great advice because we never had to remember times, just look at our notebook.

As Donya made subsequent visits, she updated Mary's prognosis. Donya's initial prediction of three months moved to possibly more than that during her first follow-up visit. After the UTI, she said, "I think you have weeks." A few days after that she downgraded to "less than weeks." Lynn contacted her family and started using her sick leave to stay by Mary's side and to be with family members as they made their way to Louisiana to say their goodbyes.

Mary asked Lynn to call the funeral home in Ohio to make sure that all the arrangements she had made before moving were still in place. Because Mary wanted to be buried next to Russ, she had planned to be transported to the Ohio funeral home that had previously taken care of so many members of her family. Mary wanted Lynn to alert the funeral home that they'd be pressed into service on her behalf sometime soon. My trouper wife made that very difficult phone call quickly and professionally, and afterward informed her mom that everything was ready.

The funeral director called Lynn a few hours later to explain that the funeral home in Louisiana responsible for transferring Mary's body to Ohio was very expensive. Did she mind if he made a few calls and tried to find a cheaper alternative? Lynn assented. A couple hours later, a white van pulled into our driveway. Assuming that it was the hospice medicine van, which came almost daily, I went outside to get the delivery. Two people exited the vehicle, a man in a shirt and tie and a woman in a skirt suit; both looked very professional. I walked up to them, and by way of greeting the young man asked, "Is this the residence of Mary Hathaway?"

"Yes," I responded, "What can I do for you?"

"Is she here?" he continued.

"Yes. Are you dropping off medicine?"

"Uh, no . . . we're here for the body."

In the beat of silence that followed, I felt several emotions run through me, including one that overwhelmed the rest. I burst out laughing, I just couldn't help it. Both were looking at me like I was crazy, so I said the first thing that came to mind. "Well, y'all are a little early. She's inside and she's alive."

Their crazy looks were immediately replaced by abject horror—they were speechless. I don't think I can articulate how hysterical this moment was for me. Of all the farcical possibilities! The woman remained speechless while the man stammered, then apologized profusely, and then both started babbling at once about the phone call they got from Ohio, about how it wasn't communicated that this was a pre-planning situation, that they'd call Ohio back for correct details, and so on. They retreated for the van, and I waved goodbye while skating the razor's edge between uncontrollable laughter and unabashed weeping. I channeled my "yoga warrior" and used controlled breathing to tamp down my feelings before returning inside.

Mary continued to travel between "normal" reality and the alternate one that was all her own. As the days went on, she seemed to spend more and more time in the latter. While there, she would speak using incomplete statements or pose what seemed to be open-ended questions. Lynn and I hung on every word Mary said, but with critical words missing or insufficient information to provide context, it was impossible to figure out what, if anything, we should do in response.

Are you at the end yet?

I'll tell you how I feel. I feel . . .

What about the . . .

Where do you keep him?

Oh, that was a good . . .

Anybody have a black eye?

Are you coming on the trip?

Do you have any clothes?

How much do you have to buy to stay?

Exhaustion started seeping in. It was impossible to get a full night's sleep while keeping up with her anti-itch regimen. In addition, Mary would often call Lynn's name or mine, or would shout out those incomplete statements or questions. Even the sleep we did get was tinged with vigilance, like listening for dropped glasses, only more so. We were no longer worried that Mary would fall because the hospital bed had safety rails, but we were compelled to be available for the times that Mary needed us.

Up to this point in my life, only while I navigated the bad miles of a marathon had I relied solely on my mental and spiritual drive to keep me going. For the first time outside of a marathon, I re-found this gritty determination. I felt resilient, but previously I'd only needed to deploy this coping strategy on the scale of minutes to hours. This process was much longer than that. I resolved to pace myself while struggling with new tightropes: We wanted Mary to be pain free but didn't want her itchy. We wanted Mary comfortable but present. We wanted her satiated, but she increasingly didn't want to eat.

* * * * *

Several days later, Mary didn't recognize Ashley when she came to bathe her. Mary was belligerent and impolite, not the woman I knew at all. "How do you know my name?" she bellowed when Ashley greeted her. Mary muttered and said no a few times while Ashley went about her business. She was almost done when Mary started calling for help. When I entered the room, it was clear that Mary didn't know me either. I helped Ashley put a new sheet on the bed, said calming things to Mary, and explained what we were doing and why, but she fixed me with a nasty, silent look.

Afterward, Ashley told me, "I know that this seems upsetting, but it's normal when my patients don't recognize me anymore. That happens most of the time. Mary's just not happy today and is letting us know, but this is nothing. I've been clocked, punched, kicked, scratched, and called horrible names. It's just part of the process." Later that afternoon, Mary told Lynn that Ashley and I were monsters and that we had beat her up. I couldn't help feeling hurt, just as I couldn't help bursting out in laughter at the funeral attendants in the driveway. Her testimonial was one of the last things she ever said.

The next night, Mary began having death rattles. I contacted the on-call hospice nurse about what to do, and she suggested administering the Atropine that hospice had delivered to us previously. "Is this it?" I asked the nurse. "Well, most of the time it's close to the end, but some people can have death rattles for up to six weeks." The drug ameliorated the rattles, and after Mary's breath returned to pseudo equilibrium we went to bed, me in our bedroom and Lynn in the chair next to her mom, the spot she had slept in the previous two nights.

At 5:30 the next morning I returned to Mary's room after a fitful night's sleep. The rattles were getting worse again, so Lynn administered more Atropine as I went to the kitchen to make coffee. Lynn and I proceeded to guzzle coffee for the caffeine lift while sitting in our respective chairs, with our slurps and Mary's labored breathing the only sounds.

"It's okay to go, Mom," Lynn said gently.

Mary hadn't been conscious for thirty-six hours, and even that glimpse had been amorphous, but we kept talking to her as we usually did because the hospice staff had assured us that somewhere in there Mary could still likely hear us.

I was not thinking that death was imminent. I knew from reading and from talking to the hospice staff that as a person approaches death their limbs get cold. Mary's were hot. They had gotten cold for a short time two days before, but then had heated back up—they were hotter than usual, not colder. Hospice talked about how a person's veins came closer to the skin surface near death, and hers were not more visible than usual. So there we sat, mustering the energy to wake up, when Mary stopped breathing. We each put our cups down, stood up, and grabbed a hand.

"That's apnea, right?" I asked Lynn.

"I don't think so, I think this is it."

Mary took one breath after about seven seconds and stopped again. Ten seconds after that, there was a single gasp. And that was it—at 6:41 A.M. on October 12, Mary was gone. And in a moment, so were all the tightropes we had been walking. We were in free fall.

If the cage I felt like I was in sparked the beginning of the journey for three hundred, then being released from it would help me finish. In Mary's honor. Because I knew how to feed the coil of rage inside my grief. Drive. Hike. Search. Find. Breathe crisp air. Enjoy the high sky. Focus. Nail it.

7

THREE HUNDRED

"I've got to get out of this house. Let's go birding."

It was the morning after Mary died, and we were sitting in our living room drinking coffee together. Even though I was with Lynn, part of me felt alone. No matter how closely you work together at the end of someone's life, a significant component of dealing with a loved one's death is an individual experience. I also felt verklempt. We were a team without a game. There wasn't anything left to *do*—so we had to just *be*.

There had been things to do in the immediate aftermath of Mary's last breath. I called hospice as Lynn made phone calls to her siblings. Donya was at our house within fifteen minutes of my call and tended to Mary's body, while Hurricane stayed curled up under Mary's bed and refused to come out. Hospice contacted the funeral home, and two employees came to remove her from the house about ninety minutes after she died. One of them was from the pair that had come a few days earlier; she regarded me with slight nervousness as she approached but relaxed once she realized I wasn't mad about the mix-up. After Donya had fully accounted for all the medication we hadn't used, packed it up, and left, there really was nothing to do. Hospice came and retrieved their hospital bed later that afternoon, and the two of us wandered around the house, shell-shocked. The dog was as lost as we were.

We had almost a week before we needed to leave for Ohio for the funeral. Lynn hadn't been out of the house in almost two weeks, so I could understand her wanting to get away from ground zero. All year long, birding had given us structure and solace, and a way to just be. So we loaded up our binoculars and heavy hearts, and with little fanfare and almost no conversation we headed for

Cameron Parish to bird for the first time since exiting the boat in Venice thirty-three days before.

Although I hadn't been paying attention recently, a quick look on LA-BIRD and eBird showed that William Matthews had recently seen an adult male Vermilion Flycatcher on Wildlife Drive in Pool Unit D in Lacassine NWR. Since we needed the Vermilion Flycatcher, we headed for Lacassine first. We began searching immediately when we reached Pool Unit D because William had reported the vermilion in the first leg of the rectangular-shaped drive. We immediately saw an Eastern Phoebe, cardinals, and a Marsh Wren, but did not locate our target. We moved on to the tree line on the third leg of the pool unit, where there were more Eastern Phoebes, a Gray Catbird, and a couple of Blue-gray Gnatcatchers. Lynn and I pished up a storm at this corner, which seemed birdy, and in almost no time an immature male Vermilion Flycatcher flew up to displace a nearby phoebe who was sitting atop a metal cattle gate. We didn't do the usual new year bird dance, but we were both as close to happy as we could get.

We birded our way out of Lacassine, hoping for but not finding an American Bittern along the way, and then headed for Peveto. It was hot for mid-October, and we battled humidity and temperatures in the mid-80s while we birded the woods. Deerflies and mosquitos found and feasted on us, while we found relatively few birds. This bird-bug scenario reminded me more of birding Peveto in August than near the peak of fall migration. The only surprise occurred when we pulled into the parking area, where a pair of turkeys was camped out near the pavilion. As far as I was aware, turkeys did not inhabit Peveto. Although we already had this bird, it was great to see a couple up close. However, their lack of fear of humans made me realize quickly that these turkeys were likely domesticated and thus would not count on an eBird list.

We finished our day by birding Little Chenier Road; located five miles south of Pintail Loop off Highway 27, Little Chenier Road cuts a rare (in this area) east-west path through the coastal prairie. A ridge partway down the fifteen-mile road sports groves of mature trees, and the changing habitat can yield a lot of bird species. This area represents an underappreciated but outstanding location to bird. We logged ten species of wading birds, though not the American Bittern, and redundantly but appreciatively two more Vermilion Flycatchers.

The very next day, having gained permission, we crashed a Baton Rouge yard to see a banded Rufous Hummingbird. While sitting on the grass together and getting great looks at the hummer flashing its orange and green colors as it repeatedly visited a feeder, Lynn wryly observed that we had driven five hundred miles the day before to get a single year-list bird, while today we drove only five miles to get another. With this "easy get," I was sitting at 295 bird species and Lynn was at 292.

With one last nature-inspired hoorah before going to Ohio, we went kayaking in Irish Bayou Lagoon and birded the lagoon and Bayou Sauvage NWR, including South Point. During this trip, Lynn caught bass for the first time in several years, likely because of the influx of fresh water into the lake courtesy of the August floods. We also recorded thirty-one bird species on this trip, including a Nelson's Sparrow that Lynn needed.

After that, we packed our binoculars, along with some of Mary's things that she wanted us to give to relatives, and headed up to Ohio. We spread the eighteen-hour drive over two days, and I spent a lot of time on that drive just looking out the window. The changing terrain and increasing fall colors the farther north we traveled provided an art show of sorts, which helped quell the hurricane of emotions swirling through my heart.

The funeral was surreal; it seemed almost varnished and so removed from the reality of holding someone's hand while they died. I was used to attending funerals and feeling like the process drew me closer to that person, almost like I was entering a close circle of the deceased and their loved ones. This funeral felt entirely different. I'd been used to just the three of us, and the turnout was so much bigger than just me, Lynn, and Mary.

Being surrounded by so many people who loved Mary was wonderful, but I almost felt like I was inside a tiny circle and looking out—it was like grieving from the inside out. The funeral wasn't unpleasant, it just felt a lot less intimate. I realized that I had actually experienced an initial closure when the two funeral attendants had carried Mary's body out the door. I also realized that I would have given anything to buy out another shelf of LFVWO. I would have cherished the nasty vibes or surprised looks of any cashier, and I wouldn't have said a word in response, if I only had the chance.

* * * * *

Between the two of them, Robby Bacon and Melvin Weber have birded Louisiana for ninety-plus years. On October 21, the pair found a Black-throated Blue Warbler in Peveto, near the water drip. They reported their find, and in response Dave Patton and Mac Myers chased this bird later that day and found it. They also located a Black-throated Gray Warbler in the process.

Lynn and I set off for Peveto the very next day with high hopes of snagging at least one of these birds that I never expected we'd be able to put on our year list. We were chatting about something I don't even remember when a police car jammed up our rear bumper with red and blue lights flashing. "Oh no," Lynn said, "I was speeding and I didn't even realize it!"

In every community there are surefire spots where police officers give speeding tickets. And usually, if you are familiar with the terrain, you know where those spots are and act accordingly. We knew that the elevated part of I-10 between Baton Rouge and Lafayette was a famous speed trap, especially coming off the elevated area, when the speed limit hasn't yet increased from 60 to 70 mph. A police car was parked right at the base of the bridge, and Lynn passed that police car going the speed she typically clocks in a 70 mph zone.

Lynn pulled over immediately, and we didn't have to wait long. The officer practically leapt out of his car and approached Lynn with an angry look clouding his young face.

"Did you know you were going 75 mph in a 60 mph zone?" he barked, "That is *way* too fast!"

"I'm sorry," said Lynn.

"Well, you get a ticket for that!"

It only took about two minutes for him to print one, which he handed Lynn brusquely and with an admonition to pay better attention to the speed limit.

"I thought about telling him that I've been feeling awfully absent-minded ever since mom died, but I really was speeding and I really am sorry," Lynn said, "so I'll just take the ticket and pay it." It was the first speeding ticket Lynn had gotten in all the years she'd lived in Louisiana. She did not exceed the speed limit for the rest of our trip to Peveto.

When we arrived, the tame turkeys were still at the parking area. They seemed even more people-oriented than last time; they watched us as we parked, then actually took a couple of steps toward us when we exited our truck. We quickly made our way to the water drip, where we encountered several birders looking for the warblers, but no one had spotted them despite hours of searching. We joined the cause and focused our time around the water drip. Eventually we birded other trails in the sanctuary, and I was happy to add a first-ever-for-Peveto Brown Creeper to our site list, but we left empty-handed after multiple passes and lengthy stationary campouts at the water drip, replete with occasional turkey gobbling sounds in the background.

The trip was not an entire bust, however. Van was stationed at the water drip when we first arrived. I asked him about the turkeys, and he just shook his head. "Those things totally fail the bread test,"[1] he muttered, "I think someone dropped their pets here." I asked if he'd seen anything notable, and he volunteered the location of a much-needed Say's Phoebe that he and his group had just spotted. The Say's was hanging out with a flock of Scissor-tailed Flycatchers at the stingray plant, less than a half mile from where we stood. This facility, located on the corner of Highway 82 and Gulf View Road, the turnoff street to get to Peveto, was surrounded by chain-link fence and barbed wire, the kind of structure that flycatchers like.

We made our way there and initially saw a couple of scissor-tails, but nothing else. We dialed up the Say's Phoebe call and played it a couple of times, and the Say's swooped in immediately to investigate, along with a few more scissor-tails. This ten-minute stop netted us one Say's Phoebe, one Eastern Phoebe, and eight scissor-tails. It was the ninth time that we had observed one or more Scissor-tailed Flycatchers in 2016. I was not one bit tired of them. I am not sure if I've ever seen that shade of salmon in their lower flanks or underwing anywhere else in nature.

Lynn and I began our trek home along Highway 82 and stopped to bird Four Magic Miles, scrutinizing every flock of birds we encountered. In the third flock, mixed in with some Laughing Gulls, was a single Franklin's Gull, slightly smaller, more slightly built, and grayer than the hundreds of Laughing Gulls it stood with. I pointed out the Franklin's to Lynn, and with that bird we edged ever closer to the magic number.

* * * * *

There are different kinds of birders—some love all birds equally, some love all birds but have particular specialties, and some birders are focused on one type of bird. I've noticed that birders who worship hummingbirds are a tribe within birders. Margaret and John Owens are a case in point. When they posted that they had a Calliope Hummingbird in their yard, I got in touch and asked them if we could yard crash. They assented immediately. We drove to the pretty neighborhood tucked into tall pine trees just south of I-12 in Covington. They opened their door as I raised my knuckles to knock, welcomed us warmly, and led us to a vantage point in their backyard in sight of the hummingbird feeder that the Calliope was frequenting. They then left us alone for a few minutes. Lynn got out the digital camera and got it ready. Margaret had said that as sunset approached, the Calliope came much less often, and we were starting to fight daylight. After only three minutes the Calliope flashed his purple gorget while taking a quick swipe at the feeder. I was elated—bird number 299! He returned several times within the next ten minutes, and Lynn was able to get identifiable pictures.

Margaret and John came out to observe with us and regaled us with stories of their hummingbirds. This one was a returnee to their yard, based on the band Nancy Newfield had placed on it previously. Eight different hummingbird species had been recorded in their yard. The Owens' yard was famous enough that National Geographic's Filipe Deandrade filmed an episode on hummingbirds there. Margaret said that someday she hoped to log every one of the thirteen hummingbird species that had ever been found in Louisiana; she'd take any new state species, too. The Owens offered us coffee and muffins after the successful sighting, but we declined. As we had embarked on this quick trip relatively late in the day, we still needed to get home to get ready for work the next morning. Margaret asked us to sign their guest book. As Lynn and I penned our names in a volume listing hundreds of visitors spanning at least ten years, I marveled at the passion of this couple, not just for hummingbirds but for hospitality as well.

The fall LOS meeting was held in Cameron on October 29. We had signed up for the meeting before the pelagic trip, not realizing that we'd both be on the cusp of three hundred (and sans Mary). As usual, there were two all-day field trips to choose from, one to the eastern side of the town of Cameron, and the other on the west side, in which you ride the ferry across the Calcasieu Ship Channel to bird Peveto, Lighthouse Road, Holly Beach, and Highway 82, including Four Magic Miles.

I chose the eastern side of Cameron with some trepidation. Steve and Donna were leading the trip, and I had 120 percent confidence in them. However, I was largely unfamiliar with spots on the eastern side of Cameron Parish. I figured that it would be really fun to learn a few new places to bird, despite the fact that we would not set foot in any of the Cameron Parish hot spots I was used to, including the Cameron Courthouse wetlands, where I was counting on an American Bittern. I was fairly confident that a full day of birding in Cameron Parish with Steve and Donna would add at least one bird to my list. I began wondering which bird would be number three hundred. Lincoln's Sparrow? Ash-throated Flycatcher? It was a fun game to play, and I wasn't nervous about getting to three hundred—it was only October 29 and I had much of the year to go.

Lynn and I drove to Lake Charles on Friday night and checked into a hotel about forty-five minutes from the field trip rendezvous point, the Cameron Motel parking lot. We got up on time and packed up, but we somehow managed to lose a couple of minutes between breakfast and swinging out of the parking lot. When Lynn headed south on Highway 27 and I punched in the Cameron Motel address, I blanched when the trip time showed fifty-four minutes. We were set to arrive at the motel at 6:37, and the field trip was set to depart at 6:30. I cussed briefly while Lynn smiled and put the pedal to the metal. "I'm going to get us there. We're not going to be late," she said confidently.

With no cars on the road, we were able to start chewing time off the fifty-four-minute trip. Lynn was talking about how her grandfather the race car driver had taught her that steering fast into turns was a good thing to do if you wanted to win a race. My pulse quickened only slightly as centrifugal force pinned me into the passenger seat while Lynn expertly handled curves, chuckling quietly in the darkness. We streaked past a rare convenience store, and Lynn said, "Oh God—was that a cop car in that parking lot?" She slowed down just in case, but it was indeed a cop car and it was indeed too late. Even as Lynn decelerated toward the speed limit, the blue lights half a mile behind us cut a strobe pattern through the darkness. The officer closed the distance within a minute.

"Oh *no!*" Lynn cried, "I can't believe it!" She pulled over immediately and hung her head. Unlike Officer Angry, Officer Boudreaux was downright cheerful for barely past six in the morning. "Where are y'all going?" he asked.

"Well, we're headed for the Louisiana Ornithological Society meeting in Cameron this morning, sir. We're a little late, and I'm trying to get us there on time." Lynn spoke in forthright charm mode.

"Where are y'all from?" he followed.

"Baton Rouge, sir."

"What time does this thing start?"

"6:30."

Officer Boudreaux looked at his watch and said, "Yeah, I guess y'all are running a little late. I stopped a guy a few minutes ago going to the same place! Y'all know you were speeding, right?"

"Yes, sir."

"I had you going 71 in a 55. Can I see your driver's license, registration, and insurance, please?" Lynn handed it over, and he said, "I'll be right back."

As soon as he left, Lynn looked at me and said, "What if he sees I have a speeding ticket from last weekend? Oh man, do you think he'll give me another ticket? Do you think that the other ticket is in the system yet?" I had no idea. I had never known anyone who received two speeding tickets in six days. But I hoped that maybe since it had been so recent the first ticket hadn't shown up yet, and I told her so. We both sat up straight as Officer Boudreaux came back, handed Lynn all her stuff, and then gave her a ticket. Lynn slumped when she took it.

"I gotta give you that, your speed was just a little too high," he said, "but hey, if you call this number," he said, pointing to the ticket, "you should be able to get consideration for this being your first offense." Bingo, I thought, the previous ticket was not showing yet.

"Can you give me some consideration now?" Lynn asked.

Officer Boudreaux smiled broadly and said, "Nah, already written. But I tell you what—do you know the district attorney in Baton Rouge?"

"No . . . ," Lynn replied—like how would she, in a metropolitan area of over eight hundred thousand people?

"Well, too bad, because if you did, you could just call him and get this speeding ticket wiped out! Hey, maybe you should give it a shot anyway!"

Officer Boudreaux waved at us as we launched again for the Cameron Motel, but this time at 55 mph. When we were pulled over, we'd had an ETA of 6:33 A.M., which I thought was within the safe zone. Now our ETA was showing 6:42 and we couldn't speed to make up time. I emailed Steve to tell him that we'd be a few minutes late and that hopefully we'd be able to make contact so that we could catch up with them if they left before we arrived. I heaved a sigh of relief when he wrote back fifteen minutes later to tell me that he would let me know the first destination if we didn't make it before their party departed, but they weren't in a big hurry and we would likely be there well before the group left the parking lot.

We rolled in to the Cameron Motel at 6:42 on the dot. Thank you Louisiana Standard Time—the party was still in the parking lot. Lynn and I vaulted out of the truck and jumped into the crowd milling in the middle of the area. I saw Steve immediately, and he gave me a nod hello and a smile. He was right; the birding party had not yet organized into a caravan. Christine Kooi greeted me with a question: "Marybeth, how many do you have?" I answered 299 right away, knowing exactly what she was asking. Upon hearing my answer, Mary Mehaffey jumped into our conversation with aplomb.

HUNDRED

"I'm at 294 myself," she said, "and I'm hoping to add more to my year list today!" When Lynn shared that she was at 296, Mary said, "Yes, I've been following you on eBird, I am right behind you in rank! What birds do y'all need?" We recited lists, confined to what was possible that day. Mary had a few birds that we had and vice versa; she needed the Black Scoter, Bay-breasted Warbler, and Long-billed Curlew that we had, and she had the Lincoln's Sparrow and White-tailed Kite that we needed.

"One year, I was birding a lot and Jay Huner contacted me," Mary said, "and he told me that I ought to try for three hundred bird species. We wound up in a friendly competition that year. He'd go up on me a bird or two, and then I'd get out in the field and sometimes would pass him up by a bird or two. I thought that ultimately we'd be tied, and it seemed to be going that way, but at the very end of the year Jay went out and wound up beating me by one. It's fun, going for three hundred. You both are going to make it."

Donna and Steve sounded the call, and the fifteen of us packed into our vehicles and headed for the first stop of the day, the Cameron jetty. We parked and started birding at the observation tower, but the adjacent beach and mudflat sported very few birds, so we decided to walk the beach to the east. Along the way there were several shorebird, gull, and tern flocks. I am not a gull expert; they are among the toughest bird species to master because the first-year plumage of one gull species can be very close in appearance to the second-year plumage of another, etc. When you're down to the color of the tenth primary (flight feather) to figure out the species of gull you have, that's a level of bird nerddom I have not yet reached. Steve and Donna of course had. They easily picked out several immature Lesser Black-backed Gulls among the throng of Laughing Gulls. I could at least tell the Franklin's apart myself, and there were several of them as well. The day was shaping up to be gorgeous, with the early morning light almost reminiscent of the sweet light late in the day; the photographers in our group had fantastic rich colors to take advantage of among the confluence of water, sand, beach grass, and birds.

After walking almost a mile and scoping several flats of birds, we were headed back toward the observation deck when a Long-billed Curlew flew by from behind us. The bird did not seem daunted by our presence and almost seemed to be showing off its gorgeous tawny-brown color as it flew down the beach, right along the waterline, passing within twenty feet of our group before landing in the surf about fifty feet away from us. As our group ventured slightly closer to the stationary bird and the whir of clicking shutters ensued, Mary Mehaffey, who was right next to us, looked at Lynn with a big smile and a sparkle in her eyes. "Gotcha girl!" she declared.

And it was all over. Lynn's spine stiffened a little, she stood up a tad straighter, and even though she smiled, I actually watched her brain saying, "Oh, so you just came up on me a bird? Competition?! It's so *on* right now!" Lynn had already told me that we might as well keep going once we hit three hundred. Put up the best number you can this year and then you have something to shoot for when you retire and decide to try again, she said. But the encounter with Mary meant that Lynn would not only be birding hard for my bird total, she would be doing it for hers too. I was super excited. If anything would be better than seeing my three hundredth bird today, this was it.

Steve and Donna led us past the observation deck onto the jetty beach. They stationed us in front of an expanse of beach grass and executed tag team pishing; their combined squeaks, hisses, and kisses were so good that every Seaside and Nelson's Sparrow in the area paid admission for the show. I'd never seen so many of each species at once. Although we already had the Nelson's Sparrow for the year, it had been a typical *Ammodramus* encounter, a furtive glance. Having an individual of one of these species rise up out of the grass and sit out for you is great. Having eight to ten of both species sit out at the same time is fantastic.

While the sparrow show was going on, Steve and Donna got word that Jay Huner and Mike Musumeche had just heard a Black Rail at Broussard Beach, first identified by sound by Erik Johnson a couple of days before. They informed us that when we were done with the sparrows, our next stop was Broussard Beach. Once we arrived we had to locate an old pink tricycle that had been left adjacent to a path in the beach grass. The Black Rail was being heard in a field of tall beach grass immediately to the north of this tricycle. Within ten minutes our caravan was en route. Donna made it clear that in this special case, if she absolutely had to, she would be willing to use playback, sparingly, on the black rail. I was surprised but appreciative; Donna hates using playback the way I hate shopping at Walmart.

We arrived at about 9:30 and began a group search for the pink tricycle. We located it quickly, with help from Mary and Cham Mehaffey, who without our knowledge had hightailed it out of Cameron jetty and gotten to Broussard well in front of our caravan. As soon as they saw us in the vicinity, they called us over to the tricycle. "We heard the Black Rail!" Mary declared, "it's over there." She pointed to a spot about forty feet from where we stood.

The group of us moved a little closer to the thick beach grass in the direction in which Mary pointed, assumed human statue formation, and listened hard into the ether. I heard nothing but wind caressing grass for about ten minutes. Then, from deep in the thickest part of the beach grass, I heard the third note only of the distinctive call of a Black Rail. It was a thin note, but to my ear identifiable. "See?" Mary said.

I whooped silently. Black Rail! This was *so* not a bird I had considered would *ever* make it onto our year list, a heard-only lifer for me. Donna continued to listen though. She was not convinced that the note was in fact the Black Rail. And if the trip leader is unconvinced, it is not a bird that you can count. We waited some more, and then Donna sighed deeply, got out her phone, and played a few seconds of Black Rail calls. We heard nothing in response. She tried a second time. Nothing again. She put the phone in her pocket and kept listening.

I was starting to stress out. I felt damn confident that I'd heard the single note and that it had been a Black Rail, and for me this bird represented the magical three hundred mark. And I really, and I mean really, wanted to get to that significant milestone on this significant species.

All of a sudden I heard the full call of the Black Rail, low and immediately to my left; I looked toward the sound and saw Donna with her head down, drawing the phone out of her pocket. "Oops, my phone has a mind of its own," she said, shutting down the Black Rail recording. Three seconds later came the blissful, full three-note call of a Black Rail from the exact spot the single note had emanated from earlier, about twenty feet away from us, in the thickest part of the beach grass. Donna smiled and our entire group, with subdued but collectively happy noise, acknowledged that most beautiful sound. "Ha, I butt-dialed a Black Rail! How about that!" Donna said.

At approximately 9:50 A.M. on October 29, I became the fifth birder in the state of Louisiana to cross the three hundred species bird mark in 2016.

We stayed at Broussard Beach for another ten minutes while Donna posted our find on LA-BIRD and Steve told us the story of Black Rails in California, and how they could be found at the edge of certain marshes as the tide was rising. "One time I was calling a Black Rail and it seemed to get closer and closer but I couldn't find it visually," Steve said. "I finally looked down and there it was, standing on my boot!"

As soon as we got back into our truck to head for Willow Island with the rest of the caravan, Lynn grabbed something from the back seat and told me to close my eyes. She placed it on my lap and told me to open them. I was looking at a black, hooded sweatshirt with a line of birds across the chest and the single word *Ornithologeek*. "Congratulations on three hundred!" she told me.

I felt happy and accomplished in making it to three hundred, but I wasn't elated. I thought of Mary and wished I could have shown her a picture of the bird we heard only that got me to three hundred. She likely wouldn't have been impressed with its appearance, but I know that she would have been excited about the accomplishment. When I set out in January to get to three hundred, I envisioned that getting there, if I actually did, would feel like a major victory. On this account, making it to the three hundred milestone was anticlimactic. Grief was seemingly modulating my emotions; on this journey to three hundred, that I thought was inside a bigger journey, but which outlasted the initial one, I had hit a major milestone. Next stop: getting Lynn to three hundred.

At Willow Island, our group saw Inca Dove, Yellow-bellied Sapsucker, Scissor-tailed Flycatcher, and Sharp-shinned Hawk, among others. On our way back to our vehicles we watched a White-tailed Kite fly in a long arc across the sky and over the ball field north of our vantage point. I was almost the last person in the group to spot it, with other members giving me landmarks as they traced the trajectory of the bird. I finally located it as it flew over one of the light posts and was able to watch the rest of its long arc. Mary Mehaffey checked in with Lynn and me individually during the "flyby" to ensure that we both saw the kite. There was no doubt a competition brewing between Lynn and Mary, but it was clearly a friendly one. Lynn ended the day with 298 species.

The next Saturday, we headed for the Yellow Rails and Rice Festival in the Jennings area, organized by Steve and Donna. The festival had started on Wednesday and most festival participants had already completed the marquis event: while riding on a combine with a farmer who is harvesting rice, you watch the area right in front of the combine blades as the farmer and a bird guide identify all the rail species that run and/or fly to get away from the jaws of the harvester. The most common rails in these fields are Sora and Virginia, with occasional King and Yellow Rails also present. Most of the festivalgoers, having seen all four species of rails between Wednesday and Friday, had headed for the Cameron coast or the piney woods in the center of the state on day-long field trips. Lynn and I were two of only eight birders present in the rice fields on this last day of the festival. I was excited because we'd get lots of chances to ride the combine for Yellow Rail.

Fog is a normal thing to contend with in the rice fields in the fall, and Saturday morning was no exception. Donna and Steve thus took our small group to bird nearby Turf Grass Road while we waited for the fog to lift and the moisture to lessen, which is when the rice farmer would fire up the combine and start harvesting. It was fun to bird a familiar location with Steve and Donna, as they have their own way to bird and their own cadence in which to do it. They are more deliberate than Lynn and I, and their carefulness paid off, as we added two new birds to our place list, if not our year list. They located two Say's Phoebes, one on each side of the farmstead on Turf Grass Road, and a male Vermilion Flycatcher perched on the lowest rung of a barbed wire fence just north of the farmstead on the east side of the road. I was enjoying the brilliant red of this bird when Steve said, "Hey, if y'all look up at the power line, there are two Brewer's Blackbirds right next to the power post."

The early morning light silhouetted the pair, but their not moving meant we could all change our location to use the low hanging sun to our viewing advantage. I silently cheered while Lynn and I stood next to each other watching the small yellow eyes of the male of the pair blaze out from his glossy black body. Woohoo! With this species, Lynn was on the brink, at 299 and counting.

The fog began to lift, but we still had about an hour to kill before the farmer got cutting, so on the way back to the rice fields Steve and Donna stopped at an old house seemingly in the middle of nowhere. They explained that this old house was free to whoever paid to move it—and until then, if ever, it sat empty and alone. Our bird trips took us by many such dwellings, and Lynn has shared that she's always wondered about the stories behind these places. "One day, this house was brand new, and someone lived in it and loved it. What set of circumstances led from that point to this one?"

The house was in an agricultural area that contained some rice fields and some fallow fields—it was the only sign that a human had ever lived here. Next to it was a tight grove of pine trees. Steve and Donna explained that contained within this grove was a family of Barn Owls. We were going to try to locate them. The pair lined us up in a configuration reminiscent of the "looking for a dead body" arrangement that Terry Davis employed at the Shreveport Airport. We then walked through the pine grove, front to back. We located a couple of birds, including Eastern Phoebe, Pine Warbler, and House Wren, but no owls. We stayed in the same line, executed an about-face, and made the trek back to front. Right at the end of the pine grove, about fifty feet before leaving its bounds and encountering the slumbering house, we flushed two Barn Owls. Lynn and I had gotten good looks at Barn Owls at the "guy with shotgun on lap" house on Turf Grass Road earlier in the year, but those observations had taken place in the dark. We had an even better look in the daylight.

After a quick pit stop at the rice processing facility in Thornwell, our group headed for the rice fields. Once there, we were greeted by a group of bird banders who had strung nets along the back corner of the rice field, the part of the field that would be harvested last. Their purpose was to capture and band as many rails as possible. We waved to the banders as we approached the combine, and they assumed strategic positions along the length of net to facilitate fast removal and banding. I immediately jumped into the cab of the combine with the farmer, who introduced himself and explained that he wasn't *the* farmer, but first cousin of the farmer. The farmer's son played college football, and the farmer was at his football game. Not wanting to disappoint the birders, he had asked Rick to drive the combine instead, and Rick was happy to do so, and happy to share his knowledge of birds.

Lynn was not on the combine with me, but was instead in a side-by-side Utility Task Vehicle (UTV) driven by Steve. He maneuvered the vehicle in a parallel configuration with the combine and ran at the same speed, to be in position to view any rails that flew toward the UTV. We made two passes through the field, scattering sparrows but nothing else. Then we changed places, with Lynn in the cab and me in the UTV. Two more passes with sparrows and nothing but sparrows.

Just after Lynn exited the combine, a horrific metal on metal screech brought the machine to an abrupt halt. Rick had driven the combine too close to the banding nets to make a regular turn. Undaunted, he had put the big machine in reverse but had left part of the threshing implement in the engaged position. The result was that the cover plate was bent to hell and had partly detached from the combine. Rick had to go back to the shop to get tools to straighten and reattach it.

I heaved an internal sigh of frustration as Steve and Donna explained the situation and, with broad smiles, told us to go eat lunch and return in ninety minutes, which was when Rick estimated that he'd be operational again. After eating some outstanding seafood and Cajun fare at Nott's Cajun Restaurant in Lake Arthur, we returned to the field to find the combine fixed and plowing away. The harvester had whittled the uncut rice to a small corner, which meant that the last few passes through this field should be fruitful for rails (or railful).

Lynn and I got in Steve's UTV together and rode parallel to the combine. We had gone only about three hundred feet when a brown-orange rail rose out of the rice and flew low before landing in a trough between plowed field rows about one hundred feet in front of us. Steve stopped the UTV and we all piled out. Steve was armed with a net; he was going to try to find the Virginia Rail that had just landed, net it, and send it to the banding station. He also wanted us to form a human line at the harvest edge, which would drive the rails away from us and into the net for banding. He told us to clap, which would also drive the birds toward the net.

I stood at the plowed edge of the field as the combine lumbered by, clapping and feeling a little bad for the stress that the rails must be experiencing, when a number of rails rose up out of the field. Steve immediately yelled, "*Yellow rail!*" Lynn and I first tracked his finger and found the bird, then looked through our binoculars to note the white secondary (middle part of the wing) patches, tiny beak, and tan-beige mottling as the bird flew before dropping out of sight into amazingly short grass. Then we high fived. At approximately 3:00 P.M. on November 5, Lynn became the sixth birder to cross the magical three hundred mark in Louisiana in 2016.

LAGNIAPPE

After we both crossed over three hundred, we were in lagniappe territory, and the challenge shifted from reaching a specific numerical milestone to a free-form "just how many birds we can get?" My strategy for the rest of the year was to execute spur of the moment chases anywhere in the state that a new bird would take us and to take one more crack at the Shreveport area. The Cross Lake Mew Gull trip in January and the Yates Unit Willow Flycatcher and Bell's Vireo caper in June had been spectacularly successful, and I wanted one more try to hit several new spots that looked promising to yield additional species. We decided to make this trip during my birthday weekend. I set about checking frequency histograms in eBird and doing some in-depth reading of *The Birder's Guide to Louisiana* to get ready.

Our friends Irina Shport and Kathryn Barton, though not birders, had cheered us all year long and were especially invested in our eBird rank in the state of Louisiana. The previous year, fifteen eBirders had eclipsed the three hundred mark. I really wasn't going for ranking but for species numbers. But Irina in particular was pushing us to stay in the top ten. Although rank was a secondary consideration, I did begin to watch who was in the top ten, especially who was immediately in front of us and who was immediately behind us; we were hovering in fifth to seventh place, depending on the day.

In November we took several fortuitous trips to pick up the Black-chinned Hummingbird in Robb Brumfield's yard in Baton Rouge, a Broad-billed Hummingbird in Covington courtesy of Claire Thomas, and Ash-throated and Brown-crested Flycatchers on Recovery Road. I was excited that the latter two species cooperated with copious calling, which assisted in separating them for identification purposes. In early December our second trip to find the Ringed Kingfisher, who appeared to be spending her second consecutive winter at Lake Martin in St. Martinville, was successful. We located her by her raucous sound and found her perched on a short, leafless cypress tree branch twenty-five feet above the water. When she dive-bombed and hit the water, the sound she made was spectacular, like a Belted Kingfisher on major steroids. She made off with a decent-sized fish and perched farther away to consume it as Lynn got grainy but identifiable pictures.

A couple of days before our departure for Shreveport, I emailed Charlie Lyon:

Hi Charlie!

Hopefully you remember me—my name is Marybeth Lima and you were kind enough to take me and Lynn Hathaway out on your boat this past January to see the Mew Gull. I remember you saying during that trip that you were planning to do some birding in Arkansas—I also see from eBird that you've been very successful in this endeavor!

We have been successful too in our goals—long story short, we were on a mission to join the "300 club" in Louisiana in 2016, and we both made it! Now we're trying to see how high we can get before December 31, so that we'll have a number to try to beat some day long in the future when we retire (currently I'm at 308 and Lynn's at 305).

We are headed to Shreveport this weekend to try to locate birds we don't yet have on our year list. We're going to Sentell Road to try for Horned Lark and Western Meadowlark and whatever else might show up (Fox Sparrow, Harris's Sparrow, Sprague's Pipit, Bewick's Wren)—we're also trying Red River NWR Headquarters Unit and a few other assorted areas based on your super helpful Guide to Louisiana Birding for the aforementioned (and some of the below mentioned) birds.

However, there's nothing like current intelligence and/or favorite spots for local targets. That's why I'm checking in. If you know of any recent locations where the aforementioned have been spotted recently, or reliably in the past (I'm not seeing much on eBird; there have been a dearth of sparrows reported), and others like Red-breasted Nuthatch (I have but Lynn does not), Common Goldeneye, Purple Finch, Henslow's Sparrow, Lincoln's Sparrow, American Woodcock, or Short-eared Owl, I'm all ears!

Please let me know if you have any intel if you have time.

Thanks so much and hope all is well,

Marybeth

Charlie wrote back within twenty-four hours, gave me his cell number, and told me to call him in the morning between 8:30 and 9:30 A.M. I called him at 8:31 (was I a little excited?). Charlie said that he was just leaving for work and to call him back in five minutes. I did, and Charlie got right down to business after a simple hello.

"You can search for Red-breasted Nuthatch, Purple Finch, and Fox Sparrow at the feeders at Walter Jacobs Memorial Park. As far as I know, the Purple Finches aren't down yet; we need a good cold front to bring them down. The Fox should be easy there. Red-breasteds are wanderers and they're not here every year, but this year appears to be irruptive and they are around.

"Good thought on Sentell Road for the Horned Lark and the Western Meadowlark. Sentell is also the best place for Sprague's Pipits. If you get out walking in some of those fields you might be able to locate one. Check in the alfalfa fields near DixieMaze Farms. Farmer John owns the fields and is fine with you walking them. Look for Lapland Longspur there as well.

"Lincoln's Sparrow? Well, you'll have a chance on the Chocolate Trail in Red River NWR, but they're mostly gone now, they're spotty at best, but present. You have a better shot at those in south Louisiana. Read in my book—it'll tell you where to go. You may as well cross Grasshopper Sparrow off your list, it's too wet for them right now."

As I scribbled notes as fast as I could, I heard a bell sound occasionally, just like one hears in the hospital, those robotically musical sounds that indicate a doctor being paged. Charlie seemed to ignore them. I was amazed not only at the amount of information coming my way, but also the recall of this guy—he essentially went through each of my targets, not in any particular order as far as I could tell, and often gave multiple locations on where to look for each.

"Common Goldeneye? In Cross Lake, but you won't be able to access that. Merganser Pond on Highway 71, the book will tell you how to get there, also has Common Goldeneye, but we're past prime time for it. Again, this bird is better in south Louisiana right now. Go to South Point and walk that levee along the southern edge of Lake Pontchartrain the second or third week of December. Y'all have kayaks? Oh, for sure, do that!

"Bewick's Wren? You can check any brushy pile in the area for them. The Yearwood Loop is great for Bewick's, especially the road to Bayou Pierre Wildlife Management Area. There's a barn area there with cattle and cows, with an old feedlot and barn. The brush there is prime for Bewick's. Just play a tape of their call right from the road and you'll very likely get them there."

All of a sudden Charlie stopped talking, and there was a pregnant pause. I used it and my own version of shorthand to catch up to him. "Say," he said, "you're not going to pass up Rosemary Seidler, are you?" I laughed. Rosemary was the top ranked eBirder in the state.

"No, she's at least twelve birds ahead of me, and while I have about that many targets for this trip, if I hit half of them it will be a miracle. No, I am not even going to get close to Rosemary."

"Well good," he responded, "because if you passed her and it was because I told you where all these birds were, she wouldn't be too happy with me. She's been spending a lot of time in Arkansas with me and the Trahans this year. It's been fun, birding up there, we're spending time in some new places and we're logging data that the state doesn't have to this point. Not sure we're going to hit three hundred, I doubt it, but we'll try for it." Then he jumped back in.

"Harris's Sparrow? Well, that's a tough one. Last year we didn't get any coming down into the state because our winter was too warm. I've only seen one this entire year, in Arkansas; like those Purple Finches, they need a good cold front to bring them down. Really, you ought to go to that same area I was telling you about for the Bewick's. Stop next to the silos. I believe it is the best spot right now for Harris's Sparrow as well. And if there are Lincoln's Sparrows around, this is also a great place for those too. Also, if you drive past those silos, there are some fields on the left, and if they're not cut, they're a great spot for Short-eared Owl at dusk. Another spot for the owls is on Atkins Clark Road toward Lock & Dam 5. Again, drive that area at dusk—just be aware that there's a kooky guy that hangs out there sometimes, he's probably harmless, just weird, but be careful.

"Let's see, you said Henslow's Sparrow. I've got a slam dunk spot for that one! You go to Bayou Bodcau Wildlife Management Area, and you cross over the dam there. As soon as you get to the other side, there's a road on the right called Duck Dam Road. Pull off on that road, park where you can, and then get out and walk the pine tree, grass line edge, right at the base of the levee. The combination of two- to five-year-old pines with tall grass is perfect for Henslow's Sparrows. I've had LeConte's there too. The last time I was out there, I had twelve Henslow's right along that edge."

By the end of the call I had a new name for Charlie Lyon: Dr. Encyclopedia. I also felt uber-prepared for the trip.

We left right after work that Friday and headed for Shreveport. We even ventured off the beaten path long enough to drive through the famous Christmas lights display in Natchitoches. After settling into our hotel in Shreveport at about 10:00 P.M., I set the alarm for zero dark birdy. Shreveport was the headquarters for this trip because it was centrally located with respect to our target areas, which were north, east, and south of the city.

Because Sentell Road sported at least two birds that appeared to be straightforward gets, we headed north first. I shivered as we transitioned from the hotel to the truck. The temperatures were barely above freezing, and Shreveport was noticeably colder than our residence some two hundred miles to the south. It would definitely have been considered a cold front in Baton Rouge, but in Shreveport it was weather as usual. I set the truck's heater on the highest setting and put my seat heater on high to warm up.

As soon as we turned onto Sentell Road from Highway 3049, I rolled down my window to hear what was calling. There seemed to be lots of sparrow chips and robin whinnies, so we stopped the truck to bird the trees adjacent to the road. There was not much of a shoulder, but Lynn did a nice job of balancing pulling off the road enough to avoid being hit by other vehicles without pulling off so much that we were stuck in the ditch. We needn't have worried, there was almost no traffic on this rural motorway. After quickly noting Dark-eyed Junco, White-crowned, White-throated, and Chipping Sparrow, along with Downy Woodpecker and American Goldfinch, we got back into the truck and headed for agricultural fields a little farther down the road.

We stopped in the middle of the road at the sign of the first large ag field. We scanned the field with binoculars and found nothing but Killdeer, so we quickly moved to the second field a few hundred feet down the road. This time, standing in the dirt between mounded rows on the fallow field, about three hundred feet away from us, we located two Horned Larks. Score! Lynn got out the scope so that we could observe the birds close up. There was also a meadowlark in the field. I got excited, since Eastern and Western Meadowlarks were possible and we didn't have the latter, but as I scoped the bird, the buffiness on its underparts and white malar looked eastern to me. We returned to the truck and moved to the next field, repeating our scans.

After almost three hours of birding this road, we had located more than thirty Horned Larks along with lots of Killdeer and American Crows, whose large-flock presence reminded me of Midwestern agricultural fields. We had located several small flocks of meadowlarks, where we had identified a number of Western Meadowlarks, replete with yellow malars and less contrasting back colors. A dozen American White Pelicans in V-formation drifted over us as we walked the fields adjacent to DixieMaze Farms for the Sprague's Pipit. While we did not locate one, I was very excited to come away with the two new birds for this trip that I thought would be easiest to get.

We then jaunted over to Walter B. Jacobs Memorial Park, hoping for the Fox Sparrow and Red-breasted Nuthatch, and hoping against hope for the Purple Finch. We spent almost an hour at the feeders and on the trails but were unsuccessful in locating any target species, though we did spot two cooperative White-breasted Nuthatches. Mindful of the relatively short length of daylight at

this time of year, we abandoned that spot and ate wish sandwiches while truck-
ing south for Red River NWR.

From the winter 2013 LOS field trip guided by Terry Davis, I remembered
the site immediately. It was a decent hike from the headquarters to the Chocolate Trail, where four years previously Terry had located Fox and Harris's Sparrows for us, both lifers for me at the time. Still mindful of daylight, we set out for
the Chocolate Trail, birding at a speed slightly faster than usual. Sparrows were
everywhere, especially white-throateds and Dark-eyed Juncos. On Lake Trail,
which featured an expanse of tall, dry grass and bare-branched trees that led to
a tall tree line to our right and the river to our left, I thought I heard a familiar
smack call that was unlike other sparrow chip notes I was hearing. I dialed up
the Fox Sparrow call and played it. Immediately, one responded, flying in and
showing off beautiful rufous-reddish breast spots. *Ha!* Take that, Walter Jacobs!

We hiked another half mile and started to traverse the Chocolate Trail, but
unfortunately the trail was so flooded that we were able to hike only about 40
percent of it. Although the trail itself was very birdy, we did not locate a Harris's
or Lincoln's Sparrow. Our bird count for this two-hour trip was almost forty
species, with the best bird being our new-for-the-year Fox Sparrow.

We blitzed south and began to bird the Yearwood Road Loop in late afternoon. We were armed with specific directions to the tenth of a mile that were provided in *A Birder's Guide to Louisiana* and were buttressed with recent intel courtesy of Charlie. At the hedgerows on both sides of the road 2.5 miles after turning right (south) onto Yearwood Road from Highway 1, a place specifically mentioned in the book for Bewick's Wren and White-crowned and White-throated Sparrows, we stopped to try our luck for the Bewick's. The hedgerows indeed held the sparrow species mentioned, in addition to Ruby-crowned Kinglets, Yellow-rumped Warblers, and an Eastern Phoebe. I played the Bewick's Wren call and immediately one torpedoed out of the hedgerow on the left-hand side of the road, flew right at the iPhone in my hand while calling back emphatically, and veered away at the last second before jetting into the hedgerow on the other side of the road and out of sight. Lynn and I both whooped as we racked up bird number four of the day. We continued our birding trek by following the book's loop description.

Even supplemented with the positive report from Charlie's phone call, one would not expect that his information and the following three sentences from his book would lead to birding paradise: "At 5.8 miles, a gravel road comes in from the right (Red River PR-412). Turn here and enter the relatively new Bayou Pierre Wildlife Management Area. At 6.3 miles, a group of silos on the left, along with the remnants of an old stable, are the haunt of Barn Owl and Bewick's Wren."[1] For me, this picturesque little strip of road and the rusty, abandoned silos are absolute birding nirvana. If I had to choose a single place in northwest Louisiana to bird, this spot would be it.

We did not find any Barn Owls, but we had another Bewick's Wren, a Fox Sparrow, bunches of Savannah Sparrows and juncos, lots of cardinals, Yellow-rumped Warblers, White-throated Sparrows, and a few White-crowned as well, in an absolutely massive, dense thicket on the right side of the road, right across from the silos. Several American Robins, as well as Downy Woodpecker, Yellow-bellied Sapsucker, and Golden-crowned Kinglet, were in the trees that dotted the landscape behind the thicket. After fully exploring the thicket and the grassy field and trees behind it, we ventured across the road to the silos. As we walked around the short fence toward the silos, an American Woodcock rose up out of the six-inch high grass and fluttered low along the fence line before landing in another covered spot fifteen feet away.

Lynn and I looked at each other without speaking. I simultaneously laughed out loud and choked up at the sight of this otherworldly looking bird and its labored airtime. I had a roil of emotion, a sense of death and life, of nature taking back an area once commanded by humans, of adventure and action, and of the knowledge that we were having an absolutely sublime day of birding with a higher number of new birds than I ever thought I'd see in a day in December when well over the three hundred-species mark.

After searching the area around the silos, as well as inside them, we returned to the super-birdy thicket, where the Fox Sparrow and Bewick's Wren were still visible or calling. Lynn dialed up the clear, beautiful notes of the Harris's Sparrow song and let them play for a few seconds. After a couple of rounds of the Harris's call, with good breaks in between, we heard a bird whistle back. It sounded a lot like a Harris's Sparrow—a whole lot like one. But we just weren't sure. A visual identification would have clinched it, because it is almost impossible to mistake this large sparrow with its black throat and face. However, we observed White-crowned Sparrows in the area in which the bird seemed to be calling from, and the first part of the White-crowned call can sound an awful lot like a Harris's Sparrow. We waited and watched, and waited and watched some more, before ultimately deciding that we just didn't know. Ditto with a bird that we were 99 percent sure was a female Purple Finch but which showed itself once, quickly, and was never visible again. We birded this spot until dusk and then cruised the roads around adjacent ag fields searching for the Short-eared Owl. Unsuccessful in this endeavor, we called it quits and returned to Shreveport, where we dined at locally famous Frank's Pizza Napoletana and spent the night at our hotel, which unfortunately had walls far too thin to shield us from the voracious couple staying next to us.

We got started slightly later on Sunday and headed east for Bayou Bodcau Wildlife Management Area. Our target was the Henslow's Sparrow that Charlie had told us about. We followed his directions to the letter and birded the pine tree–savanna grass line from the edge of the road to the edge of the water, about a half mile in all. Although it was a good ten degrees warmer than the previous day, which I welcomed, the wind was about ten miles an hour stronger as well, and this state of affairs was not optimal, because the birds were mostly hunkered down and out of sight. We didn't see any Henslow's Sparrows on the way out, despite netting five other sparrow species, and were about halfway back to the car on the return trip when we spotted a single sparrow. The bird perched silently at the forest edge on a thin branch about six inches above the top of the grass, its small pink beak and yellow-green head working like little beacons, screaming, "I am the target bird you've been looking for!" Charlie Lyon had seen a dozen Henslow's when he last walked the trail. We had only one, but one is all you need to have it count on the list.

We pit-stopped at Bayou Pierre WMA and the silos on our way home, looking once again for the Purple Finch and Harris's Sparrow. Although we located neither, we saw almost every species we had observed the day before, including the Fox Sparrow and Bewick's Wren. I marveled once again at the beauty of this tucked-away spot and its superior bird density.

Lynn and I ended the weekend in Shreveport with 311 and 314 birds respectively. Collectively, our three trips to Shreveport put fifteen birds on our year list that we didn't get in any other place. We had nineteen days left in our year. I didn't expect to pick up anything new during the White Lake CBC I was doing in Vermilion Parish the next week, and I planned to double down on chasing any bird I saw on my target species email alerts.

* * * * *

I got an email while on the way back to Baton Rouge from Shreveport that Erik Johnson, the better half of our two-person CBC team, was unable to join me for White Lake. The thought of attempting a CBC individually was daunting, so count leader Michael Seymour and I each attempted to recruit another birder to take Erik's place. That week, I contacted several of my friends, none of whom were able to accommodate the short notice. Then I got a call from Michael.

"I got you someone!" he reported cheerfully.

"Great," I responded, "who?"

"Van!" he said.

I hung up the phone in disbelief. OMG, I am about to bird with god. Not exactly—but if the Ivory-billed Woodpecker is known as the lord god bird, I am about to spend a day alone with the lord god birder. The best. I was simultaneously thrilled and quaking in my boots. Thrilled in thinking about everything I would learn by having the chance to spend a day alone with him. And quaking because I'm fully aware of all the weaknesses I have as a birder.

I thought about every blackbird call I've ever screwed up, and there have been many. How I struggle to separate Short-billed and Long-billed Dowitchers, or White-rumped and Baird's Sandpipers. How once in a while I can trip over the identification of a female House Sparrow or pull complete blanks on immature gulls. And so on. I thought about studying and then thought to myself, I am as good as I am, and there isn't a whole lot I can do in the next twenty-four hours to fix that.

We met the next morning at 4:15 at the Trader Joe's parking lot, where I climbed into Van's car and we began our trek to meet the other White Lake CBC birders at the McDonald's in Kaplan. Van's easy conversation about all things birding made the drive seem fast. I asked questions—I figured that if you ever have a question to ask about birding, who better than Van? He told me about CBCs and how they're really great historical running totals on the one hand, but not entirely accurate on the other, because the level of noise in the data is incredibly high. It is possible to use them to figure out if bird populations are going up or down, but one also has to factor in complexities.

He told me about his role as state keeper of eBird checklists, and how he has his filters set to the day on certain species in various parishes. He told me that even parish filters can be frustrating because parts of a parish might contain a particular species of bird, but other parts of the same parish would not, so he checked the specific within-parish location of many checklists submitted so he'd be sure that birders weren't making mistakes. He told me about the fascinating distribution of particular species in Louisiana, like the Fish Crow, and how in coastal Cameron Parish there are nothing but Fish Crows, whereas on Grand Isle there are no Fish Crows. There are Fish Crows in Jefferson Parish, the parish that contains Grand Isle—but none on Grand Isle, which is why parish level filters are not always precise enough.

I asked him about species changes in the state over his almost forty years birding in Louisiana, and he confirmed that there are a number of species once considered rare for the state that are making inroads by spreading to the east and north, birds like the White-tailed Kite and Crested Caracara. The one bird that has made a significant decline that he mentioned is the Groove-billed Ani. "They were common in Cameron in the 1980s," Van said, "but the acacia bushes they love have almost been wiped out by people, and now they're almost never seen." I could relate. In all my years of birding in Louisiana, I had never seen a Groove-billed Ani. He said the very same thing about Cameron Parish that Donna had, that it was depressing to bird there because the species numbers and diversity were nothing like they had been during the late 1970s.

"Just as one example," he said, "you know that meadow at Peveto, the one surrounded by barbed wire on the eastern side of the woods?" When I nodded, he continued, "That meadow used to be forest, the entire thing. To bird Peveto well, with the woods we have now plus every tree that was in that meadow, would take seven hours. Those woods held so many amazing rarities. One good thing is that when private owners destroyed that part of Peveto, the Baton Rouge Audubon Society got serious and bought the property. But still, Peveto is nothing like it once was."

When I asked him which bird he thought would be Louisiana's newest addition to the state checklist, he readily answered, "Black Phoebe. I'm guessing it will be one of those species that is most quickly expanding its range toward us from the west. It could also be the Green Kingfisher or Golden-fronted Woodpecker. Who knows? It could be something else."

At Kaplan, we met briefly with Michael and the other CBC birders and then took off for a birding-before-dawn start on Joe Road. On the short ride from the restaurant to our count area, Van explained that dawn was absolutely the best time to bird and if he had to give up a couple of hours of birding in the middle of the day in order to make sure that he got a dawn start, he would make that trade every time. He also showed me the checklists he had printed out for our day, which featured the most likely birds we'd see in Vermilion Parish at the end of the second week in December. Instead of compiling one large list of everything in our count area, his plan was to start a new checklist every time we hit the five-mile mark on the odometer, so that the checklists would have maximal meaning in eBird.

At Joe Road, we exited the vehicle and listened into the darkness; as the charcoal gray sky began to lighten by the minute, we began ticking off heard birds. Van was able to pick out more sounds than I in the dawn cacophony. He took his time to parse out Wilson's Warbler and Hermit Thrush chips from the other ten or so species calling and to teach them to me.

Daylight soon added a second sense to our repertoire, and with that we were off to fast counting: thousands of Snow Geese, White-faced Ibis, and Red-winged Blackbirds joined hundreds of White Ibis, Greater White-fronted Geese, and Mallards flying overhead. I counted ibis and Van counted geese and blackbirds, while we both counted less frequently occurring bird species. I was amazed at how fast and easily he estimated impressive numbers of flyover birds. "How do you count large flocks so quickly?" I asked.

"Well first, chill out. You want to be as accurate as possible, but remember that the nearest order of magnitude is okay for these abundant species—there is no Nobel Prize for counting birds. Then, you need to get into the habit of estimating the area which holds ten birds by ten birds—that's your one hundred bird grid size. If you can estimate that area by sight, then you can quickly estimate the number of birds in a big flock. Why don't you try it on that flock of dark ibis[2] right there?"

I did, and when the flock finished going by I announced, "120."

"I had 160," he responded with a smile, "keep practicing."

After recording staggering numbers of birds at the Joe Road dawn flyover spot, we began our bird survey along each assigned road. We had an overarching strategy and then a specific one. The overarching strategy involved splitting our part of the fifteen-mile-diameter CBC circle, a sixth of the entire count area, into smaller areas and then birding those areas in geographic order to minimize driving and maximize time on task. Within those specific areas, we birded from the vehicle constantly and exited every quarter mile or so to survey.

To this end, Van brought a contraption I'd never seen before. It was a recorder box with speakers that you could attach to branches. A snake also adorned the box and jiggled in plastic yellow splendor. When I asked about it, Van grinned and said that he'd observed numerous bird species respond to the sound emanating from the speakers, find the snake at the center of the action, and proceed to attack it.

The first time Van employed the recorder, I was absolutely impressed. Instead of a simple Eastern Screech-Owl call, this recording included at least five additional bird species' scolding calls, with occasional vocal additions from several more. The speakers put out some decent volume, and pretty soon every bird around had answered the clarion call. It brought in Ruby-crowned Kinglets and Blue-gray Gnatcatchers like crazy. The trick with this avian pied piper was to make sure that we didn't over count zipping Carolina Chickadees or Yellow-rumped Warblers. The other trick for me was to not mistake the calls of birds in the recording with actual birds in the field. I was fooled several times by sound and the way that it can bounce off trees and other objects and seem like it's coming from another direction.

We managed to fit in several short conversations while birding from the vehicle between survey stops. When I told Van I was trying to amp up my year list in Louisiana, he asked me what I needed, and I told him I doubted I'd get anything that day but that I needed the American Bittern and Lincoln's Sparrow. "Hmm . . ." he said, "Lincoln's is pretty doubtful, but the bittern is a possibility."

My birding acumen from a vehicle had gotten better over the years, but it was no match for Van's. At one point he saw two birds on the side of the road while we were driving by that launched into a low branch on a nearby tree. "I think those were Vesper Sparrows," he said, stopping the car and getting out to look. "Yep," he said, peering through his binoculars, "that's very common behavior for Vesper Sparrows." I was flabbergasted by the identification he made from the briefest of looks at several hundred feet away.

We passed several rice fields, and when we got out to scope them Van said, "Let's find some Cackling Geese!" Now that was a bird I needed! He told me that in rice fields in the winter, you needed to locate Greater White-fronted Geese, because Cackling Geese tended to flock among them. I did not know this fact. We searched rice fields all day long and found Greater White-fronted Geese in many, but did not locate a Cackling Goose among them. Still, it was a great tip to learn.

At midmorning we got out to survey a marshy area sandwiched between a road and a rice field. "Hmm...," Van said, "this looks like pretty marginal habitat for a bittern, but let's give it a shot." We got out and took a look and listen, and then he dialed up an American Bittern call. He gave it a few seconds and stopped it. After listening into nothing but wind, he played it again. A few seconds after the second call ceased, the old water pump grunt of an American Bittern sounded off. We simultaneously stood up straight and looked at each other with smiles. "I really didn't think this was good enough marsh!" Van said, "It just goes to show you, it's always worth a try!"

I was excited when our journey brought us to the stakeout spot for the Couch's Kingbird that I'd seen the previous year on this same CBC route; Lynn and I had visited here in January to put this bird on our year list. When we pulled even with the wetland area where I'd spotted the kingbird before, I drew in a gut-punched breath. It had been destroyed: bare, muddy ground had replaced the trees and the sea of cattails. There were no birds on this lot. I got out and surveyed the area with my mouth open and my spirits low; there was at least some suitable habitat around this area, I thought, trying to make myself feel better. Maybe the Couch's had returned and was frequenting an adjacent property.

I was about to tell all this to Van, but a bearded man with a friendly face and wearing a white tank top despite the December temperatures had rolled down the window of his truck as he pulled even with us. There was a tiny, unique-looking, plump dog on his lap.

"Hey y'all," he said by way of greeting, "It's December 14th, the day you always come and walk my oak trees."

"Oh, which trees do you mean?" Van asked.

"The ones down the road a bit. I always say yes every year when you ask, and thanks for asking. I got lots of birds in my trees, and I like it that you count them."

Van thanked him for cooperating and briefly talked about the importance of Christmas Bird Counts while I surreptitiously began looking around at the habitat adjacent to the former Couch's Kingbird house turned muddy mess. Van asked him his name and the guy responded, "My name is Jack. Say, you know birds. Last week, I saw one of them Mexican . . . Mexican . . ."

"Black-bellied Whistling-Ducks?" Van supplied. This supposition made sense, I thought, a lot of locals called Black-bellied Whistling-Ducks Mexican ducks, and they'd certainly be around at this time of year.

"No, it was not a duck . . . oh I remember—a Mexican eagle!"

I was confused, but Van didn't miss a beat, "Ah, a Crested Caracara."

"A what?"

"Here, I'll show you," Van went to the back of his car and pulled out a Roger Tory Peterson bird guide, flipped to the right page, and placed it at the threshold of the rolled-down window. Jack looked down and studied it hard, while the dog stayed plastered to his lap and regarded Van with doe eyes.

"Well, that *mostly* looks like the bird, but not entirely," Jack said, "the head looks right, but I'm not sure about the legs."

"Tell you what," Van replied, "why don't you keep the book? The next time you see one, you can look it up and compare it to the book, so that you're sure."

"Really?" Jack sounded excited. "I could use this to figure out some of the birds in my backyard too." Van smiled.

"What kind of dog do you have, is it a Chihuahua mix?" I asked.

"I have no idea. I picked her up on the side of the road one day. I think someone dropped her and hoped she'd get saved. Precious is the best little dog ever." Jack rubbed the dog's neck. "She is one heck of a duck hunter, let me tell you. Precious follows me everywhere and can find a duck I've shot hundreds of yards away—she knows exactly where they drop and she can carry a duck bigger than herself back to me so fast." The last part of what he said seemed redundant to me—I wasn't sure that Precious was bigger than a Bufflehead. Jack's pride in her, like his pride in his bird-ladened oak trees, was obvious. As he waved goodbye and drove past us, I told Van about the destroyed lot, and we took a quick survey up and down the road, but no Couch's was present.

While we looked, I said, "I thought I was the only one who gave away bird guides!" Over the years I've given away at least five to people I ran into in various places who seemed super interested in birds but didn't have any background. "Well, education is really important" Van responded. "I buy used bird guides four at a time on Amazon for a penny apiece and pay the shipping. I always carry them around in my car and I give them away to anyone who shows interest. I've shared a truckload of guides over the years. The only way we're going to save our birds is if the local people who live and work around them understand them too." Score one for the lord god birder, giving away bird bibles from the back of his old Subaru Outback.

We picked off chunk after chunk of our CBC map zone throughout the afternoon and didn't add many new species, though we buttressed our numbers of many. I continued to test my counting skills and compared numbers with Van. I was spot on with well-spaced bird flocks of twenty but tended to run about half of what he counted on the bigger flocks. Van continued to give me pointers on things like depth of a flock and counting a representative density with the ten by ten bird grid. He must have told me five times to chill out because no one wins the Nobel Prize in bird counting.

The cloudy, foggy, low sky and windy conditions reminded Van of the many CBCs he'd conducted in Crowley. "We won't hit one hundred bird species today," he said, "but I bet we would have if the weather had been more cooperative." We'd seen almost no people during our day of counting, but in late afternoon a man driving by stopped when he saw us and asked what we were doing.

"Bird surveys," stated Van.

"Okay, have a great day," the guy said, and drove off.

"When someone asks you that," Van told me, "never say 'bird-watching' or 'birding.' Always say 'bird surveys.' This makes what you're doing scientific—which it is—and makes birding the serious pursuit it is."

We decided to end the day looking for Short-eared Owl. Erik and Marty Guidry, who had birded this spot in the count the five previous years, had gotten

Short-eared Owl every other year. If their pattern held, this was an on year. Van was less optimistic than I.

"If you are hoping to get one of these with me, Marybeth, you have hitched your cart to the wrong wagon. I have only seen one Short-eared Owl in this manner in all my years of birding in Louisiana. This is not a high probability venture because even though the habitat looks right, the Short-eared Owl usually comes to fields like this when Northern Harriers leave it for the day, and while we have seen harriers today and even one on this field, it's not like there are a bunch around here patrolling. Plus, by the time you actually get to see the owl, it's so dark you can barely see it anyway. It's not the most satisfying way to observe this bird."

We waited and watched as the color of the sky reversed its dawn trajectory. When it got to slate charcoal, Van called it quits for the day. We decided to pit-stop in the field before leaving so that we wouldn't need to stop on our way back to Baton Rouge. As I was finishing business behind a tree, Van started yelling for me. I jumped up and ran while zipping my fly. Had he seen a Short-eared Owl? I drew even with him and breathed, "Whatjaget?"

"American Woodcock! It came up right from my feet and flew that way," he pointed. We stood there in the barely visible light, and after about thirty seconds he said, "Look!" I followed his finger and saw another woodcock fluttering nearby. Although Van didn't say another word, I could actually hear his smile. I hoped he could hear mine, it was every bit as loud. The woodcock was our last counted bird of the day, the ninety-ninth species we observed.

Our return trip to Baton Rouge was just as fast as the trip out because we kept talking birds. While briefly discussing duck hunters, when I mentioned that none will eat a spoonbill, which is duck hunter language for a Northern Shoveler, Van's response was, "Well no wonder! I wouldn't eat one either. You never know where a duck like that has been. Most ducks love the weeds and eat plants, so similar to grass-fed beef, they taste pretty good. Northern Shovelers love sewage ponds. I remember seeing thirty-five thousand shovelers at the Rayne sewage treatment pond and fifteen thousand at the Crowley treatment ponds." I grimaced at the thought of ducks swimming in such environs, and at the same time I was impressed with the sheer number of ducks he'd observed at once. I'd never seen anything like that.

Back at the Trader Joe's parking lot, while I moved my stuff from Van's car to mine, he said, "Marybeth, you have decent birding skills and you have a talent with your ear. You should keep birding because you can get even better. If you are interested, I'll put you on my birding list. If you can make my trips, many are short notice, you'd be welcome to join us. Hopefully I won't drive you crazy with too many emails."

I told Van that I'd love to be put on his list. Although I didn't literally jump up and down while telling him yes, I was completely doing so inside my head, saying, "Seriously? I just passed the bread test!"

* * * * *

Four days later I took advantage of a target eBird alert and Van's tip about Cackling Geese. Lynn and I headed first for Pintail Loop, where we scored a lifer Tundra Swan swimming in the water inside the last leg of the loop. We specifically made the trip looking for this rarity, which had been posted on LA-BIRD and was being regularly seen. I was thankful for the large target and pointed out the swan to birders looking for it from the car that pulled up behind us as Lynn took pictures. We then headed to Illinois Plant Road, where Cackling Geese were being reported in rice fields immediately to the west of the road, just north of Lacassine NWR. I told Lynn that just as you have to kiss a lot of frogs before you find your prince or princess, you have to search a lot of geese-laden fields before you find a Cackling. Thanks to Van's tip, by scouring the areas in and around the Greater White-fronted Geese, we eked out two Cackling Geese.

When Karen and Bob Pierson reported Purple Finches at their feeder in Baton Rouge on December 20, we jumped at the chance to see them. I emailed them and within two hours had an open invitation to come see their finches, plus their three wintering hummers (two Rufous and a Black-chinned) if we wanted. We wanted! I let them know that we were coming late that afternoon. As soon as Lynn got home from work, we headed for their house on the eastern side of the city. We battled horrific traffic that was typically bad to start with, but was made even worse by the August flood aftermath and holiday shoppers. We arrived at their place at about 4:30, and Karen led us to her backyard.

"I was going to call you and tell you not to come; we haven't seen them today. We had a Cooper's Hawk swoop through today and get a bird," she said, pointing to downy feather remains right near the feeder, "and they have stayed away."

Karen played the Purple Finch call, but it brought in nothing. As we were waiting, Bob drifted in and said hello while Karen explained, "We have a goal of seeing one hundred bird species in every state and every province in Canada. We are almost there, we just have a few states to go. We're headed for Alberta and Saskatchewan next year to try to complete those lists. We have 680 birds on our North American bird list, although with the ABA[3] just adding Hawaii to North America, we'll be over 700 since we spent five weeks there and have a number of species from Hawaii to add.

"I have an idea," she continued, "let me see if I can call in these birds with a screech-owl call." She dialed up a recording quickly, and similar to Van's from the previous week, it featured an Eastern Screech-Owl and several other mobbing species. "Wow, that's a great recording!" I said, as cardinals and Mourning Doves began funneling toward the recorder. "Thanks," she said, "I'll send it to you, if you'd like."

We did see one of the Rufous Hummingbirds while we waited, but no Purple Finches. Dusk came and went, and as we returned to our vehicle Karen told us that we had an open invitation to drop by anytime to check the feeders, even if they weren't home. She promised to call if the finches returned to the feeder. Within ten minutes she had emailed me the outstanding mob call tape. I once again marveled at the hospitality of birders.

Two days after that, having been invited by Van, Lynn and I joined him and Marco Rego to visit the Denham Springs water treatment plant. Ironically, there were no Northern Shovelers on the ponds. We observed mostly Ruddy Ducks and Lesser Scaup, got great views of male and female Redheads, and made some close-up observations of Canvasback, the first time we'd seen this species since the faraway flock we'd observed on Charlie's boat on Cross Lake. Best of all, we all saw a skittish female Common Goldeneye, her silvery back the perfect color complement to the grayish sky and water's reflection on the overcast day.

It was December 22, and while the birding was going great guns, I felt like I was in a strange place with the impending holidays. I admit that I don't have a great attitude about the holidays anyway. I don't like the commercial nature of them, and cynically, part of me feels like the holidays create extra things to do during what would otherwise be a restful break between semesters. Even more cynical on my part is the concept of good cheer—which I really believe in as a principle; it's the idea that you only pay attention to it in December that I don't like. As far as I'm concerned, good cheer should be the default all year long. Plus, I detest Christmas music sung by pop stars, and it's impossible to avoid because it pollutes the ether like kudzu strangles natural landscapes. I would take the mating call of a Yellow-headed Blackbird over Bruce Springsteen horking out "Santa Claus Is Coming to Town" any day of the year. Even at high noon on Christmas day.

I try not to be a scrooge, but it takes conscious effort on my part. Lynn loves Christmas, including Christmas music by pop stars. But this year was different—the loss of Mary weighed on us, and especially on Lynn. For the first time ever, we didn't put up a Christmas tree. I would have taken the initiative and put one up, but Lynn told me that she didn't want one. I was ready to do whatever would make her feel better on her first Christmas without either parent alive, and she told me she'd let me know when she figured it out, but she wasn't sure yet. I knew that I wasn't back to my normal self yet either, but I was okay. The birds seemed to be lighting my way, so I just flew with it.

All of a sudden, I had 318 bird species, and Lynn was at 314. All of a sudden, I was in second place in the state with Lynn, Van, and Jay Huner in the mix and Rosemary Seidler only a couple of birds ahead of me. All of a sudden, Irina was urging us for a top five finish, or better yet, a top three. Lynn was saying that we should bird everything possible to try to get me to number one.

Before this year, I would have said that I didn't think we'd ever finish in the top ten eBirders in Louisiana because there are so many great birders in the state—but so many of those great birders had shared their time and talents, their boats and yards, and their special spots with us throughout the year. And although I wasn't going for ranking, just species numbers, all of a sudden I was competitive with Rosemary for number one. I had laughed off Charlie when he had asked a couple of weeks before if I was going for it. Two weeks ago, it had seemed impossible—and I really wasn't going for it. Now I thought maybe, just maybe, with a perfect run of birds, perhaps I could.

We decided to take a day trip to Grand Isle on December 23. Our primary purpose was chasing birds; the Grand Isle CBC had taken place a couple of days earlier and a team consisting of Cathy DiSalvo, Rosemary Seidler, and Joan Garvey recorded a Groove-billed Ani in some scrub right along Highway 1. We wanted to take a crack at the ani and at the beach; there was a not-often-seen Red Knot flock that was wintering on Grand Isle. I knew it wasn't a high probability, but the knot and the ani were two birds I needed within a fairly confined area. We also had possibilities for the bittern and the Red-breasted Nuthatch that Lynn needed. A secondary purpose was for Lynn to fish; she'd had precious little chance to do so in 2016, and I was always game to bird from a kayak.

It might seem crazy to drive nearly three hours one way, explore for five or six, and then return home, but once you get used to such jaunts they're actually pretty enjoyable, and this time was no different. The drive to Grand Isle from Baton Rouge got interesting on the corner of I-10 and I-310, which sported two pairs of nesting Bald Eagles. We then executed the short, counterintuitive jig west on Highway 90, where an eclectic mix of commercial properties was engaged in active warfare against nature taking over, including Frank's Lounge, famous for its Bloody Marys. We did not stop for them, but continued onto Highway 308 East, tracing the northern edge of Bayou Lafourche before crossing it on a drawbridge and beginning our run down Highway 1, where the bayou became wider and where large, wingspread shrimp boats moored near the banks or chugged up and down the middle. After we passed through small towns with big names like Golden Meadow and Cut Off, the new Leeville Toll Bridge provided an elevated view of a vast expanse of marsh that is slowly succumbing to open ocean. At the base of this bridge we turned left to continue on Highway 1 South, where the views on either side of the barely-above-sea level road were vast fields of marsh grass that changes colors with the seasons the way that leaves do farther north. Every so often, the skeleton of a live oak tree punctuated this flat landscape, almost as if to say, "I was here, and freshwater was at one time too." This seven-mile stretch before hitting Grand Isle proper is my favorite leg of the trip, because all the promises of what you might find are literally and figuratively right in front of you. The electrical lines on either side of the road hosted numerous Belted Kingfishers, while the connecting posts featured Osprey. Brown Pelicans and Double-crested Cormorants flew overhead in large "X" patterns across the sky.

We stopped at Elmer's Island first, whose beach had recently been closed forever to vehicles. Although I had driven that beach many times with our truck, and enjoyed doing so very much, I wasn't sorry. All the birds that nested on the almost two-mile-long shore were very vulnerable to high frequency vehicular and human traffic. Being allowed to traverse this area only by foot seemed to balance the scales. We did not walk the beach, however; we took to our kayaks after checking the marsh and mudflats on the entry road and at the foot of the beach— no bitterns or knots—and paddled to the end of the beach at Caminada Pass.

The kayak trip was longer than it looked, but I was captivated by the cloud pattern in the sky, which almost formed a huge doughnut over the horizon. We moored on the spit of beach at edge of the pass, and I got out to explore the strip of sand that ran along the last quarter mile of the pass. From past experience, I knew the best birds on the beach typically hung out at this end point. A scan up the beach's edge revealed a dearth of birds, and I was disappointed to not find anything. While panning back toward where I stood, I ran by a gray football-shaped raptor and my heart sank—Peregrine Falcon! This majestic bird, currently engrossed in consuming the bloody remains of something, a coot maybe, had cleared the beach of avian activity. Normally I'm thrilled to see this bird, but the fact that it had ruined my (admittedly low) chances of a year list Red Knot was disappointing.

I made my way back toward Lynn to tell her so, but before I got there the top of her pole careened over and she whooped, "I got a big one!" I ran the last part of the way and arrived just in time to help push off the kayak she had jumped into so that she wouldn't "get spooled,"[4] because this fish was running. I could hear the scream of the line.

"Get it!" I encouraged while looking at Lynn's thousand-watt smile. It was the happiest I'd seen her in a long time. It took a good half hour, with the fish dragging Lynn and her kayak a few hundred yards around the pass, but eventually she brought in a Redfish more than three feet long and weighing approximately thirty-five pounds. After I took pictures, she carefully returned the fish to the sea, where it would continue to breed to make more Redfish. With this catch and release, Lynn's day was officially made.

"Okay, let's go find that ani!" she stated. We paddled double time back to the truck, loaded up, and headed for the brushy scrub between the main drag and the levee to the Gulf, almost smack-dab in the middle of Grand Isle.

The ani is a fascinating bird. Their vocal repertoire is unlike any bird's I have ever heard, and their look is pretty unique as well. They remind me of roadrunners, which makes sense because both birds are part of the cuckoo family. Anis seem to like to skulk about in heavy cover, and when they do show themselves, they shimmer in and out of sight by barely appearing in front of dense foliage, then fading back so that they almost disappear like a magic trick. I once watched spellbound with my mom as a family of eight Groove-billed Anis executed this behavior in Santa Ana NWR in south Texas.

I was hoping for a glimpse of this shimmering bird as an early Christmas present, but alas, it was nowhere to be found. We birded the target area carefully for a while but eventually abandoned it for the state park because daylight was as short as it would be all year and we wanted to check the park for knots. The beach at the state park sported inspiring numbers of Black Skimmers, Brown Pelicans, and Laughing Gulls, but a dearth of shorebirds. We proceeded to bird the beach and struck out on the Red Knot.

As we pulled out of the state park with windows down on the truck, Lynn thought she heard something promising for the American Bittern. I hadn't heard anything, but the lush, thick marsh grass on either side of the entry road was likely habitat. Lynn killed the engine and played the bittern's chuck notes on her iPhone. After a couple of minutes we both heard a chuck in response. Lynn was giddy. I was pretty sure that we had just heard a bittern, but like Donna, who wasn't absolutely sure about that first Black Rail call, I wasn't either, and I wanted to be absolutely sure. Lynn rolled her eyes at my reticence but played the tape again. We waited in silence for a good minute, she played the call again briefly, and we waited in silence some more. Then two chuck calls on her side of the truck broke the silence—there it was! Lynn was so excited—"See?" she exclaimed. I nodded while springing goose bumps along my arms. I was so excited that this bird did not wind up as her nemesis. Just for good measure, the cooperative bird pumped once more as we made the left turn out of the park.

Now fighting daylight, we returned to the ani spot instead of searching the woods for the Red-breasted Nuthatch, since the latter species was being spotted occasionally in New Orleans and the Northshore area and we'd have better probability there. A recheck of the ani spot produced Savannah Sparrows, cardinals, and after about a half hour an entire wedding party, with bridesmaids and groomsmen decked in pink and red accents. We called it quits and returned to Baton Rouge. Despite not adding a bird to my list, I had a wonderful day on the water and the beach. Lynn's day was decidedly sublime.

Bob and Karen followed up with us about their Purple Finches. The birds had not yet returned to the feeders, but the Piersons had done some scouting for the upcoming Baton Rouge CBC. They emailed us precise directions to a spot we never knew about in one of the richest suburbs in the city, a spot where they'd seen two pairs of Purple Finches. On the morning of the 24th we made the fifteen-minute drive to where Buccaneer Street dead ended into a pumping station. At this juncture, we observed a high tree line, some scrub around the station to our right, and a bayou flowing immediately in front of us.

We noted about a dozen species, then played Bob and Karen's super screech-owl recording to see if we could dial up anything else. We spent almost twenty minutes at that spot before finally bringing in one female Purple Finch, which had us both cheering. During this twenty-minute period we identified twenty-two species and had at least five neighbors check on us to make sure that we were not up to anything nefarious. On the drive back to the house Lynn turned to me and said, "Let's go to the beach for Christmas." And so we did.

Although Lynn had to work on the 29th, we returned to Louisiana a couple of days before that to chase birds. Rosemary's year total was 321, and I was right on her tail at 319.

A Groove-billed Ani had just been reported in the tall grass of a field down in Plaquemine Parish where birders would occasionally stop to see a flock of twenty to twenty-five Swainson's Hawks that patrolled the area. We decided to return from Dauphin Island via Plaquemine Parish. We used GPS coordinates to get to the field, found the fence where the ani had been spotted, and parked the truck as far off the Highway 23 shoulder as possible before exiting. I was birding as usual, but we had Hurricane with us, so Lynn birded with her binoculars in one hand and the leash in the other. We patrolled the fence line looking for the ani and occasionally playing its call. The spot itself was a really awesome birding area except for the eighteen-wheelers blowing by on a regular basis. I wished for less noise and a safer place to park, but you take the places as they are. We did log a number of raptors, mostly Red-tailed Hawks and Turkey Vultures, and we did see one Swainson's Hawk. No ani, though. We packed it in after birding the hundred-yard strip for almost an hour and headed due north for New Orleans.

Ed Wallace had just located a Red-breasted Nuthatch in City Park, courtesy of a Joan Garvey post. Lynn said that she wanted to go home, but it was fresh intel and it was December 27 and we were running out of days in the year to see the Red-breasted Nuthatch, so why not? It was almost on the way home anyway.

We followed Ed's directions and found the grove of pine trees in the middle of the Frisbee golf course. We parked as close to this course as possible; I kept Hurricane and walked her around the green space adjacent to the truck while Lynn walked across the street into the pine grove. She returned ten minutes later with a scowl on her face; she kept shaking her head no and looking down. I thought to myself, Why did you come back so fast, you barely took time to look? I opted for the more diplomatic, "You're back awfully fast." Lynn's grimace instantaneously morphed into her best thousand-watt smile.

"*Because I already got it!*" she declared triumphantly. She explained that she was trying to stop me from seeing her beaming smile so I'd be fooled—and I was. "There are two of them in there!" she continued.

"I wanna see!" It was my turn to express childlike excitement. My January 4th Red-breasted Nuthatch that started this whole journey for three hundred had been a heard-only bird.

"Okay," said Lynn, "let me show you where. I'm going to take pictures too."

Lynn led the way back into the pine grove. I had the dog in one hand and my binoculars in the other. As soon as she hit play on the tape, an emphatic "yank, yank, yank" came in return. Lynn shut off the tape immediately as a Red-breasted Nuthatch landed on a pine tree trunk some twenty feet away from us to investigate. While the bird regarded us silently, another continued yanking from afar. I thought I could detect perhaps a second distant call, but I wasn't sure. Then the silent bird began yanking and the second one flew in and joined it. Lynn started snapping pictures. I watched with great happiness even as Hurricane pulled my arm against the length of her tether. All things considered, this bird seemed an appropriate bookend to our long, simultaneously difficult and wonderful year.

* * * * *

As it happened, the Red-breasted Nuthatches hanging out in the middle of a Frisbee golf course in City Park in New Orleans were not quite the end of the year. The very next day we executed one more Cameron Parish pilgrimage, where we picked up a male Cinnamon Teal on Pintail Loop and a Lincoln's Sparrow on Fabacher Road in Calcasieu Parish. The latter bird made me extremely proud—of myself for identifying it by its smack call, and of Lynn, who somehow managed to get identifiable photographs despite the bird's affinity for ground cover. We both laughed up a storm when we birded for the last time in Louisiana for the year: late that afternoon in Oak Grove Sanctuary, who should come calling but another pair of Red-breasted Nuthatches?

After the 28th, I didn't really feel like there was much else I could do. I could have continued to chase low-probability birds, but why? I was so happy with 321 species—so very much higher than the 292 I thought we could do at best. Rosemary kept rolling and wound up first in the state with 327 species, her last bird a Couch's Kingbird on December 29. She rocked first place—no one could touch her, including me. Van breezed into a tie with me in second place with a Henslow's Sparrow on a CBC on December 30. Lynn was next in fourth with 319. Jay Huner had 313. Ten birders exceeded the 300 species mark in Louisiana in 2016, including Mary Mehaffey, who finished in eighth place with 307 species.

Lynn and I returned to the beach for New Year's, where we joined Linda and Sarah, Kathryn and Irina, and other friends for our annual polar bear plunge into the Gulf. This ritual of washing off the old year and bringing in the new helped me to close out this journey inside a journey. My mom was so proud of us. I think Mary would have been too.

My passion for birding began with tiny, tectonic shifts; it has burgeoned into a tidal wave by virtue of being nurtured by the good hearts of people, buffeted by winds of life experience, and fed by surges of wild, natural places. Surfing this tidal wave has made me appreciate all aspects of life, both my own and that of the larger ecosystem of which I am part. Birding makes everything around me "fall away" and I am utterly myself and in the moment, without defense, and often without awareness of the tethers of human constructs. It is, I suppose, a form of escapism, but really it feels more like a coming to than a going away. In this space I can see infinity in a ditch, stillness in movement, divinity in compromise. In this space I am simultaneously grounded and flying.

EPILOGUE

I KNOW WHY THE CAJUN BIRD DANCES

The Louisiana Waterthrush is a warbler that spends most of its time on the ground. This bird passes through south Louisiana during spring migration and sometimes gives birders fits because it can be difficult to tell the Louisiana Waterthrush apart from the Northern Waterthrush. There are a few good clues to differentiate them.

When looking at one of these birds, I use the term I created to remember their difference: "northern streaker," meaning that the Northern Waterthrush's breast has more defined streaks (and a higher number of streaks) than the Louisiana Waterthrush. I used to say "white northern streaker" because many times the Northern has a lighter (white) breast than the Louisiana, whose breast tends to be a buffier or cream color. However, breast color is not a surefire field mark, so I eliminated "white" from that little reminder. The Louisiana Waterthrush also has a more pronounced supercilium (eyebrow) that flares at the back of its head.

The songs of the two species are similar, but the beginning three notes of the Louisiana's song are more musical sounding than the Northern's. This is easy to remember, since Louisiana is the birthplace of jazz. There is one more feature that makes it easy to tell the two waterthrush species apart. Both warblers are tail pumpers and almost always have their tails in motion, but the northern pumps its tail straight up and down, while the Louisiana pumps its tail up and down *and* side to side. This Cajun bird is a dancer—it sings and dances better than its cousin.

In the book *I Know Why the Caged Bird Sings,* Maya Angelou says that the bird sings because it has a song. Analogously, the Cajun bird dances because it has a dance. The Cajun bird also dances because it has a dance floor. And this dance floor, for a small but critical part of every year, is Louisiana.

For the Louisiana Waterthrush and hundreds of other migratory bird species that pass through each spring and fall, Louisiana's dance floor represents habitat crucial for their lives. But the birds can't dance when there is no dance floor. And Louisiana is losing dance floor every second of every day. We hear about it a lot in the state, translated into a currency that most Louisianans understand: football fields. Louisiana loses a football field's worth of land every one hundred minutes.[1] In the past eighty-five years, we have lost land area equivalent to the size of Delaware.

Life in Louisiana has taught me a lot about loss. There's loss that while really hard is a normal part of life, like Mary's death. Parts of coastal land loss in Louisiana are normal; it's typical to lose land from subsidence or natural settling, and wave action moves sand around, including off beaches.

But then there's loss that's not normal or necessary. And the larger part of Louisiana's coastal land loss is in this category. When the Mississippi River was confined by levees, the natural land-building process driven by the river was disrupted. As a result, sediment in the river now flows out into the Gulf of Mexico and over the continental shelf instead of being deposited in the delta along the coast. Oil companies have built some ten thousand miles of pipeline in south Louisiana; the act of carving through the land and wetlands for pipelines has increased saltwater intrusion and has contributed to land erosion that increases over time.

Compounding this issue is the fact that pipelines break or leak. According to the Louisiana Oil Spill Coordinator's Office, Louisiana averages fifteen hundred oil spills per year, or slightly more than four per day. They're so frequent that most spills don't even make the news.[2] Environmental losses in Louisiana are catastrophic. And the one spill that did make the news, the biggest in history, wiped out approximately 700,000 birds.[3]

I know that there is so much loss. And yet I have so much hope.

I see hope personified when I visit rural places in Louisiana in which I am a guest, and the people who live there and have never met me welcome me as a friend. I feel hope when I watch the unspoken fishing pier rules in action, the ones in which everyone knows who is fishing for fun and who is fishing for dinner, and the way that Louisianans fishing for fun will often give their catch or their leftover bait to the people fishing for dinner. I hear hope; for example, while encountering a pair of rare Whooping Cranes during a Christmas Bird Count, a local approached in a pickup truck with the greeting, "You're not going to shoot my cranes, are you?" I live hope through the privilege of teaching college students from every corner of Louisiana (and beyond) who are unified in their commitment to a better world. I know hope because the research-based plans to save the Louisiana Waterthrush's dance floor will work if they are fully put into motion.[4]

I have so much hope because Louisianans never stop. As soon as the last of Katrina's winds blew through, Louisianans with boats who were not impacted by the storm, those in Cajun country, marshaled their resources and resolve and set sail for New Orleans. In the week following Katrina, this group of men and women and their boats plucked some nine thousand people from rooftops and other flooded structures and delivered them safely to dry land. Known as the Cajun Navy, this group helped curb an already too high death toll from the storm. Hope in motion, the Cajun Navy responded after Hurricanes Harvey and Irma in 2017 and still sails today. The Cajun Airlift was formed in 2017 to assist the Houston area after Harvey and served Puerto Rico after Hurricane Maria as well.

I have hope because Louisianans can compromise. Harnett Kane said of Louisiana, "It is a place that seems often unable to make up its mind whether it will be earth or water, and so it compromises." Louisianans are the most rooted people in the United States. Compromise is part of their place-based DNA. It's not birder or duck hunter, it's both. It's not jobs or environment, it's jobs *and* environment. It's not rural or urban, it's all of us. We know resilience and how to bounce back from tough times; we've had a lot of experience in bouncing back. There's honor in compromise and there's honor in resilience, but unless we use these qualities carefully, we will lose our dance floor. All the compromise and resilience in the world can't compete with open ocean.

The first time I attended the Yellow Rails and Rice Festival, I was riding on a combine platform right next to the enclosed cab. The farmer was inside the cab, as was a birder somewhere in her eighties who climbed onto that combine with lots of determination and little assistance. During the second pass through the field, guide Kevin Colley called "Yellow Rail" and a cheer went up from inside the cab as we all clearly viewed the bird. When I looked inside, I saw the farmer and the birder, each with both arms raised and mouths wide open, raucously cheering in victory. The Yellow Rails and Rice Festival would never have happened without compromise between a farmer's work and a nature lover's play, or a bridge between urban and rural communities. Louisianans understand one love when they see it, and the birds in this case were the one love. My ultimate hope is that we all can recognize one love when we see it, because that one love represents our way forward.

AFTERWORD, 2022

As I write this afterword on a summer evening in June, the cicadas are buzz-
ing and three Mississippi Kites are using their tails as rudders to circle the sky
over my house. We have temporarily ceded our covered back porch to a pair of
Mourning Doves who took up residence on top of one of the ceiling fans. By observing the pair for the past two months, I have learned that the breeding cycle of this species seems to have no beginning or end. As soon as her offspring
fledge, mom starts laying eggs again, even as she and dad are bringing food to the
fledglings. Right now, the female is sitting on what will be her third consecutive
brood. Our gas grill, stationed adjacent to the porch and some twenty feet from
the doves' den, has suffered a similar fate. Industrious Carolina Wrens managed to wend their way into the back of the grill, building a nest on the flat cook-
ing surface. Until they are finished, there will be no grilled vegetables, veggie
burgers, or fresh-caught fish. Although we miss these creature comforts of our
homestead, Lynn and I are content to share them with our winged community.

I am so excited to have this opportunity to check in, albeit briefly, with
updates.

At the time of this book's writing, the Louisiana state bird list consisted of
482 species—it is now up to 488! Louisiana has joined the Limpkin craze, as this
once "confined to Florida" bird has opened its wings and geographical horizons
to follow invasive apple snails. The Limpkin is now fairly common in south Louisiana; I've already seen it in two parishes (Terrebonne and East Baton Rouge)
and expect to find it in more. In April 2020, Jane Patterson found Black-capped
Vireo—a state first—while birding a thin strip of land between Lake Pontchartrain and Lake Maurepas. Almost exactly a year later, this Texas Hill Country

specialty showed up in Peveto Woods Sanctuary, and many Louisiana birders were able to see it during the five-day stint it spent in the woods (though not me—hopefully next time).

As of this writing, Sarah Myers has a bird up on me once again. She and Linda Lee birded Dauphin Island's Shell Mound this past spring and found several Scaly-breasted Munia. For some reason, I find myself unwilling to yard crash a feeder for this species, and so far I am doing pretty well, ignoring the occasional teasing coming my way. Lynn and I were able to visit Yellowstone National Park in February 2020, where almost all the locals told us that we chose the right time of year to visit because the park is full of wildlife and almost devoid of people. We were hiking the Mammoth Hot Springs area when a Clark's Nutcracker flew down and landed on the branch of a tree about fifteen feet from us, at eye level. Any frustration that I had once felt over missing the Clark's Nutcracker near the road on that Colorado mountainside has since been assuaged.

I am happy to report that my mother loves this book. She read it immediately and then read it a second time, armed with a set of arrow-shaped page flags. The two of us have spent hours working through the book flag by flag (in effect, almost page by page). Through this process, she has let me know that I got a couple of things wrong about her in the book, which I have deemed "matriarchal errata." To set the record straight: when I was trying to see the aforementioned Clark's Nutcracker and left the car parked in the middle of the road while I investigated, my mother informed me that her outburst for me to return to the vehicle had nothing to do with the distant car behind us. Instead, it was the fact that I had just crossed the centerline of the road in front of our car, on a blind turn. It would have been easy, she said, for a driver coming the other way to hit me, since I was right in their lane and wasn't paying attention to the road because I was trying to find the bird. All I had to say to that was: "Oh." I was reminded once again that perspective is everything (and thanks, Mom, for always keeping me safe!). In the book, I also reported that Mom, Joan Nicolosi, Harry Moran, and I saw a lifer Chuck-will's-widow in Peveto. "I just wanted to remind you," she said, "that this bird was a lifer for all of you except me. I went to De Soto National Forest with Judy Toups and the Bushwhackers, and we saw

Chuck-will's-widows and Red-cockaded Woodpeckers galore at dawn!" She had indeed told me about that.

The biggest change for me in terms of birding has been that I finally capitulated to carrying a camera. I always avoided doing so in the past because I was worried that I would concentrate on getting the perfect picture instead of enjoying the bird. Van Remsen finally talked me into it. He told me that someday I would find a rarity, and that without photo proof, no one would believe me (or they might, but with no documentation, there would be no way to prove it). I now feel naked in the field without my Nikon COOLPIX P900 digital camera. I have gotten so much enjoyment from taking pictures of birds and have found a middle ground in which I am still enjoying birds in real time while taking their photographs when possible. I have also appropriately documented several rarities.

Not all of my updates are positive. Birder-wise, we lost Janine Robin, who showed Lynn and me the baby Eastern Screech-Owls in her backyard; she succumbed to cancer in December 2020. More broadly, most of the Louisiana coastline has been devastated by hurricanes in the past two years, including three in 2020 alone: Laura (Category 4) in Cameron Parish; Delta (Category 2), which struck six weeks later and fifteen miles from where Laura made landfall, also in Cameron Parish; and Zeta (Category 3) in Terrebonne Parish. In 2021, Hurricane Ida, a Category 4 storm, hit Lafourche Parish on the sixteenth anniversary of Hurricane Katrina. These storms did not just collectively devastate coastal habitats; the storms themselves also destroyed communities and killed people, birds, fish, and other wildlife. And of course, even more broadly, the COVID-19 pandemic has changed the entire world.

Recently, an attendee of a presentation I made about my book asked if I still had the kind of hope I expressed in the epilogue. I admit that this question is not as easy to answer in 2022 as it was in 2018 when I finished this book (and it was harder to answer in 2018 than in 2013, when I started it).

The answer is still yes. I do have hope. I draw inspiration from two cultural icons whom we have also lost since the publication of this book: John Lewis, who said, "Ours is not the struggle of one day, one week, or one year. . . . Ours is the struggle of a lifetime, or maybe even many lifetimes, and each one of us in every generation must do our part"; and Ruth Bader Ginsburg, who said, "You go on to the next challenge and you give it your all. These important issues are not going to go away." Ginsburg also stated, "Real change, enduring change, happens one step at a time."

I will close by answering the most common question I get: will there be a sequel? The answer, as best I can tell, is yes, at some point in the future. I am not sure of the structure or context of the sequel just yet, but birds and birders continue to tell me stories and I continue to bear witness and take notes.

Until next time, dear reader, I wish you good birding and great living. Keep looking up!

ACKNOWLEDGMENTS

I may be the author of this book, but I can promise that its creation is the culmination of a team effort, and I am blessed to have a huge, fabulous team, starting with the best birding partner anyone could ask for, my wife, Lynn Hathaway. She not only birds with me pretty much anytime I want, she graciously lives with my propensity for publicly sharing stories that involve her in more personal ways than she would ever voluntarily share. I read the manuscript out loud to Lynn twice for her okay to share the stories contained within it, which were improved as a result of her thoughtful suggestions and sage edits. Thank you, Lynnie, for sharing your incredible heart and generosity with me in ways that have led me to heights I never thought possible.

I am so thankful to medical personnel at the University of South Alabama Medical Center Regional Burn Unit who helped to save Lynn after the boat accident, especially Sherri Raybon and Jessie Smith. Our Dauphin Island neighbors rallied around us during the accident and continue to support us, especially Jane Moore, Elton Tanner, Ron and Jo Ann Tait, Larry and Lucinda Wallace, and Kerry Wiley. Other friends, including all mentioned in the pages of this book, and Cherie Fletcher, Shanika Thomas, and Missy Zeller, were instrumental in Lynn's healing. I am also thankful to all the staff at Clarity Hospice in Baton Rouge, who helped us at the end of Mary's life.

Writing this book took the better part of five years. People who helped me think about this work initially include Bruce Sharky, Jean Rohloff, and Donna Dittmann. I slowly took notes, jotted down thoughts, and wrote small chunks until the summer of 2017, when I felt like I had the material, time, and perspective to finish. My steadfast writing partner during this time was Irina Shport, who was as hard at work as I was, on journal articles. We wrote in the same space together, in adjoining rooms; the conversations we had during breaks, on writing, human nature, politics, identity, and understanding, helped shape the manuscript immensely. That I could walk into the next room and ask Irina a question when I was stuck was invaluable as well. Irina's *joie de vivre* pushed me to finish, and her creative suggestions on every part of this book made it infinitely better. I can only hope I was as helpful to her as she was to me. Thank you Irina, best writing buddy ever!

Some of my friends read chapters or listened to stories and gave helpful feedback, including Jennifer Baumgartner, Erik Johnson, Connie Kuns, Sarah Liggett, Martha Lund, Jean Rohloff, and Cristina Sabliov. Celeste Barlow and Irina Shport read the entire manuscript and gave great suggestions for improvement. Maggi Spurlock and members of the LSU Faculty Staff Book Group helped me with insights about Louisiana, including Dianne Lindstedt, Robert Perlis, Melissa Lee, Sheri Wischusen, Adrienne Steele, Betsy Reeves, Chelsea Duhon, Grace Fiorenza, Rachel Champagne, Summer Steib, Meredith Wilbanks, and Michelle Spielman. Linda Benedict and Emily Toth provided helpful feedback on writing, editing, and publishing. Aaron Hargrove created the illustrations contained in the manuscript, and Lynn drew the birder's guide map. I would be unable to write without yoga and acupuncture; Carmen Board and Ching Guo provide these services with verve, so that I can write accordingly. I thank Richard Bengtson, David Constant, Donna Elisar, and Angie Singleton for their long-term professional support.

I thank MaryKatherine Callaway, who asked me to write my first book for the LSU Press (*Building Playgrounds, Engaging Communities*) and who thus introduced me to "writing crossover" for popular audiences, a medium that I have discovered I love more than any other. I thank Alisa Plant, the talented editor for my first book, who roped me into writing this one just days after the first was published. And I thank Margaret Lovecraft, who served as the editor for this book, and in so doing completely elevated the work beyond the best I could do, for which I am forever grateful. Thank you for applying your craft and your heart to this work, Margaret. Your suggestions were brilliant, and so are you!

Finally, I did not realize that the copy editing process could enhance more than a book's readability until this manuscript was put into the gifted hands of Derik Shelor. The collective contributions of the entire staff at LSU Press have made this book shine. Thank y'all so much!

I am a member of many tribes, and in this book, I'd like to call out two of them. First, an engagement tribe, consisting of friends and colleagues who endeavor toward justice in their communities, including Emily Adoue, Sharon Williams Andrews, Taylor Armer, D. Boz Bowles, Christy Kayser Arrazattee, Caroline Bergeron, Judy Bethly, Ann Christy, Daniel Davison, Adriana Deras, Roxanne Dill, Ashley Flynn, Beatriz Garcia, Grant Gonzalez, Aaron Hargrove, Kristin Harper, Barrett Kennedy, Kristen Galloway La Porte, Jon Leydens, Lauren Lilly, Juan Lucena, Kristin Menson, Mary Alice Morgan, Brooke Morris, Debbie Normand, Bill Oakes, Emily Patterson, Rhoda Reddix, Peggy Reily, Troy Robertson, Madison Ruston, Cindy Seghers, Jan Shoemaker, Jeanne Steyer, Nick Totaro, Brandon Tramontana, Shane Vallery, Alexandra Williams, and Joe Zerkus. Thanks all of you for the constant inspiration! During a critical juncture, fellow engagement experts and storytellers Connie Mick and Tal Stanley reminded me of the importance of bearing witness without overbearing, and that place always involves conflict and thus demands constant work toward justice, respectively.

The second tribe is birders; I acknowledge all the birders mentioned in this book and indeed all birders, many more than I can name. Some not mentioned in these pages that I'd like to call out include Jim Boutte, Gary Byerly, Paul Conover, Allen Correll, Larry Cowan, John Dillon, Andrew Haffenden, John Hartgerink, Crystal Johnson, Rick Kittinger, Delaina LeBlanc, Laurie McDuff, Michele McLindon, Jimson Josia Mndeme, Patty O'neill, Hans Paul, Melissa Sovay, Cheri Wiese, Nancy Williams, and Martha Wright.

I thank Van Remsen for letting me touch the edges of elite birding. Though I still only aspire to be elite, the privilege of birding with Van and his avian posse has taught and continues to teach me so much. I thank Dan Lane for the simultaneously best and worst birding jokes ever, and Erik Johnson and Cameron Rutt for generously sharing their birding wisdom.

I am blessed to have a family that has provided love, support, and wisdom throughout my life. I especially thank my mother, Kay Rogers, and hope that I didn't tease her too much in the pages of this book. I have a special bond with my mom, one that is deeper because of our shared love of birds. My mother has provided a towering and constant model for the way to thrive in life with equal parts grace and grit, and with an unerring compass toward justice. She has positively and profoundly influenced my life in ways I still continue to realize. My father, John Lima, and my brother, John Jr., have also been unwavering support posts; their strong foundation helps me to stand on the solid ground of self-confidence every day of my life. I draw inspiration from many family members, including Sharon and Shirley Ferreira, Marc and Marthamarie Fuller, Roger and Dylan Hart, M. Eve Hathaway, Julie Johnson, Tom and Blanche Judd, Nancy Leaver, Elizabeth, Sarah, and Sherry Lima, Jan MacKichan, and Chris Rogers. I acknowledge my entire family (Hathaway, Lima, and Rogers clans); all are kind enough to take me on birding adventures whenever I visit. My friends are a fount of love and support. Besides those already mentioned in the pages of this book, thank you Diana Glawe, Leslie Morreale, Becky and Brian Ropers-Huilman, and Dorothy Thrasher. Those included in the book who deserve extra thanks include Kathryn Barton, Linda Lee, Carol Lee Moore, Sarah Myers, and Irina Shport.

I acknowledge loss and the difficulties associated with it, as well as those lost during the creation of this book, including Lynn's parents, Russ and Mary; Emily Callaway; Murray Forman; Bob Hamm; Deborah Marvin; Pete Morreale; Lisi Oliver; Bob Rogers; John Stowers; CW Wiley; and Malcom Wright.

Finally, I thank the great state of Louisiana, this place of compromise and conflict, where I have found my spiritual home. It is my ultimate hope that this book plays a part in helping to keep you alive and healthy so that you can continue your unique dance while providing a dance floor for all those who inhabit your borders.

APPENDIX A: FIELD NOTES

These notes were created using my own style and are not necessarily best practice. I put the date, location, and weather information at the top of the page, the distance traveled during birding, and the start and end times during which I observe birds.

This set of notes was taken on August 28, 2016, at Holly Beach, from mile marker (MM) 21 to 26, a five-mile distance. I started my checklist at 12:51 P.M. and ended at 2:30 P.M.

I list all the birds I see using four-letter alpha codes that were created by the Bird Banding Laboratory. The four-letter codes for North American birds are currently maintained by the Institute for Bird Populations and can be found at http://www.birdpop.org/pages/birdSpeciesCodes.php.

For the most part, alpha codes are easy to use because lots of birds have two-word names, and the first two letters of each word are used in the code, such as SPSA for Spotted Sandpiper. Many birds have compound names, like Great-Tailed Grackle or Boat-Tailed Grackle, whose abbreviations are GTGR and BTGR respectively. Sometimes the codes can be less clear because of similar bird names. For example, BARS on this checklist refers to Barn Swallow. If we used BASW, it might be unclear whether the abbreviation referred to a Barn Swallow or a Bank Swallow

I record all the species I observe while I bird. Rather than keeping track of the total bird count of each species in my head and recording them at the end of the observation period, I keep running tallies as I go and then circle the total of each species for entry into eBird. Species for which I see only a single individual list only the four-letter code, with no corresponding number.

12:51 / 2:30   8/28/16

Holly Beach, MM 21-26

mostly cloudy, NNE 9 mph, 82F

(16) 4 GTGR + 3 + 6 + 3
(2) BTGR
(3) 2 CONI + 1
(+) 2 BBPL + 2
    (2) SPSA
(4) 3 SNEG + 1
    BARS
(10) 8 CATE + 2
    (6) RWBL
(+5) 18 BLSK + 8 + 10 + 7
    SNPL
    (3) WILL
(3) 2 SEPL + 1
(6) 3 KILL + 2 + 1
(6) 2 RUTU + 2 + 2

    AMAV
    MIKI
    LBHE
(16) 4 SAND + 6 + 3 + 3
(10) 20 FOTE + 15 + 15 + 10
    LOSH
(12) 7 BLTE + 5
(8) 3 SATE + 3 + 2
(73) 17 ROYT + 12 + 5 +
        24 + 8 + 7
(5) 2 PIPL + 2 + 1
(+2) 15 LAGU + 10 + 2 + 8
        + 7
(2+) 6 BRPE + 6 + 10 + 2
(20) + LETE + 10 + 4 + 2

APPENDIX B:
2016 LIST OF LOUISIANA BIRDS

BIRD #	SPECIES	LOCATION	DATE
1	Pied-billed Grebe	Pine Prairie CBC, Northwest area, Evangeline Parish	January 4
2	Double-crested Cormorant	Pine Prairie CBC, Northwest area, Evangeline Parish	January 4
3	Great Blue Heron	Pine Prairie CBC, Northwest area, Evangeline Parish	January 4
4	Snowy Egret	Pine Prairie CBC, Northwest area, Evangeline Parish	January 4
5	Black Vulture	Pine Prairie CBC, Northwest area, Evangeline Parish	January 4
6	Turkey Vulture	Pine Prairie CBC, Northwest area, Evangeline Parish	January 4
7	Red-shouldered Hawk	Pine Prairie CBC, Northwest area, Evangeline Parish	January 4
8	Red-tailed Hawk	Pine Prairie CBC, Northwest area, Evangeline Parish	January 4
9	Sandhill Crane	Pine Prairie CBC, Northwest area, Evangeline Parish	January 4
10	Spotted Sandpiper	Pine Prairie CBC, Northwest area, Evangeline Parish	January 4
11	Eurasian Collared-Dove	Pine Prairie CBC, Northwest area, Evangeline Parish	January 4
12	Mourning Dove	Pine Prairie CBC, Northwest area, Evangeline Parish	January 4
13	Belted Kingfisher	Pine Prairie CBC, Northwest area, Evangeline Parish	January 4
14	Red-bellied Woodpecker	Pine Prairie CBC, Northwest area, Evangeline Parish	January 4
15	Yellow-bellied Sapsucker	Pine Prairie CBC, Northwest area, Evangeline Parish	January 4
16	Downy Woodpecker	Pine Prairie CBC, Northwest area, Evangeline Parish	January 4
17	Hairy Woodpecker	Pine Prairie CBC, Northwest area, Evangeline Parish	January 4
18	Northern Flicker	Pine Prairie CBC, Northwest area, Evangeline Parish	January 4
19	Pileated Woodpecker	Pine Prairie CBC, Northwest area, Evangeline Parish	January 4
20	American Kestrel	Pine Prairie CBC, Northwest area, Evangeline Parish	January 4
21	Eastern Phoebe	Pine Prairie CBC, Northwest area, Evangeline Parish	January 4
22	Loggerhead Shrike	Pine Prairie CBC, Northwest area, Evangeline Parish	January 4
23	Blue-headed Vireo	Pine Prairie CBC, Northwest area, Evangeline Parish	January 4
24	Blue Jay	Pine Prairie CBC, Northwest area, Evangeline Parish	January 4
25	American Crow	Pine Prairie CBC, Northwest area, Evangeline Parish	January 4

26	Fish Crow	Pine Prairie CBC, Northwest area, Evangeline Parish	January 4
27	Carolina Chickadee	Pine Prairie CBC, Northwest area, Evangeline Parish	January 4
28	Tufted Titmouse	Pine Prairie CBC, Northwest area, Evangeline Parish	January 4
29	Red-breasted Nuthatch	Pine Prairie CBC, Northwest area, Evangeline Parish	January 4
30	Brown-headed Nuthatch	Pine Prairie CBC, Northwest area, Evangeline Parish	January 4
31	Brown Creeper	Pine Prairie CBC, Northwest area, Evangeline Parish	January 4
32	House Wren	Pine Prairie CBC, Northwest area, Evangeline Parish	January 4
33	Carolina Wren	Pine Prairie CBC, Northwest area, Evangeline Parish	January 4
34	Golden-crowned Kinglet	Pine Prairie CBC, Northwest area, Evangeline Parish	January 4
35	Ruby-crowned Kinglet	Pine Prairie CBC, Northwest area, Evangeline Parish	January 4
36	Eastern Bluebird	Pine Prairie CBC, Northwest area, Evangeline Parish	January 4
37	Hermit Thrush	Pine Prairie CBC, Northwest area, Evangeline Parish	January 4
38	American Robin	Pine Prairie CBC, Northwest area, Evangeline Parish	January 4
39	Northern Mockingbird	Pine Prairie CBC, Northwest area, Evangeline Parish	January 4
40	Cedar Waxwing	Pine Prairie CBC, Northwest area, Evangeline Parish	January 4
41	Orange-crowned Warbler	Pine Prairie CBC, Northwest area, Evangeline Parish	January 4
42	Pine Warbler	Pine Prairie CBC, Northwest area, Evangeline Parish	January 4
43	Yellow-rumped Warbler	Pine Prairie CBC, Northwest area, Evangeline Parish	January 4
44	Chipping Sparrow	Pine Prairie CBC, Northwest area, Evangeline Parish	January 4
45	Dark-eyed Junco	Pine Prairie CBC, Northwest area, Evangeline Parish	January 4
46	White-crowned Sparrow	Pine Prairie CBC, Northwest area, Evangeline Parish	January 4
47	White-throated Sparrow	Pine Prairie CBC, Northwest area, Evangeline Parish	January 4
48	Song Sparrow	Pine Prairie CBC, Northwest area, Evangeline Parish	January 4
49	Swamp Sparrow	Pine Prairie CBC, Northwest area, Evangeline Parish	January 4
50	Eastern Towhee	Pine Prairie CBC, Northwest area, Evangeline Parish	January 4
51	Northern Cardinal	Pine Prairie CBC, Northwest area, Evangeline Parish	January 4
52	Red-winged Blackbird	Pine Prairie CBC, Northwest area, Evangeline Parish	January 4

BIRD #	SPECIES	LOCATION	DATE
53	American Goldfinch	Pine Prairie CBC, Northwest area, Evangeline Parish	January 4
54	Cooper's Hawk	Home, Baton Rouge	January 5
55	Snow Goose	Highway 35 mud fields, Acadia Parish	January 10
56	Mallard	Highway 35 mud fields, Acadia Parish	January 10
57	Great Egret	Highway 35 mud fields, Acadia Parish	January 10
58	Killdeer	Highway 35 mud fields, Acadia Parish	January 10
59	Dunlin	Highway 35 mud fields, Acadia Parish	January 10
60	Western Sandpiper	Highway 35 mud fields, Acadia Parish	January 10
61	Long-billed Dowitcher	Highway 35 mud fields, Acadia Parish	January 10
62	Greater Yellowlegs	Highway 35 mud fields, Acadia Parish	January 10
63	Lesser Yellowlegs	Highway 35 mud fields, Acadia Parish	January 10
64	Tree Swallow	Highway 35 mud fields, Acadia Parish	January 10
65	European Starling	Highway 35 mud fields, Acadia Parish	January 10
66	Ross's Goose	Highways 35 and 699 intersection, Vermilion Parish	January 10
67	Greater White-fronted Goose	Highways 35 and 699 intersection, Vermilion Parish	January 10
68	Northern Harrier	Highways 35 and 699 intersection, Vermilion Parish	January 10
69	Stilt Sandpiper	Highways 35 and 699 intersection, Vermilion Parish	January 10
70	Least Sandpiper	Highways 35 and 699 intersection, Vermilion Parish	January 10
71	Ring-billed Gull	Highways 35 and 699 intersection, Vermilion Parish	January 10
72	Savannah Sparrow	Highways 35 and 699 intersection, Vermilion Parish	January 10
73	Vesper Sparrow	Highway 699 and Dulva Road intersection, Vermilion Parish	January 10
74	Forster's Tern	Lapland Longspur stakeout, Shams Road, Vermilion Parish	January 10
75	Lapland Longspur	Lapland Longspur stakeout, Shams Road, Vermilion Parish	January 10
76	Eastern Meadowlark	Lapland Longspur stakeout, Shams Road, Vermilion Parish	January 10
77	House Sparrow	Lapland Longspur stakeout, Shams Road, Vermilion Parish	January 10

78	White Ibis	Highway 35 between Lapland Longspur and Couch's Kingbird stakeouts, Vermilion Parish	January 10
79	Couch's Kingbird	Couch's Kingbird stakeout, Lomire Road, Vermilion Parish	January 10
80	Blue-gray Gnatcatcher	Couch's Kingbird stakeout, Lomire Road, Vermilion Parish	January 10
81	Brown-headed Cowbird	Couch's Kingbird stakeout, Lomire Road, Vermilion Parish	January 10
82	Laughing Gull	Jefferson Davis Parish Landfill environs (Turf Grass Road area)	January 10
83	American Pipit	Jefferson Davis Parish Landfill environs (Turf Grass Road area)	January 10
84	Northern Pintail	Hacketts Corner area, Highway 27, near Cameron Prairie NWR	January 10
85	Black-necked Stilt	Cameron Prairie NWR	January 10
86	Blue-winged Teal	Cameron Prairie NWR	January 10
87	Northern Shoveler	Cameron Prairie NWR	January 10
88	Gadwall	Cameron Prairie NWR	January 10
89	American Wigeon	Cameron Prairie NWR	January 10
90	Mottled Duck	Cameron Prairie NWR	January 10
91	Green-winged Teal	Cameron Prairie NWR	January 10
92	Anhinga	Cameron Prairie NWR	January 10
93	Little Blue Heron	Cameron Prairie NWR	January 10
94	Tricolored Heron	Cameron Prairie NWR	January 10
95	White-faced Ibis	Cameron Prairie NWR	January 10
96	Roseate Spoonbill	Cameron Prairie NWR	January 10
97	Common Gallinule	Cameron Prairie NWR	January 10
98	American Coot	Cameron Prairie NWR	January 10
99	Caspian Tern	Cameron Prairie NWR	January 10
100	Sedge Wren	Cameron Prairie NWR	January 10
101	Marsh Wren	Cameron Prairie NWR	January 10
102	Common Yellowthroat	Cameron Prairie NWR	January 10
103	Boat-tailed Grackle	Cameron Prairie NWR	January 10

BIRD #	SPECIES	LOCATION	DATE
104	Red-headed Woodpecker	City Park, Baton Rouge	January 13
105	White-breasted Nuthatch	Walter B. Jacobs Memorial Nature Park, Shreveport	January 17
106	Bufflehead	Cross Lake shoreline, Shreveport	January 17
107	Brown Thrasher	Cross Lake shoreline, Shreveport	January 17
108	House Finch	Cross Lake shoreline, Shreveport	January 17
109	Canvasback	Cross Lake, Shreveport	January 17
110	Lesser Scaup	Cross Lake, Shreveport	January 17
111	Red-breasted Merganser	Cross Lake, Shreveport	January 17
112	Ruddy Duck	Cross Lake, Shreveport	January 17
113	Horned Grebe	Cross Lake, Shreveport	January 17
114	Western Grebe	Cross Lake, Shreveport	January 17
115	American White Pelican	Cross Lake, Shreveport	January 17
116	Bald Eagle	Cross Lake, Shreveport	January 17
117	Bonaparte's Gull	Cross Lake, Shreveport	January 17
118	Mew Gull	Cross Lake, Shreveport	January 17
119	Herring Gull	Cross Lake, Shreveport	January 17
120	Lesser Black-backed Gull	Cross Lake, Shreveport	January 17
121	Canada Goose	Copse of trees on Walden Road, Baton Rouge	January 24
122	Wood Duck	Copse of trees on Walden Road, Baton Rouge	January 24
123	Common Loon	Bayou Sauvage NWR; South Point	January 30
124	Brown Pelican	Bayou Sauvage NWR; South Point	January 30
125	Clapper Rail	Bayou Sauvage NWR; South Point	January 30
126	Ring-necked Duck	Bayou Sauvage NWR; Joe Madere Marsh Overlook	January 30
127	Common Grackle	Home, Baton Rouge	January 31
128	LeConte's Sparrow	Sherburne WMA Complex; South Farm, Iberville Parish	February 7

129	Pine Siskin	Sherburne WMA Complex, South Farm, Iberville Parish	February 7
130	Neotropic Cormorant	Highways 20 and 308 intersection, Thibodaux	February 8
131	Rock Pigeon	Highways 20 and 308 intersection, Thibodaux	February 8
132	Cattle Egret	Chauvin, Terrebonne Parish	February 8
133	Osprey	Bayou Sale Road, near Cocodrie	February 8
134	Sharp-shinned Hawk	Bluebonnet Swamp Nature Center, Baton Rouge	February 10
135	Barred Owl	Bluebonnet Swamp Nature Center, Baton Rouge	February 10
136	Ruby-throated Hummingbird	Bluebonnet Swamp Nature Center, Baton Rouge	February 10
137	Winter Wren	Bluebonnet Swamp Nature Center, Baton Rouge	February 10
138	Purple Martin	Peggy Street, Baton Rouge	February 18
139	Redhead	LSU Aquaculture Research Station, Baton Rouge	February 23
140	Hooded Merganser	LSU Aquaculture Research Station, Baton Rouge	February 23
141	Rusty Blackbird	Farr Park, Baton Rouge	March 5
142	Green Heron	Campus Lake, LSU, Baton Rouge	March 5
143	Black-bellied Plover	Jefferson Davis Parish Landfill environs (Turf Grass Road area)	March 12
144	American Golden-Plover	Jefferson Davis Parish Landfill environs (Turf Grass Road area)	March 12
145	Long-billed Curlew	Jefferson Davis Parish Landfill environs (Turf Grass Road area)	March 12
146	Pectoral Sandpiper	Jefferson Davis Parish Landfill environs (Turf Grass Road area)	March 12
147	Gray Catbird	Jefferson Davis Parish Landfill environs (Turf Grass Road area)	March 12
148	Field Sparrow	Jefferson Davis Parish Landfill environs (Turf Grass Road area)	March 12
149	Yellow-headed Blackbird	Route 397, near Lake Charles	March 12
150	Black-bellied Whistling-Duck	Cameron Prairie NWR	March 12
151	Fulvous Whistling-Duck	Cameron Prairie NWR	March 12
152	Glossy Ibis	Cameron Prairie NWR	March 12
153	King Rail	Cameron Prairie NWR	March 12
154	Crested Caracara	Cameron Prairie NWR	March 12
155	Greater Scaup	Holly Beach (Four Magic Miles)	March 12

BIRD #	SPECIES	LOCATION	DATE
156	Black Scoter	Holly Beach (Four Magic Miles)	March 12
157	American Avocet	Holly Beach (Four Magic Miles)	March 12
158	Piping Plover	Holly Beach (Four Magic Miles)	March 12
159	Ruddy Turnstone	Holly Beach (Four Magic Miles)	March 12
160	Sanderling	Holly Beach (Four Magic Miles)	March 12
161	Willet	Holly Beach (Four Magic Miles)	March 12
162	Royal Tern	Holly Beach (Four Magic Miles)	March 12
163	White-winged Dove	Peveto Woods Sanctuary	March 12
164	Wilson's Warbler	Peveto Woods Sanctuary	March 12
165	Great-tailed Grackle	Peveto Woods Sanctuary	March 12
166	Peregrine Falcon	Holly Beach (Four Magic Miles)	March 12
167	Surf Scoter	Route 11 about a mile from I-10, near Slidell	March 13
168	Palm Warbler	Bayou Sauvage NWR; South Point	March 13
169	Northern Gannet	Elmer's Island	March 14
170	Reddish Egret	Elmer's Island	March 14
171	Wilson's Plover	Elmer's Island	March 14
172	Semipalmated Plover	Elmer's Island	March 14
173	Marbled Godwit	Elmer's Island	March 14
174	Short-billed Dowitcher	Elmer's Island	March 14
175	Seaside Sparrow	Elmer's Island	March 14
176	Chimney Swift	Home, Baton Rouge	March 16
177	Buff-bellied Hummingbird	Bluebonnet Swamp Nature Center, Baton Rouge	March 19
178	Yellow-crowned Night-Heron	Eastover, New Orleans East	March 20
179	Tropical Kingbird	Eastover, New Orleans East	March 20
180	Swallow-tailed Kite	Route 11, Slidell	March 20

181	Barn Swallow	Rigolets kayak route, Slidell	March 20
182	Cliff Swallow	Rigolets kayak route, Slidell	March 20
183	White-eyed Vireo	Grand Isle, woods; Lafitte Woods Preserve, Landry-LeBlanc Tract	March 21
184	Yellow-throated Vireo	Grand Isle, woods; Lafitte Woods Preserve, Landry-LeBlanc Tract	March 21
185	Red-eyed Vireo	Grand Isle, woods; Lafitte Woods Preserve, Landry-LeBlanc Tract	March 21
186	Ovenbird	Grand Isle, woods; Lafitte Woods Preserve, Landry-LeBlanc Tract	March 21
187	Louisiana Waterthrush	Grand Isle, woods; Lafitte Woods Preserve, Landry-LeBlanc Tract	March 21
188	Black-and-white Warbler	Grand Isle, woods; Lafitte Woods Preserve, Landry-LeBlanc Tract	March 21
189	Prothonotary Warbler	Grand Isle, woods; Lafitte Woods Preserve, Landry-LeBlanc Tract	March 21
190	Hooded Warbler	Grand Isle, woods; Lafitte Woods Preserve, Landry-LeBlanc Tract	March 21
191	Northern Parula	Grand Isle, woods; Lafitte Woods Preserve, Landry-LeBlanc Tract	March 21
192	Yellow-throated Warbler	Grand Isle, woods; Lafitte Woods Preserve, Landry-LeBlanc Tract	March 21
193	Black-throated Green Warbler	Grand Isle, woods; Lafitte Woods Preserve, Landry-LeBlanc Tract	March 21
194	Sora	Grand Isle, woods; Lafitte Woods Preserve; Grilletta Tract	March 21
195	Northern Rough-winged Swallow	Grand Isle; Dowitcher Pond	March 21
196	Broad-winged Hawk	Grand Isle, woods; Lafitte Woods Preserve, Landry-LeBlanc Tract	March 22
197	Solitary Sandpiper	Grand Isle, woods; Lafitte Woods Preserve, Landry-LeBlanc Tract	March 22
198	Worm-eating Warbler	Grand Isle, woods; Lafitte Woods Preserve, Landry-LeBlanc Tract	March 22
199	Black Skimmer	Grand Isle State Park	March 22
200	Virginia Rail	Big Branch Marsh NWR	March 24
201	Great Horned Owl	Big Branch Marsh NWR	March 24
202	Red-cockaded Woodpecker	Big Branch Marsh NWR	March 24
203	Whimbrel	Jefferson Davis Parish Landfill environs (Turf Grass Road area)	March 31
204	Buff-breasted Sandpiper	Jefferson Davis Parish Landfill environs (Turf Grass Road area)	March 31
205	Wilson's Snipe	Jefferson Davis Parish Landfill environs (Turf Grass Road area)	March 31
206	Merlin	Jefferson Davis Parish Landfill environs (Turf Grass Road area)	March 31

BIRD #	SPECIES	LOCATION	DATE
207	Eastern Kingbird	Jefferson Davis Parish Landfill environs (Turf Grass Road area)	March 31
208	Bronzed Cowbird	Route 397, near Lake Charles	March 31
209	Yellow-billed Cuckoo	Cameron Prairie NWR	March 31
210	Indigo Bunting	Peveto Woods Sanctuary	March 31
211	Orchard Oriole	Peveto Woods Sanctuary	March 31
212	Great Kiskadee	Hidden Ponds RV Park, Sulphur	March 31
213	Chuck-will's-widow	Home, Baton Rouge	April 1
214	Swainson's Hawk	I-10, mile marker 46	April 2
215	Philadelphia Vireo	Peveto Woods Sanctuary	April 2
216	Swainson's Thrush	Peveto Woods Sanctuary	April 2
217	Blue-winged Warbler	Peveto Woods Sanctuary	April 2
218	American Redstart	Peveto Woods Sanctuary	April 2
219	Sandwich Tern	Holly Beach (Four Magic Miles)	April 2
220	Great Crested Flycatcher	Home, Baton Rouge	April 3
221	Wood Thrush	Home, Baton Rouge	April 16
222	Mississippi Kite	Sherburne WMA; Whiskey Bay Rd.	April 16
223	Acadian Flycatcher	Sherburne WMA; Whiskey Bay Rd.	April 16
224	Summer Tanager	Sherburne WMA; Whiskey Bay Rd.	April 16
225	Scarlet Tanager	Sherburne WMA; Whiskey Bay Rd.	April 17
226	Least Tern	Jefferson Davis Parish Landfill environs (Turf Grass Road area)	April 17
227	Dickcissel	Jefferson Davis Parish Landfill environs (Turf Grass Road area)	April 17
228	Purple Gallinule	Lacassine NWR, Pool Unit D	April 17
229	Kentucky Warbler	Lacassine NWR Headquarters and Visitor's Center	April 17
230	Upland Sandpiper	Jefferson Davis Parish Landfill environs (Turf Grass Road area)	April 24
231	Bank Swallow	Jefferson Davis Parish Landfill environs (Turf Grass Road area)	April 24

232	Cave Swallow	Highway 165 bridge at I-10, Iowa	April 24
233	Common Tern	Holly Beach (Four Magic Miles)	April 24
234	Eastern Wood-Pewee	Peveto Woods Sanctuary	April 24
235	Veery	Peveto Woods Sanctuary	April 24
236	Cerulean Warbler	Peveto Woods Sanctuary	April 24
237	Magnolia Warbler	Peveto Woods Sanctuary	April 24
238	Blackburnian Warbler	Peveto Woods Sanctuary	April 24
239	Chestnut-sided Warbler	Peveto Woods Sanctuary	April 24
240	Yellow-breasted Chat	Peveto Woods Sanctuary	April 24
241	Rose-breasted Grosbeak	Peveto Woods Sanctuary	April 24
242	Blue Grosbeak	Peveto Woods Sanctuary	April 24
243	Painted Bunting	Peveto Woods Sanctuary	April 24
244	Baltimore Oriole	Peveto Woods Sanctuary	April 24
245	Black-crowned Night-Heron	Lighthouse Road, Cameron Parish	April 24
246	Semipalmated Sandpiper	Lighthouse Road, Cameron Parish	April 24
247	Common Nighthawk	Lighthouse Road, Cameron Parish	April 24
248	Scissor-tailed Flycatcher	Lighthouse Road, Cameron Parish	April 24
249	Prairie Warbler	Lighthouse Road, Cameron Parish	April 24
250	Bobolink	Lighthouse Road, Cameron Parish	April 24
251	Golden-winged Warbler	Peveto Woods Sanctuary	April 24
252	Least Bittern	Thornwell–Southern Jefferson Davis Parish shorebird census area	April 28
253	White-rumped Sandpiper	Thornwell–Southern Jefferson Davis Parish shorebird census area	April 28
254	Wilson's Phalarope	Thornwell–Southern Jefferson Davis Parish shorebird census area	April 28
255	Inca Dove	Thornwell–Southern Jefferson Davis Parish shorebird census area	April 28
256	Hudsonian Godwit	Highway 717, western edge of Vermilion Parish	April 28
257	Black Tern	Holly Beach (Four Magic Miles)	May 4
258	Least Flycatcher	Peveto Woods Sanctuary	May 4

BIRD #	SPECIES	LOCATION	DATE
259	Warbling Vireo	Peveto Woods Sanctuary	May 4
260	Gray-cheeked Thrush	Peveto Woods Sanctuary	May 4
261	Tennessee Warbler	Peveto Woods Sanctuary	May 4
262	Nashville Warbler	Peveto Woods Sanctuary	May 4
263	Bay-breasted Warbler	Peveto Woods Sanctuary	May 4
264	Blackpoll Warbler	Peveto Woods Sanctuary	May 4
265	Western Kingbird	Lighthouse Road, Cameron Parish	May 9
266	Yellow Warbler	Lighthouse Road, Cameron Parish	May 9
267	Swainson's Warbler	Sherburne WMA; Whiskey Bay Road	May 23
268	Bachman's Sparrow	Kisatchie National Forest, Wild Azalea National Recreation Trail	May 23
269	Eastern Screech-Owl	Blackwell Lane, Folsom	June 1
270	Northern Bobwhite	Matt Pontiff Roadrunner Loop	June 3
271	Common Ground-Dove	Matt Pontiff Roadrunner Loop	June 3
272	Greater Roadrunner	Matt Pontiff Roadrunner Loop	June 3
273	Barn Owl	Jefferson Davis Parish Landfill environs (Turf Grass Road area)	June 3
274	Magnificent Frigatebird	Grand Isle beach	June 10
275	Gull-billed Tern	Grand Isle beach	June 10
276	Snowy Plover	Grand Isle State Park	June 11
277	American Oystercatcher	Queen Bess Island, Grand Isle	June 11
278	Monk Parakeet	Roosevelt Mall, City Park, New Orleans	June 15
279	Willow Flycatcher	Red River NWR; Bayou Pierre Unit Yates Tract	June 18
280	Bell's Vireo	Red River NWR; Bayou Pierre Unit Yates Tract	June 18
281	Lark Sparrow	Highway 537, Plain Dealing	June 18
282	Wood Stork	Highway 71, Port Barre	June 18
283	Wild Turkey	Sherburne WMA Complex; South Farm, Iberville Parish	August 17

284	Brown Booby	Causeway Bridge, mile marker 6.6, near New Orleans	August 23
285	Olive-sided Flycatcher	Peveto Woods Sanctuary	August 28
286	Alder Flycatcher	Peveto Woods Sanctuary	August 28
287	Canada Warbler	Peveto Woods Sanctuary	August 28
288	Great Shearwater	Plaquemines Parish: inshore from South Pass to 14 miles into the Gulf of Mexico	September 10
289	Cory's Shearwater	Plaquemines Parish: Gulf of Mexico, 14–18 mi SE of South Pass	September 10
290	Pomarine Jaeger	Plaquemines Parish: Gulf of Mexico, 14–18 mi SE of South Pass	September 10
291	Long-tailed Jaeger	Plaquemines Parish: Gulf of Mexico, 14–18 mi SE of South Pass	September 10
292	Bridled Tern	Plaquemines Parish: Gulf of Mexico, 14–18 mi SE of South Pass	September 10
293	Northern Waterthrush	Plaquemines Parish: Red Pass	September 10
294	Vermilion Flycatcher	Lacassine NWR, Pool Unit D	October 13
295	Rufous Hummingbird	Shirley Avenue, Baton Rouge	October 14
296	Nelson's Sparrow	Lake Pontchartrain kayak route, New Orleans	October 15
297	Say's Phoebe	Stingray plant, Highway 82, Cameron Parish	October 22
298	Franklin's Gull	Holly Beach (Four Magic Miles)	October 22
299	Calliope Hummingbird	Cardinal Road, Covington	October 23
300	Black Rail	Broussard Beach, Southern Cameron Parish	October 29
301	White-tailed Kite	Willow Island, Southern Cameron Parish	October 29
302	Brewer's Blackbird	Jefferson Davis Parish Landfill environs (Turf Grass Road area)	November 5
303	Yellow Rail	Rice fields, Thornwell	November 5
304	Black-chinned Hummingbird	Tulane Drive, Baton Rouge	November 12
305	Ash-throated Flycatcher	Recovery Road, New Orleans East	November 16
306	Brown-crested Flycatcher	Recovery Road, New Orleans East	November 16
307	Broad-billed Hummingbird	Swallow Street, Mandeville	November 29
308	Ringed Kingfisher	Lake Martin, St. Martinville	December 3
309	Horned Lark	Sentell Road, Belcher	December 10

BIRD #	SPECIES	LOCATION	DATE
310	Western Meadowlark	Sentell Road, Belcher	December 10
311	Fox Sparrow	Chocolate Trail (also known as the Lake Trail), Headquarters Unit, Red River NWR	December 10
312	Bewick's Wren	Yearwood Road Loop, Shreveport	December 10
313	American Woodcock	Yearwood Road Loop, Shreveport	December 10
314	Henslow's Sparrow	Bodcau Dam Road, Benton	December 11
315	American Bittern	White Lake CBC, Liberty Square area, Vermillion Parish	December 14
316	Tundra Swan	Cameron Prairie NWR	December 18
317	Cackling Goose	Illinois Plant Road, north of Lacassine NWR	December 18
318	Common Goldeneye	Denham Springs Water Treatment Plant	December 22
319	Purple Finch	Buccaneer Avenue, Baton Rouge	December 24
320	Lincoln's Sparrow	Fabacher Road, Calcasieu Parish	December 28
321	Cinnamon Teal	Cameron Prairie NWR	December 28

NOTES

PREFACE

1. To see the current state bird checklist, see http://losbird.org/la_checklist_2016.pdf.

1. LISTING TOWARD LISTING

1. For details on this reintroduction effort, see http://www.wlf.louisiana.gov/wildlife/whoop ing-cranes.

2. The book *The Big Year* uses the actual names of the three birders competing for the North American big year record, while the movie does not. In the movie, Greg Miller's name is Brad Harris.

3. A parish is the same thing as a county. Louisiana is the only state in the nation that has parishes; Alaska has boroughs instead of counties, and the rest of the states are carved into counties. The origin of parish goes back to our French heritage. Parish derives from the French word *paroisses*.

4. According to eBird (https://ebird.org/barchart?byr=1900&eyr=2018&bmo=1&emo=12&r= US-LA-023), as of August 25, 2018. This species count will likely increase over time as new birds are recorded in the parish.

5. A chenier is a group of trees, typically in a coastal area. Chenier is the French word for oak.

6. Verbal communication during a RGVBF field trip at Southmost Preserve, Brownsville, Texas, November 9, 2013. Karlson was one of the guides for this field trip.

7. https://knowla-dev.tulane.edu/entry/tarzan-of-the-apes.

2. FOR THE LOVE OF IT

1. People can be trained to band birds, catching and then carefully placing a metal or plastic band on a bird, typically on its leg. The band comes with a number, and a trained bander can enter

information about the bird, such as its age and weight, into a website (see the Bird Banding Laboratory for details, https://www.usgs.gov/centers/pwrc/science/bird-banding-laboratory). Later, others who encounter the bird can use the band number to look up information on the bird and add new information. Bands have provided researchers with many insights about birds, including their travel patterns and longevity. If you find a banded bird, you are encouraged to report it to the aforementioned Bird Banding Laboratory and the U.S. Fish and Wildlife Service at https://www.fws.gov/birds/surveys-and-data/bird-banding/reporting-banded-birds.php.

2. Florence Williams, *The Nature Fix: Why Nature Makes Us Happier, Healthier, and More Creative* (New York: Norton, 2017), 86.

3. Researchers have found adverse impacts on birds with respect to noise. Some studies are described in a January 9, 2018, *Washington Post* article by Sarah Kaplan entitled "Some Birds Are So Stressed by Noise Pollution It Looks like They Have PTSD," https://www.washingtonpost.com/news/speaking-of-science/wp/2018/01/09/some-birds-are-so-stressed-by-noise-pollution-it-looks-like-they-have-ptsd/?noredirect=on&utm_term=.f8b44d3e6294. Numerous other studies on these impacts can be found in the scientific literature.

4. Hunters played a role in early federal efforts to conserve land through the establishment and ongoing support of National Wildlife Refuges and Wildlife Management Areas. All hunters sixteen and older are required to purchase a federal duck stamp (currently $25), which provides funds to protect land and purchase or lease additional acreage for conservation. More than 1.5 million duck stamps were purchased for the 2017–18 season, resulting in approximately $36 million for conservation. For further information on the duck stamp program, see https://www.fws.gov//birds/get-involved/duck-stamp.php.

5. J. Christopher Haney, Harold J. Geiger, Jeffrey W. Short, "Bird Mortality from the *Deepwater Horizon* Oil Spill. II. Carcass Sampling and Exposure Probability in the Coastal Gulf of Mexico," *Marine Ecology Progress Series* 513 (October 22, 2014): 239–252.

6. Arlie Russell Hochschild, *Strangers in Their Own Land: Anger and Mourning on the American Right, A Journey to the Heart of Our Political Divide* (New York: New Press, 2016). I highly recommend this book, which is set in Lake Charles, Louisiana, and which provides tremendous insight and understanding no matter where one falls on the political spectrum.

3. BIRDING FROM THE INSIDE OUT

1. Playback is a technique used by some birders to locate birds. It involves playing the recorded songs and calls of a particular bird species to elicit a response from that same species; many times a specific species will come out into the open in response to playback, making it easy for birders to view. Playback can also be done using a recording of a predator bird species, such as Eastern Screech-Owl or Northern Saw-whet Owl. Many adjacent species in the area will "mob" in response

to a predator call to try to flush the predator from the area. The use of playback is allowed in birding, and there are specific recommendations developed by the American Birding Association involving length and volume of playback, as well as situations and places in which to use it (see http://www .sibleyguides.com/2011/04/the-proper-use-of-playback-in-birding/ for details). The use of playback can be controversial; some birders advocate for its use while others believe that it can be detrimental to birds. The rules regarding playback are conclusive, while research regarding the impact of playback on birds is inconclusive. Some birders in this book are proponents of playback; others generally are not. Lynn and I use playback and also follow the rules regarding it.

2. Steve Lerner, *Diamond: A Struggle for Environmental Justice in Louisiana's Chemical Corridor (Urban and Industrial Environments)* (Cambridge, Mass.: MIT Press, 2006).

3. We quietly played the call inside the truck so that no birds would hear the recording; birders are not supposed to use playback inside National Wildlife Refuges.

4. https://www.youtube.com/watch?v=eRMceoRQXQU.

5. Compression is important for burns because it helps scars heal faster and better.

4. THE YEAR OF THE DAY TRIP

1. An irruption refers to the influx of a population of birds into a particular area in which they are not typically found.

2. This abandoned area has been reclaimed by the community as a locally infamous skateboarding location.

5. THE QUEST FOR THREE HUNDRED: THE MARATHON

1. You "yard crash" when you visit someone's yard to find a bird that they have in their yard that you wish to see.

2. https://www.lsu.edu/mns/news/2016/05022016-big-day-account.php.

3. A hat trick is a term used in hockey, for when a player scores three goals in a game. Here, I am using hat trick to indicate that we got three species during a trip.

4. The bail is part of the reel on a fishing pole; the reel includes a crank and a spool to hold fishing line, and a bail, which is a semicircular metal piece that has an open and closed position. In the open position, fishing line unspools from the reel without resistance.

5. Cajun waders are short, white, rubber boots that are commonly worn by fisherfolk and other working people in Louisiana. They are also worn in coastal Alabama, where they have a different nickname: bayou Reeboks.

6. *sp.* is an abbreviation for the word species (often pronounced "spuh"). It is used when you can

narrow down a particular bird identification to a general category, like a duck or sparrow, but you cannot narrow it down any further than that.

7. Any bird found up to 200 nautical miles off the coast of a particular state is considered a bird observed in that state. One nautical mile is 1.15 miles, so any bird found up to 230 miles offshore can be counted. Because the trip we planned was a day-long trip starting and ending in Venice, we could venture as far as 50 miles offshore, well within the 230-mile state zone.

8. Scientists put tiny bands on the legs of birds, especially endangered species such as the Piping Plover, in an effort to track them. (See note 2.1 for details about banding.) Each band has a specific number that can be looked up to find descriptive information on that particular bird. The bands are small and the numbers on the bands even smaller, so attempting to read band numbers on a bird is exceptionally difficult; you need lots of magnification and some cooperation on the part of the bird.

9. In the South, a soft drink is known as a cold drink or as a coke (and coke can mean any flavor). It is equivalent to the term soda in the northeast and pop in the Midwest.

10. http://www.losbird.org/lbrc/LBRCNL2017.pdf.

7. THREE HUNDRED

1. The bread test is a slang term regarding whether a bird is wild (and thus countable) or not. For example, if you bring a loaf of bread to your local park and ducks, pigeons, and geese approach you because they're expecting you to feed them, these birds flunk the bread test.

8. LAGNIAPPE

1. Richard Gibbons, Roger Breedlove, and Charles Lyon, *A Birder's Guide to Louisiana* (Colorado Springs, Colo.: American Birding Association, 2013), 177.

2. Louisiana is an area where Glossy Ibis and White-faced Ibis are both found. We typically refer to these two species collectively as dark ibis. Careful inspection is necessary to identify the specific species, which we were not taking the time to do during the dawn flyover.

3. The ABA is the American Birding Association.

4. When a big fish is hooked and swims away, it takes fishing line with it. If the line and/or the reel is not strong enough, a fish can pull out all the line in your reel and then snap the line. That process is called "getting spooled."

EPILOGUE: I KNOW WHY THE CAJUN BIRD DANCES

1. http://www.nola.com/environment/index.ssf/2017/07/louisiana_land_loss_slows_to_f.html.

2. http://www.losco.state.la.us/about.html.

3. http://www.sciencemag.org/news/2014/10/seabird-losses-deepwater-horizon-oil-spill -estimated-hundreds-thousands.

4. http://coastal.la.gov/our-plan/2017-coastal-master-plan/.

INDEX